S0-ARE-270

A NEW COURSE IN READING PĀLI

Entering the Word of the Buddha

A NEW COURSE IN READING PĀLI

Entering the Word of the Buddha

JAMES W. GAIR
W.S. KARUNATILLAKE

MOTILAL BANARSIDASS PUBLISHERS
PRIVATE LIMITED • DELHI

5th Reprint: Delhi, 2014
First Indian Edition: Delhi, 1998

© JAMES W. GAIR
All Rights Reserved

ISBN: 978-81-208-1440-0 (Cloth)
ISBN: 978-81-208-1441-7 (Paper)

MOTILAL BANARSIDASS
41 U.A. Bungalow Road, Jawahar Nagar, Delhi 110 007
8 Mahalaxmi Chamber, 22 Bhulabhai Desai Road, Mumbai 400 026
203 Royapettah High Road, Mylapore, Chennai 600 004
236, 9th Main III Block, Jayanagar, Bengaluru 560 011
Sanas Plaza, 1302 Baji Rao Road, Pune 411 002
8 Camac Street, Kolkata 700 017
Ashok Rajpath, Patna 800 004
Chowk, Varanasi 221 001

Printed in India

by RP Jain at New Age Books Printing Unit,
A-44, Naraina Industrial Area, Phase I, New Delhi–110028
and published by JP Jain for Motilal Banarsidass Publishers (P) Ltd,
41 U.A. Bungalow Road, Jawahar Nagar, Delhi-110007

DEDICATION

svākkhāto bhagavatā dhammo,
sandiṭṭṭhiko, akāliko, ehipassiko, opanayiko,
paccataṃ veditabbo viññūhī'ti

*   *   *

sabbe sattā bhavantu sukhitattā!

PREFACE

This book had its beginnings in a set of graded readings and grammatical notes that the authors began to assemble and discuss a number of years ago, when we found that there was a lack of introductory material for Pāli that emphasized reading and a direct approach to texts that could be read by beginning students and at the same time conveyed some of the fundamental Buddhist ideas and concepts that were embodied in the Pāli tradition. Professor Karunatillake played the primary role in the original selection, which thus had a Sri Lankan Buddhist perspective. At the same time, we believed that a text of this nature should be graded in terms of grammar and as far as possible, vocabulary, since we were aiming at a beginning student, and did not want to presume any prior knowledge, as of Sanskrit. Thus we resolved throughout to treat Pāli as a language in its own right. In short, we attempted to apply the same approach that we and others had used in texts for modern spoken and written languages. Along the way to the present work, there were numerous replacements, additions, and re-orderings, along with many valuable and pleasant hours of analysis and discussion of both grammar and content. These lessons have also been used in successive forms in our Pāli classes, and the progress and the reactions of the students have been encouraging indeed. We hope that the original perspective and intent has been retained.

Too many colleagues and students have contributed comments and encouragement for us to name them, but we would particularly like to single out a few. Successive generations of students have pointed out misprints and missing items, along with unclarities or difficulties that they encountered. In particular, Kim Atkins not only fulfilled those functions, but typed a great deal of the text in an earlier form. Richard Carlson and Tamara Hudec were particularly active in the editing function as they learned. Ratna Wijetunga and L. Sumangala contributed suggestions, and colleagues and friends, such as John Ross Carter, Charles Hallisey, and John Paolillo encouraged us to bring this material to final form. Charles Hallisey also made a special contribution, by using this text in his classes at Harvard and making numerous suggestions that have found their way into this version. We also thank Professor Lakshmi Narayan Tiwari for his valuable suggestions, and Mr N.P. Jain of Motilal Banarsidass for his help in bringing this work to publication at last.

We will be happy for comments and suggestions, and hope that others will find these materials useful as we have. If it offers, even in a small way, entry for more students, whether in formal classes or not, into the language and thought of Pāli Buddhist texts, we will feel more than amply rewarded for what efforts we have put into the task.

James W. Gair
Ithaca, New York

W.S. Karunatillake
Kelaniya, Sri Lanka
July, 1994

CONTENTS

DEDICATION v

PREFACE vii

INTRODUCTION xi

PART I: THIS TEXT AND HOW TO USE IT xi

PART II: PĀLI ALPHABET AND PRONUNCIATION xiii

PART III: THE LANGUAGE AND TEXTS xvii

PART IV: SOME USEFUL SOURCES xxi

LESSON I 1

LESSON II 14

LESSON III 29

LESSON IV 45

LESSON V 63

LESSON VI 77

LESSON VII 97

LESSON VIII 109

LESSON IX 121

LESSON X 133

LESSON XI 147

LESSON XII 163

GENERAL GLOSSARY 179

GRAMMATICAL INDEX 203

BY PĀLI ENTRIES 203

BY ENGLISH ENTRIES 206

INTRODUCTION

WHAT IS IN THIS INTRODUCTION: This introduction is in four parts: The first describes the principles on which this text is organized, and suggests how it is intended to be most efficiently used. Students, especially those proceeding on their own outside of a regular class, are thus strongly urged to read that section before beginning their study. The second part deals with the alphabet and alphabetical order, with some information on the pronunciation (phonological system)system of Pāli. Interested students may investigate the latter, but all should at least become acquainted with the order of the alphabet in order to use the glossaries in this text. The third part gives some general background to Pāli language and literature, particularly those works on which we have drawn for our readings. Lastly, there is a brief list of basic sources that the student might find useful in studying Pāli, and continuing past this text.

Cumulative glossaries, and indices of grammatical forms and topics will be found at the end of the volume.

PART 1: THIS TEXT AND HOW TO USE IT

The readings and grammatical notes included in this text are intended to serve as a primer to introduce students to the reading of authentic Buddhist texts in Pāli (sometimes written as Pāḷi and in English usage commonly written simply as Pali). The emphasis throughout is thus on acquiring the ability to read, and the texts have all been selected and ordered with that goal in mind. At the same time, however, we have operated under the principle that such reading should not be a mere exercise, but should have significant and interesting content. We have thus made every attempt to make every reading, even if a selection from a larger text, self-contained and meaningful and in some sense complete in content. We have also assumed no knowledge of Sanskrit or any other Indo-Aryan language, but have approached Pāli as a language in its own right. We have also assumed a wide range of learners, ranging from the interested student of Buddhism who may be approaching the texts on his/her own, through college freshmen and graduate students. In the classes in which the successive versions of this text have been used, we have found that it can indeed be used successively by such a range of learners. We have thus attempted throughout to make the grammatical explanations as clear and non-technical as possible, though obviously a student with some general grammatical knowledge, and especially one who has had exposure to some other language with case and verb agreement may find them, and probably the readings, easier at first.

For this book to be used effectively, however, the following points about its organization and the selection of texts should be kept in mind:

1. Each lesson has three parts: (1) a set of basic readings and an accompanying glossary, (2) grammatical notes on the forms in the lesson, and (3) a set of further readings with its own glossary. The further readings introduce no new grammatical points, but reinforce those already presented. Thus the student should work out the basic readings carefully, consulting the vocabulary and the

grammar. After that he or she will have the equipment to read the further readings for necessary practice and reinforcement, usually needing only to consult the glossary for them.

2. The readings have been carefully graded, particularly for grammatical features, and the vocabulary is cumulative. Thus they should be used in the order given. Sometimes, particularly in the earlier lessons, it was impossible to avoid including some forms that we introduce later, given our principle of using only authentic texts. At the same time, we did not want to overload the earlier lessons, when everything is new, with most of the grammar. Thus when a form that is described in a later lesson occurs in an earlier one, we have simply glossed the earlier occurrence as a unit, without an explanation, saving that for later.

3. The student will note that many of the readings, particularly in earlier lessons, contain passages that are repeated with only a few changes in vocabulary in each repetition. This was in fact one element in their selection. With such readings, once the student has worked out the first part, the rest can be read by looking up only a restricted number of new items. Thus reading them need not be simply laborious exercises in decoding and looking up words, but they may be read as text, with minimal lookup. At the same time, grammatical and rhetorical patterns will be reinforced, and will be more easily dealt with when encountered later. Thus these repetitions should not be skipped. On the contrary, they can be enjoyable in that they allow the student to approach the text for content, and what is more, they do represent one rhetorical device commonly found in Pāli texts.

We may now mention one or two things that we have not taken as goals for this text.

This book is intended as an introduction to reading Pāli, not as an independent scholarly contribution to the linguistic or literary study of the language. Thus our grammar sections are intended as aids to the learner, and we have not attempted to cover in them all of the variants that one might encounter in reading further in texts. However, the student should, after completing the readings here, and acquainting himself or herself with the basic vocabulary and grammatical patterns, have sufficient background to make use of other reference sources, such as those listed at the end of this introduction, to deal with the new forms met with in future reading.

Similarly, a word needs to be said concerning our treatment of vocabulary. One cannot read Pāli Buddhist texts without encountering a number of technical terms, such as **dhamma**, **khaṇḍa**, **kamma** etc.etc. which have not only specialized, but manifold meanings within Buddhist thought. These have served as the basis for extensive commentary, elucidation and disputation within both the Pāli and the western scholarly traditions, and many of them have been the subject of more than one book-length treatment. While we are fully aware of the importance of such work, and the indispensability of a clear understanding of such terms if one is to attain a really adequate understanding of the texts, we have not attempted to make any original contributions in that direction. Thus we have glossed forms in relation to their senses in specific texts in which they appear here. The student with an interest in the range of meanings of such terms, and their precise technical sense, is encouraged to consult the many scholarly sources on Buddhist concepts and philosophy. Nevertheless, the meanings of these technical terms are best learned when encountered in a range of actual contexts, and it is our hope that the readings here will enable the student to make a start toward that end.

PART II: PĀLI ALPHABET AND PRONUNCIATION

Alphabet and Alphabetical Order:

Pāli has no script of its own, but is written in several scripts, depending on the country in which it is written and the audience for which it is intended. In the West, it is commonly written in the Roman alphabet with some modifications (diacritics), as in the works issued by the Pali Text Society, and that is the general pattern we follow here.

The alphabetical order, however, as in the major dictionaries, commonly follows an Indic pattern. Since it will be clearly necessary for the students to be accustomed to that order if they are to use such sources, we have adopted it here. In that order, the vowels precede the consonants as a set (ṃ is considered in between). The order that we use in this text is:

a ā i ī u ū e o ṃ k kh g gh (ṃ) c ch j jh ñ ṭ ṭh ḍ ḍh ṇ
t th d dh n p ph b bh m y r l v s h ḷ

Note that ṃ occurs again in parentheses after gh. The reason is that it equates with a single character that has a double use in Sinhala and some other scripts used in writing Pāli. For this book, the simple rule to follow in determining the alphabetical order is "ṃ is placed between the vowels and the consonants. It thus precedes all other consonants in the alphabetical order, unless it occurs before k, kh, g, or gh within a word, in which case it follows gh." In practice, this will give little difficulty, since the two positions are very close in the alphabet, and ṃ occurs most frequently at the end of a word or before k, kh, g, or gh. The student will also encounter some small variations in consulting other sources. Most obvious is the representation of the forms written with ṃ here. Some other texts distinguish the two uses of ṃ Some of these may use ŋ for our ṃ, and some represent ṃ before g as ṅ. (For more detail see the pronunciation section that follows.). Also, some lists put ḷ immediately after l rather than at the very end of the alphabet as here (in this, we have followed general Sinhala practice).

Pronunciation:

Since Pāli is a classical and not a modern spoken language, its pronunciation also varies from place to place. However, we do have the testimony of some indigenous grammars as to how it was pronounced, and we can gather much from our general knowledge of Indic languages. The purpose of this text is to help the student read Pāli, but some may find it helpful to be able to produce it aloud in some systematic fashion. Others may also want to listen to texts. What we give here is a general and essentially non-technical description of "classical" Pāli pronunciation. In general, this accords with the pronunciation of Sri Lankan Buddhist monks (though they may at times fail to observe orally some of the distinctions which have been lost in Sinhala, such as the aspirate/non-aspirate distinction, or alter them somewhat).

The traditional arrangement of the Pāli alphabet, as given above, is actually based on the sounds represented by the characters. This appears clearly if we arrange them as in the chart below: (the arrows will be explained later)

		3 ↓ Velar	4 ↓ Palatal	5 ↓ Retroflex	6 ↓ Dental	7 ↓ Labial
1 ⟶ VOWELS:	a ā i ī u ū e o					
2 ⟶ "PURE" NASAL:	ṃ					
CONSONANTS:						
VOICELESS NON-ASPIRATE (STOPS):		k	c	ṭ	t	p
VOICELESS ASPIRATES:		kh	ch	ṭh	th	ph
VOICED (NON-ASPIRATE (STOPS):		g	j	ḍ	d	b
VOICED ASPIRATES:		gh	jh	ḍh	dh	bh
NASALS:		(ṃ)	ñ	ṇ	n	m
8 ⟶ RESONANTS	y r l v					
9 ⟶ SPIRANTS	s h	10 ⟶ OTHER:	ḷ	ḷh		

THE SOUNDS OF PĀLI AND THEIR ALPHABETICAL ORDER

Unlike in English, the letters have a "one symbol = one sound" character, with a few exceptions to be noted.

The vowels a, i, and u, have long and short variants, with the macron symbol (¯) indicating 'long'.* Short a is pronounced roughly like the a in American 'what' or the u in British 'but'. ā is like the a in 'father'. i is like the same symbol in 'bit'; ī like the ee in seethe. u is roughly like oo in 'look' and ū like the same in 'soothe'. In all cases, the long vowels, as the name suggests, are pronounced longer than the short ones. e and o, however, do not have distinct long and short variants, but are pronounced long before single consonants or at the end of a word and short before double consonants like tt or tth or consonant clusters such as nd or ṃg. Thus the (short) e, as in ettha 'here' is like the e in 'bet, while the e in etaṃ 'this' is like the ai in 'raid' or the a...e in 'made'. Note that the aspirate consonants (those written with h) count as single, so that the e

* Where the length is a result of two words coming together (sandhi), however, we use the circumflex symbol (^), to aid the student in breaking down the forms. (See Lesson 1 Grammar, Section 5.2.)

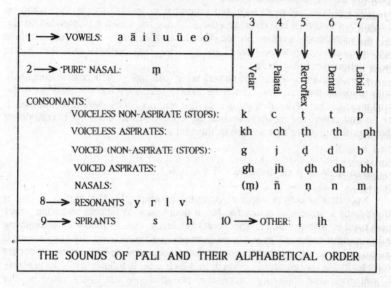

in etha 'come' is also long. The same rule holds for o. It is like the o in English 'rose' in koṭi 'end' but shorter in koṭṭeti 'beats', and thus more like the o in 'hoping', though there is no real English counterpart. One difference between English and Pāli and other South Asian languages is that the English counterparts of the long vowels are generally pronounced with an offglide at the end, so that 'say' and 'row' are not simple long e and o, but more like ey and ow. Pāli vowels, however, are pronounced "straight through", without the glide.

The labels in the chart of consonants are familiar to phoneticians, but we need not explain them all here to those unfamiliar with hat specialty, since the symbols themselves will give a sufficient clue in most cases. However, we do need to point out as we go several important distinctions that are not present in English and the familiar European languages but which do exist, or operate differently, in Indic languages such as Pāli. For now, note that the columns in the consonant chart above are arranged by the place in which the sound is articulated in the mouth. Thus the articulation goes from back to front as we proceed from left to right horizontally along each row of the main consonant block (try saying k, t, p in that order and see what is happening to your tongue and lips).

Voiced sounds are those produced with a "buzzing" action in the larynx, and voiceless sounds without it (try stopping your ears and saying b, and p and then k and g, etc). This distinction is, of course, important in English and the European languages as well. Pāli k, p, g and b are essentially like their English counterparts in 'making', 'hoping', 'good' and 'bathe'. c and j are like English ch in 'choose', and j in 'just'.

In Pāli, however, there is another distinction along this front-back axis that is unknown in the familiar European languages: the dental vs. retroflex one. The dental consonants are produced with the tongue tip on the tooth ridge just back of the upper teeth. The retroflex ones are produced further back and usually with the tongue tip curled upward. Actually, English t and d are made in almost the retroflex position, especially in words like 'to' and 'do', and are thus heard as retroflex by many speakers of South Asian languages. English has no real counterparts for the dental sounds, though t and d are far more dental in French, Spanish, and many European languages.

In Pāli and many other languages of South Asia, however, there is an important difference not found in English; that between non-aspirated and aspirated sounds (those written with -h). Aspirates are produced with an additional puff of air, or a breathy release. These aspirate consonants are, apart from the difference in aspiration, produced in the same place and manner as their non-aspirate counterparts. English p, t, and k at the beginning of words are actually quite strongly aspirated, as compared, for example, to French, and even more so to the non-aspirates of the North Indian languages. Note, however, that the aspirate consonants in Pāli count as single consonants, not clusters (as noted earlier in relation to the pronunciation of e and o). In the South Asian alphabets, in fact, they would be written with single symbols.

m is like its English counterpart in 'miss'. n and ṇ are "n-like" sounds that exhibit the same dental vs. retroflex distinction as t and ṭ or d and ḍ, and are pronounced accordingly. ñ is produced like the same symbol in Spanish 'señor'.

The symbol ṃ is more complicated in that it occurs in two places in the system we use here: between the vowels and consonants, and also as the nasal in the velar column. At the end of a word, it is pronounced like the ng in English 'sing' (to the phonetician, this is one sound, represented as ŋ). Within a word, it does not occur alone between vowels, but always immediately preceding a consonant. It then takes on the position of that consonant, and it is this "chameleon" character, together with the fact that it is the only nasal occurring at the end of a word, that accounts in part for its treatment as a "pure nasal" and thus for its special placement. Note, though, that when ṃ occurs before a velar consonant, it will thus be a velar nasal. Since there is no velar nasal in Pāli occurring elsewhere, except for ṃ at the end of a word, two distinct symbols are unnecessary. In this we have followed one Pāli manuscript tradition. Other sources, though, use distinct symbols, such as using ṃ or ŋ for the "pure nasal" but n for the velar nasal before velar consonants. Once the student is used to one system, as here, he or she should be able to adjust easily to the others. It will, however, sometimes affect the alphabetization of some items. In this text, as stated earlier, ṃ will be listed after the vowels unless it precedes a velar consonant, in which case it will follow gh. In practice, only a very few items are affected.

y and v are much like their English counterparts. r is generally produced as a "trilled" r as in Scots and some varieties of German, or the 'tapped' r of British 'very', l is like its counterparts in 'lily', and has a corresponding retroflex sound ḷ, with aspirate ḷh.

Pāli consonants may occur in clusters, such as nd, ñj, ṃg, tv, etc., and they also occur doubled, as in appa 'little', maggo 'road, path, way' rajjaṃ 'kingdom', ettha 'here' akkhiṃ 'eye' etc. Note that these Pāli are true doubled consonants, and not like the doubling in English 'silly' which actually indicates the nature of the preceding vowel, while the consonant is pronounced singly. English lacks true double consonants (except where prefixes are concerned, as in 'im-modest', 'un-natural' and 'il-logical', in some people's speech). As the examples show, the aspirate consonants in Pāli double as unaspirate+aspirate. Thus th and dh double as tth and ddh, etc.

We can now explain the arrows that we have included in the chart. The organization of the Pāli alphabet and its order, which accords with that of most South Asian alphabets and the Southeast Asian ones derived from them, is an ancient and scientific one, based on phonetic principles and going back at least to the early Sanskrit grammarians. It operates on several principles, such as vowels precede consonants as a set, voiceless precedes voiced, non-aspirates precede aspirates, non-nasals in a given position precede nasals, and the overall order is front to back of the mouth (vowels and resonants are a special case that we need not deal with here). The arrows follow these principles, and by following them in order, the overall order of the alphabet is derived. Some students may find this of help in learning the alphabetical order, but in any case it is certainly not without interest in its own right from a cultural-historical point of view.

PART III: THE LANGUAGE AND TEXTS

The Pāli Language: A Bit of History:

Pāli is fundamentally a language of Buddhism, in that virtually all texts in it are Buddhist in nature. Foremost among these are the works of the Pāli canon, the *Tipitaka* or "Three Baskets" which, particularly in the lands of Theravāda Buddhism, are taken to be the authentic pronouncements of Gotama Buddha himself. Pāli is thus the canonical and liturgical language of Buddhists in countries such as Burma, Cambodia, Sri Lanka and Thailand (in so far as Theravāda Buddhism can be said to have a liturgy), and is thus that Theravāda Buddhism has sometimes been referred to as "Pāli Buddhism." It has also, of course been referred to as Hīnayāna ("Lesser Vehicle") in contradistinction to Mahāyāna ("Greater Vehicle") Buddhism, though that is an appellation not generally favored by its adherents.

The dates and place of origin of Pāli have been the subject of considerable scholarly debate through the years, and the position that one takes on the issue may naturally be colored by one's belief as to the authenticity of the canonical texts as the words of the Buddha as originally spoken. By tradition, particularly in Sri Lanka, Pāli has been equated with Māgadhī, the Indic language spoken at the time of Gotama (Sanskrit *Gautama*) Buddha in Magadha, the northeastern Indian kingdom in which he primarily preached (though he himself came from a small kingdom in what is now Nepal). Māgadhī was an Indo-Aryan language. That is, it is a representative of the language family of which Vedic Sanskrit is the earliest extant example, and which includes Classical Sanskrit and the major later North Indian languages such as Hindi, Bengali Panjabi, Gujarati and Marathi, (along with Sinhala in Sri Lanka). Since the Indo Aryan languages form a subfamily of the Indo-European family, Pāli is ultimately related to English, and in fact to most of the major European languages, as well as, more closely, to the Iranian languages such as Avestan, Old Persian, and modern Farsi (the chief language of Iran).

Indo-Aryan Languages of the Buddha's time and for some centuries thereafter are commonly referred to as Prakrits (Sanskrit *Prākṛta*), and Pāli is thus an early Prakrit. Despite the traditional identification of Pāli as a Māgadhī Prakrit, some scholars have pointed out that it does not share many of the distinctive characteristics that we find in Magadhan inscriptions, primarily from the time of the Emperor Asoka (Sanskrit *Aśoka*) in the third century B.C., and that it does in fact show some features of the dialects of other regions. Thus it does appear to have, at the very least, incorporated some features of other languages in the course of its transmission of the texts from the time of Gotama Buddha. That date, traditionally placed in the seventh and sixth centuries B.C., has also been a matter of some dispute, but our purpose here is to present the language itself and the texts, and not to contribute to the scholarly work on those issues. Thus, as regards Pāli and its home within India, we may quote the great Pāli Scholar Wilhelm Geiger as representative of one scholar's cautious view of the tradition as balanced by observations of linguistic scholars, while reminding the reader that others have disagreed with the view expressed:

I consider it wise not to hastily reject the tradition altogether but rather to understand it to mean that Pāli was indeed no pure Māgadhī, but was yet a form of the popular speech which was based on Māgadhī and which was used by the Buddha himself.

(*Pāli Literature and Language*, pp. 5-6)

A similar measured view has been expressed by the well-respected modern Buddhist scholar, Reverend Walpola Rahula:

> It is reasonable to assume that the Buddha must have spoken one or more of the dialects current in the 6th century B.C., in Magadha. In a way, any one or all of them may legitimately have been called Māgadhī. Although we know nothing definite about those dialects today, we may reasonably guess that they could not have been basically very different from one another. But whether the dialect the Buddha usually spoke was exactly the same as the language of the Tipiṭaka as we have it today is another matter.
>
> What we call Pāli today is not a homogeneous but a composite language, containing several dialectal forms and expressions. It is probably based on the Māgadhi which the Buddha generally spoke, and out of it a new artificial, literary language later evolved.
>
> "Pali as a Language for Transmitting an Authentic Religious Tradition"*

Those who wish to know more may consult the sources, including some of those mentioned following this introduction; suffice it to say here that for the devout Buddhist, the Pāli texts of the canon do indeed represent the actual words of Gotama Buddha himself, whenever they were delivered.

The Literature of Pāli:

Pāli texts fall into two major divisions: The canon and the non-canonical literature. The texts in this volume are taken for the most part from the canon, along with a few other works to be mentioned later. But what do we refer to as the canon? We can answer this by addressing two related questions: first, how were the texts transmitted; and, second, how are the works in the texts organized.

One thing is clear: The texts were transmitted orally for a number of centuries, Along the way, there were three main councils that contributed to their codification. The first took place at Rājagaha (Sanskrit *Rājagṛha*) shortly after the death of the Buddha, placed by Sri Lankan tradition as 543 B.C., though that too has been much disputed. At that council, the major divisions known as the *Vinaya* and *Sutta* (which we will characterize later) were settled, as recited by the disciple Ānanda. The Second council, at Vesālī (Sanskrit *Vaisālī*), was called about a hundred years later, largely because of dissension, particularly concerning the Vinaya. The third council, at Pāṭaliputta (Sanskrit *Pāṭaliputra)*, took place under the Emperor Asoka (Sanskrit *Aśoka*) (264-227 B.C.). Here the

* in Gatare Dhammapala, Richard Gombrich, and K.R. Norman eds. *Buddhist Studies in Honour of Hammalava Saddhatissa*, University of Sri Jayawardenepura and Lake House Publishers, Sri Lanka, 1984

canon as we know it was essentially completed and formalized, and included a third division, the *Abhidhamma*. This council also "refuted wrong views", and it was there that the Theravāda school was founded and the decision taken to send missions abroad, including the mission of the monk Mahinda that brought the doctrine to Sri Lanka The generally accepted view is that the canon was reduced to writing only in the first century B.C. (At the Aluvihāra in Sri Lanka). In fact, its oral transmission helps to account for some of the characteristics of the texts, particularly the degree of repetition found in them, making oral transmission easier (and a feature which, as stated earlier, we have attempted to put to good use as a teaching device here).

The most widely known traditional division of the texts that are considered to belong to the canon, as representative of the Buddha's actual teaching, is the *Tipiṭaka* ('Three Baskets) one. According to this classification, there are three main divisions or Pitakas, the *Sutta, Vinaya,* and *Abhidhamma,* which can be generally characterized as follows:

I. The *Sutta Piṭaka* contains the *Dhamma* (General teachings of the Buddha) proper, sometimes referred to as such. It contains five *Nikāyas,* or collections of *suttantas* (Dialogues of the Buddha) These are defined and arranged essentially by their form, as follows:

a. The *Dīgha Nikāya,* ("Long" Collection) contains the longest suttas (=Sanskrit *sūtra*)

b. The *Majjhima Nikāya*("Middle" Collection) contains suttas of middle length.

c. The *Saṃyutta Nikāya* ("Linked" or "Grouped" Collection) in which the suttas are arranged by topic. It is this collection that contains the Buddha's first sermon, the *Dhammacakkapavattanasutta,* with which we conclude the readings in this book.

d. The *Aṃguttara Nikāya* (or The "Gradual", or "by one limb more" Collection) in which the sections are arranged in ascending order according to numbers that figure in the texts themselves.

e. The *Khuddaka Nikāya* ("Short" or "Small" Collection). The exact contents of this collection varies somewhat between Sri Lanka, Burma, and Thailand, but it includes the *Dhammapada* and the *Jātaka* verses (Only the verses, not the stories to which they relate are canonical; the stories are considered commentarial). It also includes the hymns of the monks and nuns *(Theragāthā* and *Therīgāthā*) along with a number of other works, such as the *Suttanipāta* and some works that might be loosely categorized as "prayer books".

II. The *Vinaya Piṭaka* dealing with Monastic Discipline.

III. The *Abhidhamma Piṭaka.* Scholastic and partially metaphysical in nature, it contains much philosophical treatment of the Buddha's teachings. It is generally considered the most difficult of the texts, and a mastery of it is thus highly regarded by Buddhist scholars.

In addition to the above, there is the *Mahāparitta*, a text recited by monks at *paritta* (Sinhala *pirit*) ceremonies invoking the auspiciousness and protection of the Dhamma.

There is another traditional classification of the canon is into five divisions, *(Nikāyas)*. These are the five divisions of the Sutta Piṭaka of the Tipiṭaka, with the Abhidhamma and the Vinaya folded into the Khuddaka Nikāya.

In addition to the canonical texts, there is a considerable body of non-canonical literature in Pāli, continuing up to the present time. A large part of it would fall under the heads of commentarial literature or chronicles. The remainder includes various types of works, including narrative and instructional works and some grammars. In addition, there are a number of inscriptions, most of them in Southeast Asia.

There is a large body of commentarial literature in Pāli, continuing over many centuries. The most famous commentaries, or *aṭṭhakathās*, were written by a monk named Buddhaghosa, who lived in the 5th century A.D. He was born in South India, but went to Sri Lanka, where he wrote his commentaries, apparently basing much of his work on earlier Sinhala commentaries subsequently lost. He was also the author of the famous *Visuddhimagga* 'Path of Purification', a compendium of Buddhist doctrine. The well-known Jātaka stories are actually commentarial literature as well; that is, they form the commentaries on the Jātaka verses that are included in the canon. and this *Jātakaṭṭhakatā* has also been attributed to Buddhaghosa. In addition to the commentaries, there are other forms of commentarial literature, including *ṭikās*, subcommentaries on the commentaries.

The Chronicles include the *Dīpavaṃsa* (4th or early 5th Century A.D.) and the *Mahāvaṃsa* (probably the early 6th Century), and present the history of Sri Lanka from a Buddhist-Monastic perspective. These chronicles were continued by the *Cūlavaṃsa* which continued until the arrival of the British in Sri Lanka. In fact, they are being continued even today.

Among the remaining works, there are two of particular interest here, since we have drawn some readings from them. One of them, the *Milindapañhā* (sometimes in the singular *Milindapañho*) 'Questions of King Milinda' dates from before Buddhaghosa's commentaries. It may have been translated from Sanskrit, and was also translated into Chinese. It consists of a series of dialogues between two people. One is King Milinda (Greek Menander), a second century king of the Graeco-Bactrian kingdom remaining from Alexander the Great's incursions into what is now Afghanistan and the northwest Indian subcontinent. The other participant is Nāgasena, a learned monk, who expounds Buddhist doctrine in answer to the King's questions. The penetrating nature of the King's questions and the clarity and wit of Nāgasena's answers and explanations, make this a lively as well as instructive introduction to Buddhist doctrine, and one that is accessible to the student at a fairly early stage.

The other text on which we have drawn is *Rasavāhinī*, compiled in Sri Lanka, probably in the 14th Century. It is a compilation of 103 legends and stories which, though purportedly instructional in nature, are couched in a flowing, lively style.

PART IV: SOME USEFUL SOURCES

The following is a brief list, with some annotations, of works that the student might find it useful to consult in looking for further information on grammatical or lexical points in this text, or in approaching further reading.

Buddhadatta, Mahathera A.P. *Concise Pali-English Dictionary.* Colombo Apothecaries, 1957. (Reprinted Motilal Banarsidass, Delhi 1989). A very handy concise dictionary. Although it lacks the full scholarly apparatus, such as the listing of variants, etc. of the fuller dictionaries below, it is handy to use, and the definitions, though brief, capture well the essence of the terms.

There is also an *English-Pali Dictionary* by the same reverend author. (Pali Text Society 1955, reprinted Motilal Banarsidass, Delhi 1989).

Geiger, Wilhelm. *Pāli Literature and Language.* Originally published by the University of Calcutta 1943, but reprinted by Oriental Books and Munshiram Manoharlal, New Delhi. A translation by Batakrishna Ghosh of the author's work in German. A basic scholarly source on the language, it is technical and concentrates on historical phonology and morphology. It includes an extensive index of forms that makes it very useful for finding variants. It also contains a brief survey of the literature.

Hazra, Kanai Lal. *Pāli Language and Literature: A Systematic Survey and Historical Study. Vol 1: Language: History and Structure, Literature: Canonical Pāli Texts; Vol 2: Literature: Non-Canonical Pāli Texts.* D.K. Printworld (P), New Delhi 1994. A recently appearing detailed and extensive survey. It includes an account of the history of the language and its structure, primarily from a historical perspective, but it is especially useful as a reference for the entire range of Pāli textual material, both canonical and non-canonical,

Müller, Eduard. *A Simplified Grammar of the Pali Language.* Bharatiya Vidya Prakashan, Varanasi, India. A shorter and simpler grammar than Geiger's, but also gives many variants, along with paradigms of basic forms. Like Buddhadatta's Dictionary, its concise nature makes it a good source for the "first look up" of some unfamiliar form. (Reprinted)

Nyanatiloka. *Buddhist Dictionary, Manual of Buddhist Terms and Doctrines.* Third revised and elarged edition edited by Nyanaponika. Colombo: Frewin, 1972 (first published 1952). A very useful compendium of the Buddhist terminology, including both terms and their relationships.

Rahula, Walpola Sri. *What the Buddha Taught* (revised edition). Grove Press, New York 1974 (first published 1959) A clear and well-written introduction to Buddhist doctrines. Includes a glossary of terms.

Rhys Davids, T.W. and W. Stede. *Pali-English Dictionary*. Pali Text Society, 1921-25, (reprinted Munshiram Manoharlal, New Delhi 1975). Generally referred to as the "PTS Dictionary". Much fuller than Buddhadatta's with many variants and etymological information. It also makes more distinctions concerning the technical nature of terms. The fullest available dictionary (except for those completed parts of the CPD of Trenckner et al)

Trenckner, Andersen, Smith et al. *A Critical Pāli Dictionary* (The CPD). Copenhagen 1924-. A full-scale dictionary, and a major scholarly work, but still incomplete. In fact, only the very first part of the alphabet has appeared, so that it is of limited use to the student, despite the value of the completed parts to the scholar.

Warder, A. *Introduction to Pali*. Pali Text Society, 1963. An introductory text differently organized than the present one. Less centered on reading and more on grammar, it contains a number of very useful grammar sections, and its grammatical Index makes it useful as a reference source. It also includes a very useful chart of verb forms (pp. 375 ff.)

LESSON I

1. Buddhaṃ saraṇaṃ gacchāmi
dhammaṃ saraṇaṃ gacchāmi
saṃghaṃ saraṇaṃ gacchāmi

Dutiyaṃ pi buddhaṃ saraṇaṃ gacchāmi
dutiyaṃ pi dhammaṃ saraṇaṃ gacchāmi
dutiyaṃ pi saṃghaṃ saraṇaṃ gacchāmi

Tatiyaṃ pi buddhaṃ saraṇaṃ gacchāmi
tatiyaṃ pi dhammaṃ saraṇaṃ gacchāmi
tatiyaṃ pi saṃghaṃ saraṇaṃ gacchāmi

2. ...Cittaṃ, bhikkhave, adantaṃ mahato anatthāya saṃvattatîti.
...cittaṃ, bhikkhave, dantaṃ mahato atthāya saṃvattatîti.
...cittaṃ, bhikkhave, aguttaṃ mahato anatthāya saṃvattatîti.
...cittaṃ, bhikkhave, guttaṃ mahato atthāya saṃvattatîti.
...cittaṃ, bhikkhave, arakkhitaṃ mahato anatthāya saṃvattatîti.
...cittaṃ, bhikkhave, rakkhitaṃ mahato atthāya saṃvattatîti.
...cittaṃ, bhikkhave, asaṃvutaṃ mahato anatthāya saṃvattatîti.
...cittaṃ, bhikkhave, saṃvutaṃ mahato atthāya saṃvattatîti.

Nâhaṃ, bhikkhave, aññaṃ ekadhammaṃ pi samanupassāmi yaṃ evaṃ adantaṃ, aguttaṃ, arakkhitaṃ, asaṃvutaṃ, mahato anatthāya saṃvattatîti yathayidaṃ, bhikkhave, cittaṃ. cittaṃ, bhikkhave, adantaṃ, aguttaṃ, arakkhitaṃ asaṃvutaṃ mahato anatthāya saṃvattatîti.

(-A.N.)

3. ...Micchādiṭṭhikassa, bhikkhave, anuppannā c'eva akusalā dhammā uppajjanti, uppannā ca akusalā dhammā vepullāya saṃvattantîti.

Nâhaṃ, bhikkhave, aññaṃ ekadhammaṃ pi samanupassāmi yena anuppannā vā kusalā dhammā n'uppajjanti, uppannā vā kusalā dhammā parihāyanti yathayidaṃ, bhikkhave, micchādiṭṭhi.

Micchādiṭṭhikassa, bhikkhave, anuppannā c'eva kusalā dhammā n'uppajjanti, uppannā ca kusalā dhammā parihāyantîti.

Nâhaṃ, bhikkhave, aññaṃ ekadhammaṃ pi samanupassāmi yena anuppannā vā akusalā dhammā n'uppajjanti, uppannā vā akusalā dhammā parihāyanti yathayidaṃ, bhikkhave, sammādiṭṭhi.

Sammādiṭṭhikassa, bhikkhave, anuppannā c'eva akusalā dhammā n'uppajjanti, uppannā ca akusalā dhammā parihāyantîti.

(-A.N.)

4. (Bhikkhu...)[1]

...anuppannānaṃ pāpakānaṃ akusalānaṃ dhammānaṃ anuppādāya chandaṃ janeti; vāyamati; viriyaṃ ārabhati; cittaṃ paggaṇhāti; padahati;

....uppannānaṃ pāpakānaṃ akusalānaṃ dhammānaṃ pahānāya chandaṃ janeti; vāyamati; viriyaṃ ārabhati; cittaṃ paggaṇhāti; padahati...

....anuppannānaṃ kusalānaṃ dhammānaṃ uppādāya chandaṃ janeti; vāyamati; viriyaṃ ārabhati; cittaṃ paggaṇhāti; padahati...

.....Uppannānaṃ kusalānaṃ dhammānaṃ ṭhitiyā asammosāya bhiyyobhāvāya vepullāya bhāvanāya pāripūriyā chandaṃ janeti, vāyamati; viriyaṃ ārabhati; cittaṃ paggaṇhāti; padahati...

(-A.N.)

GLOSSARY [2]

akusala	bad, inefficient, sinful
agutta	unguarded
añña	other
attho	advantage, meaning, aim, purpose
adanta	untamed
anattho	disadvantage, pointlessness
anuppanna	not having come into being
anuppādo	not coming into existence, hence non-existing
arakkhita	unprotected, unwatched
asaṃvuta	unrestrained
asammoso	non-bewilderment, non-confusion
ahaṃ	I
ārabhati	begins
(viriyaṃ...)	takes effort, strives
uppanna	having come into being, hence existing
uppajjati	arises, is born, comes into existence
uppādo	arising, coming into existence
eka	one, single, only
eva	verily, indeed (emphatic particle-see this grammar 3)
evaṃ	thus
kusala	virtuous, good, efficient, skilled
gacchati	goes
gutta	guarded, protected
ca	and, also (see this grammar 3)
cittaṃ	mind
ceva	=ca + eva

[1] Take bhikkhu as subject of each of the following sentences in turn.
[2] For the alphabetical order in this and other glossaries, see the Introduction, Section II: Alphabet and Pronunciation..

chando	desire, resolution, will
janeti	generates, causes to be born
ṭhiti	persistence, continuity
tatiyaṃ	third time (accusative of tatiya, 'third', used adverbially)
-ti	a form of iti, the quotation marker (see this grammar 3.3)
danta	tamed
dutiyaṃ	second time (accusative of dutiya,
dhammo	doctrine, physical or mental element
na	not (see this grammar 6)
nâhaṃ	=na + ahaṃ
nuppajjati	=na + uppajjati
paggaṇhāti	uplifts, takes up, makes ready, holds out/up
padahati	exerts, strives, confronts
parihāyati	decreases, deteriorates
pahānaṃ	avoidance, destruction
pāpaka	sinful, evil, wicked
pāripūri	fulfillment, completion
pi	emphatic particle (see this grammar 3)
buddho	a Buddha, one who has reached enlightenment
bhāvanāya	Dative form of bhāvanā 'development'
bhikkhave	Oh, monks (vocative plural of bhikkhu)
bhikkhu	(Buddhist) monk
bhiyyobhāvo	increase, growth (from bhiyyo 'greater' + bhāvo 'state')
mahato	great, big (dative singular of mahanta, 'great, big')
micchādiṭṭhi	incorrect views
micchādiṭṭhiko	he who has incorrect views
yathayidaṃ	that is to say, namely, to wit (from yathā 'thus' +idaṃ 'this')
yaṃ	which, that (see this grammar 4)
yena	by which (Instrumental of ya/ yaṃ) (see this grammar 4)
rakkhita	protected, watched
vā	or (see this grammar 3)
vāyamati	strives, endeavors, struggles
viriyaṃ	effort, exertion, energy
vepullaṃ	fullness, abundance
saṃgho	community, association, esp. the community of Buddhist monks
saṃvattati	leads to, is conducive to (with dative of object)
saṃvuta	restrained, controlled

samanupassati	sees, perceives correctly
sammādiṭṭhiko	he who has right views
sammoso	bewilderment, confusion
saraṇaṃ	refuge, protection

GRAMMAR I

1. NOUNS

1.1 Pāli nouns occur in:

1.11. A Stem Form, which can be considered the base from which the other forms are derived.

1.12 Three Genders: Masculine, Feminine, and Neuter. Although there is some correlation between the gender of Pāli nouns and "natural" gender, i.e., nouns referring to masculine beings are commonly masculine and those referring to feminine beings commonly feminine, the correlation is far from absolute. In particular, nouns referring to groups and to inanimate things and to concepts are unpredictable with regard to gender. Thus senā 'army' is feminine, dhammo 'doctrine' is masculine, and ratti 'night' is feminine.

1.13. Two Numbers: Singular and Plural

1.14. Eight Cases: Nominative, Accusative, Instrumental, Genitive, Dative, Ablative, Locative, and Vocative.

1.141. The most common use of the nominative is as the subject of a sentence:

bhikkhu vāyamati 'A *bhikkhu* strives'

1.142. The accusative is generally used as the object of a verb:
bhikkhu *cittaṃ* paggaṇhāti 'A bhikkhu uplifts *the mind*.'

1.143. The vocative is used in calling or addressing:
bhikkhave! 'Oh, monks!

1.144. The other cases are commonly the equivalent of English prepositions. As a general guideline, we might note that the dative case often (but not always) translates as English 'to' or 'for', the Ablative as 'from', the locative as 'in', the genitive as 'of' (or the possessive 's), and the instrumental as 'with' (as in "with a hammer") or 'by' (as in "by that means"). However, these represent only some of the most general senses and uses of the cases, and others will appear as we proceed.

1.2. Four common types of nouns appear in this reading: Masculine -a stems, Neuter -a stems, and Feminine -i or ī stems:

NOTE: Nouns used as examples in paradigms in the grammars, like the ones that follow, will generally be cited according to their stem form. In the glossaries in this book, the gender of nouns will be given separately only for a few nouns with special characteristics. Instead, the gender of a noun will generally be indicated by the way in which it ends, and there will be a standard way of indicating each class. Usually, this will be the nominative singular unless otherwise noted. Thus, for example, nouns ending in

-o, -aṃ and -i in the glossaries will belong to the masculine -a stem, the neuter -a stem and the feminine -i stem classes respectively.

The student should also expect some fluctuation in the endings of specific nouns with regard to gender, since nouns often shifted from one class to another in the history of Pāli. For example, some nouns given as masculine here may appear with neuter endings in some texts,so that dhammo, given here in the masculine form in which it usually occurs with the plural dhammā , may appear in some texts with the neuter plural ending: dhammāni. Even where there is no change in gender, there may be alternate endings that appear in different periods and texts.

In the paradigm below, and in others that follow, forms separated by / are alternants. Forms in parentheses ( ) are alternate forms which are less common, or generally found in later or commentarial texts rather than in canonical texts. Although we do give alternate endings when forms are introduced, and have attempted to give all of those that the student is likely to encounter, we have not striven for utter completeness so as to give all of the alternants for each class of nouns that occurred during the history of the language. One who has passed beyond this introductory text, and is reading Pāli texts on his/her own may thus need to consult one of the more complete grammars available as the need arises. The same applies to the alternate forms of verbs.

1.21. Masculine -a Stems. These have a stem in -a.

EXAMPLE: dhamma 'doctrine, quality (and many other senses)'

	Singular	Plural
Nom(inative):	dhammo	dhammā
Acc(usative):	dhammaṃ	dhamme
Gen(itive):	dhammassa	dhammānaṃ
Dat(ive):	dhammāya/-assa	
Inst(rumental):	dhammena	dhammehi(-ebhi)
Abl(ative):	dhammā(-asmā,-amhā)	
Loc(ative):	dhamme(-asmiṃ,-amhi)	dhammesu
Voc(ative):	dhamma (-ā)	dhammā

1.22. Neuter -a Stems. These also have a stem in -a. In glossaries, they will end in the Nominative Singular -aṃ Note that neuter nouns of this class differ from the masculine ones above only in a few forms. The nominative and the accusative are the same for all neuter nouns.

EXAMPLE: rūpa 'form, image'

	Singular	Plural
Nom:	rūpaṃ	rūpāni
Acc:		
Gen:	rūpassa	rūpānaṃ
Dat:	rūpāya / -assa	
Inst:	rūpena	rūpehi (-ebhi)
Abl:	rūpā (-asmā,-amhā)	
Loc:	rūpe (-asmiṃ,-amhi)	rūpesu
Voc:	rūpa (-aṃ)	rūpāni

1.23. Feminine -i and ī Stems: These actually represent two classes, but they are almost the same.

1.231 -i stems have a stem and nominative singular in -i.

EXAMPLE: ratti 'night'

ratti 'night' (feminine -i stem noun:)

<table>
<tr><th></th><th>Singular</th><th>Plural</th></tr>
<tr><td>Nom:</td><td>ratti</td><td rowspan="2">rattiyo / -ī</td></tr>
<tr><td>Acc:</td><td>rattiṃ</td></tr>
<tr><td>Gen:</td><td rowspan="5">rattiyā
(rattiyaṃ)</td><td rowspan="2">rattīnaṃ</td></tr>
<tr><td>Dat:</td></tr>
<tr><td>Inst:</td><td rowspan="2">rattīhi/-ībhi</td></tr>
<tr><td>Abl:</td></tr>
<tr><td>Loc:</td><td>rattīsu</td></tr>
<tr><td>Voc:</td><td>ratti</td><td>rattiyo / -ī</td></tr>
</table>

1.232 -ī stems are the same as the -i stems except for the nominative singular, which has -ī :

EXAMPLE: nadī 'river'

<table>
<tr><th></th><th>Singular</th><th>Plural</th></tr>
<tr><td>Nom:</td><td>nadī</td><td rowspan="2">nadiyo / -ī</td></tr>
<tr><td>Acc:</td><td>nadiṃ</td></tr>
<tr><td>Gen:</td><td rowspan="5">nadiyā
(nadiyaṃ)</td><td rowspan="2">nadīnaṃ</td></tr>
<tr><td>Dat:</td></tr>
<tr><td>Inst:</td><td rowspan="2">nadīhi/-ībhi</td></tr>
<tr><td>Abl:</td></tr>
<tr><td>Loc:</td><td>nadīsu</td></tr>
<tr><td>Voc:</td><td>nadi</td><td>nadiyo / -ī</td></tr>
</table>

2. VERBS

Verb forms will be introduced gradually here, as they appear in readings.

2.1. Root and Present Stem: Among the forms of a verb are a root and a present stem. The root is the form generally considered to be the form that underlies all other forms, and from which they are derived. However, the degree of formal resemblance between those forms and the root may range from close to quite distant:

Thus:	Root	Present Stem
	pat 'fall"	pata-
	jiv 'live'	jīva-
But:	nī 'lead'	naya-
	gaṃ 'go'	gaccha-
	ṭhā 'be, stand'	tiṭṭha-

More will be said concerning these relationships later.

2.2 The Present Tense: The present tense is formed by adding the following endings to the present tense stem:

	Singular	Plural
First Person ("I, we")	-:mi (-ṃ)	-:ma
Second Person ("you")	-si	-tha
Third Person ("he,she, they")	-ti	-nti

NOTE: Verbs will be entered in the glossaries under the third person singular form; hence labhati, nayati, etc.

Here and throughout, a colon (:) beginning an ending means that the last vowel of the form to which the ending is added is lengthened. Thus -a-becomes -ā-, etc.

Thus, for the verb labh- 'obtain, receive', present stem labha-:

	Singular	Plural
1 Pers:	labhāmi	labhāma
2 Pers:	labhasi	labhatha
3 Pers:	labhati	labhanti

labh- is of a type referred to as an "-a stem" verb, since its present tense stem ends in that vowel. We will meet other types later.

3. POSTPOSED PARTICLES (CLITICS)

3.1. Pāli has many particles that occur following a word and often attached to it. The technical term for these is "clitic". Five such clitics occur in this lesson:

pi	'again, also' (often with emphasis)
(i)ti	'quotation marker'
eva	'very, certainly'
ca	'and'
vā	'or'

3.2. ca generally, and vā commonly, are repeated with each element conjoined:

bhāsati *vā* karoti *vā* '(whether) says or does'

saccañ*ca* dhammañ*ca* 'doctrine and truth'
(ṃ+c --> ñc, see 5.3 below)

brāhmaṇassa *ca* putto gahapatikassa *ca*
'a brahman's son and a householder's'

Note that, as the last example demonstrates, these forms generally occur after the first word in a constituent that they conjoin.

3.3. The quotation marker (i)ti follows something said or thought. While it may occur following the object of verbs of saying, thinking, or sometimes, perceiving, it may also serve by itself to indicate that what precedes has been said, as in the examples in this reading, where the Buddha is being quoted.

When (i)ti follows a word ending in a vowel, that vowel is lengthened, and the (i) of (i)ti is lost (see 5.2 below)

4. RELATIVE PRONOUN

4.1. The relative pronoun has the stem ya-. The case forms of the masculine and neuter relevant to this lesson are as follows (other forms will be given later):

	Masculine	Neuter
Nominative.	yo	yaṃ
Instrumental.	yena	yena

4.2. The relative pronoun may be used like the English relatives (i.e., "who, that, "etc.) to introduce a relative clause modifying a noun that it follows (but not necessarily immediately), as in the examples in this reading:

aññaṃ ekadhammaṃ...yaṃ evaṃ... saṃvattatīti
another single thing that thus leads (to)...

aññaṃ ekadhammaṃ...yena... dhammā upajjanti
another single thing by which doctrines (or elements) are born.

Note that the relative pronoun generally takes the case proper to its function in its own clause as in the examples above.

More commonly, however, Pāli relative clauses are formed by a somewhat different correlative construction using a relative pronoun. These will be described in a later lesson.

5. SANDHI

When two words or parts of words come together, one or both may change in shape at the juncture. The technical term for this is "sandhi." Within a word, it is internal sandhi, between words external sandhi.

In Pāli, external sandhi is not thoroughgoing, (unlike Sanskrit), but generally affects only closely connected forms, often specific frequently used combinations. Three sandhi effects are relevant to this lesson:

5.1. When two vowels come together, the first may be lost. In this text, the loss will be marked with an apostrophe:

ca + eva---> c'eva
na + atthi---> n'atthi

5.2 When two similar vowels come together, the result may be a long vowel rather than the loss of the first. Similarly, when the quotation marker (i)ti is added, a preceding vowel lengthens, and the i in parentheses is lost. Such vowel lengthenings resulting from sandhi will be marked in this text by ^ rather than ¯. This represents no pronunciation difference; they are read the same, but it will make them easier to identify, and help in looking up forms. (When the student progresses to texts as usually printed, this aid will not be available, but hopefully s/he will be by then accustomed to the types of sandhi found.)

na + ahaṃ ---> nâhaṃ
saṃvattati + (i)ti ---> saṃvattatîti

5.3. When a nasal precedes another consonant, it may assimilate to it and become the nasal produced in that position (See the Introduction, Section II: Alphabet and Pronunciation.):

saccaṃ + ca ---> saccañca

6. NEGATIVES

6.1. na may negate sentences. If the following word begins with a vowel, the a of na is commonly dropped, though it may lengthen if that vowel is a-":

na + atthi ---> n'atthi 'is not'

but:

na + ahaṃ ---> nâhaṃ 'not I"

Note that even though na negates an entire sentence, it does not necessarily occur near the verb, unlike English "not":

nâhaṃ............samanupassāmi 'I do not perceive.'

6.2. a- negates words (like English un- or in-). Before a vowel, it occurs as an-.

a + sukho 'happiness' ---> asukho 'unhappiness'
an + attho 'meaning, objective ---> anattho 'pointlessness,

NOTE: In this book negatives in a- or an- are henceforth not listed separately in the lesson glossaries, unless their meaning is not directly derivable from their parts. Thus, a student encountering asukho in a reading and not finding it in the glossary, should look under sukho.

7. AGREEMENT OF ADJECTIVES

Adjectives agree in gender, case, and number with the nouns that they modify:

kusalo dhammo 'good doctrine' (masculine nominative singular)
akusalā dhammā 'bad factors' (or 'doctrines')
(masculine nominative plural).
cittaṃ *adantaṃ* 'subdued mind' (neuter nominative/sccusative singular)

Note that although adjectives often precede the noun that they modify, the opposite order is possible, as in the last example above. In that case, the adjective is often derived from a verb, and there may be a special sense like that in English "a/the mind which is subdued" or a/the mind when (it is) subdued".

The agreeing endings for adjectives will be given later. For the present, we simply note the agreement.

8. ACCUSATIVE OF DESTINATION

With a verb of motion, the destination is regularly in the accusative:

buddhaṃ saraṇaṃ gacchāmi 'I go to the Buddha-refuge.

9. CONJOINING IN SERIES

Items in a sentence, or even whole sentences, may be conjoined simply by giving them in sequence, without ca or any other equivalent of English "and":

kusalānaṃ dhammānaṃ ṭhitiyā asammosāya
bhiyyobhāvaya vepullāya
'for the persistence, non-confusion, increase,
(and) fulfilment of good elements (or 'doctrines')'

chandaṃ janeti; vāyamati; viriyaṃ ārabhati.
'generates resolution, strives, (and) takes effort.'

10. COMPOUNDS

In Pāli, as in English, compounds may be formed by joining two nouns:

itthi 'woman' + saddo 'sound'---> itthisaddo 'the sound of a woman'
puriso 'man'+ rūpaṃ (physical) form'---> purisarūpaṃ 'the form of a man'

Note that the first member of a compound is regularly in the stem form. For masculine and neuter nouns, this will usually be the same as the vocative singular.

NOTE: In this text, compounds will be given as such only if their meaning is not directly deducible from their parts and the context in which they occur. Thus itthisaddaṃ and itthirūpaṃ are given, since they also have the special senses 'the word "woman"' and 'the beauty (i.e., 'good form') of a woman', but itthigandho is not. Thus the student must learn to recognize compounds by looking up their parts. This is an important skill, since compounding is very frequent in Pāli and in some kinds of texts very long and complex compounds are found.

FURTHER READINGS I

1. Nâhaṃ,bhikkhave, aññaṃ ekadhammaṃ pi samanupassāmi yo evam saddhammassa sammosāya antaradhānāya saṃvattati yathayidaṃ, bhikkave, pamādo. pamādo, bhikkhave, saddhammassa sammosāya antaradhānāya saṃvattatîti.

Nâhaṃ, bhikkhave, aññaṃ ekadhammaṃ pi samanupassāmi yo evaṃ saddhammassa ṭhitiyā asammosāya anantaradhānāya saṃvattati yathayidaṃ, bhikkhave, appamādo. appamādo, bhikkhave, saddhammassa ṭhitiyā asammosāya anantaradhānāya saṃvattatîti.

Nâhaṃ, bhikkhave, aññaṃ ekadhammaṃ pi samanupassāmi yo evaṃ saddhammassa sammosāya antaradhānāya saṃvattati yathayidaṃ, bhikkhave, kosajjaṃ. kosajjaṃ, bhikkhave, saddhammassa sammosāya antaradhānāya saṃvattatîti.

Nâhaṃ, bhikkhave, aññaṃ ekadhammaṃ pi samanupassāmi yo evaṃ saddhammassa ṭhitiyā asammosāya anantaradhānāya saṃvattati yathayidaṃ, bhikkhave, viriyārambho. viriyārambho, bhikkhave, saddhammassa ṭhitiyā asammosāya anantaradhānāya samvattatîti.

Nâhaṃ, bhikkhave, aññaṃ ekadhammaṃ pi samanupassāmi yo evaṃ saddhammassa ṭhitiyā asammosāya anantaradhānāya saṃvattati yathayidaṃ, bhikkhave, anuyogo kusalānaṃ dhammānaṃ,[3] ananuyogo akusalānaṃ dhammānaṃ. anuyogo, bhikkhave, kusalānaṃ dhammānaṃ, saddhammassa ṭhitiyā asammosāya anantaradhānāya samvattatîti.

(A.N.)

2. Nâhaṃ, bhikkhave, aññaṃ ekarūpaṃ pi samanupassāmi yaṃ evaṃ purisassa cittaṃ pariyādāya[4] tiṭṭhati yathayidaṃ, bhikkhave, itthirūpaṃ.

Itthirūpaṃ, bhikkhave, purisassa cittaṃ pariyādāya tiṭṭhatîti.

---

3 Genitive Plural: here it has the sense 'in, with reference to'

4 Read pariyādāya tiṭṭhati as 'having overcome, remains' or 'overcomes and remains.' Forms lik pariyādāya will be discussed in a later lesson.

Nâhaṃ, bhikkhave, aññaṃ ekasaddaṃ pi samanupassāmi yaṃ[5] evaṃ purisassa cittaṃ pariyādāya tiṭṭhati yathayidaṃ, bhikkhave, itthisaddo.
Itthisaddo, bhikkhave, purisassa cittaṃ pariyādāya tiṭṭhatîti.

Nâhaṃ, bhikkhave, aññaṃ ekagandhaṃ pi samanupassāmi yaṃ evaṃ purisassa cittaṃ pariyādāya tiṭṭhati yathayidaṃ, bhikkhave, itthigandho.
Itthigandho, bhikkhave, purisassa cittaṃ pariyādāya tiṭṭhatîti.

Nâhaṃ, bhikkhave, aññaṃ ekarasaṃ pi samanupassāmi yaṃ evaṃ purisassa cittaṃ pariyādāya tiṭṭhati yathayidaṃ, bhikkave, itthiraso.
Itthiraso, bhikkhave, purisassa cittaṃ pariyādāya tiṭṭhatîti.

Nâhaṃ, bhikkhave, aññaṃ ekaphoṭṭhabbaṃ pi samanupassāmi yaṃ evaṃ purisassa cittaṃ pariyādāya tiṭṭhati yathayidaṃ, bhikkhave, itthiphoṭṭhabbaṃ.
Itthiphoṭṭhabbaṃ, bhikkhave, purisassa cittaṃ pariyādāya tiṭṭhatîti

Nâhaṃ, bhikkhave, aññaṃ ekarūpaṃ pi samanupassāmi yaṃ evaṃ itthiyā cittaṃ pariyādāya tiṭṭhati yathayidaṃ, bhikkhave, purisarūpaṃ.
Purisarūpaṃ, bhikkhave, itthiyā cittaṃ pariyādāya tiṭṭhatîti.

Nâhaṃ, bhikkhave, aññaṃ ekasaddaṃ pi samanupassāmi yaṃ evaṃ itthiyā cittaṃ pariyādāya tiṭṭhati yathayidaṃ, bhikkhave, purisasaddo.
Purisasaddo, bhikkhave, itthiyā cittaṃ pariyādāya tiṭṭhatîti.

Nâhaṃ, bhikkhave, aññaṃ ekagandhaṃ pi samanupassāmi yaṃ evaṃ itthiyā cittaṃ pariyādāya tiṭṭhati yathayidaṃ, bhikkhave, purisagandho.
Purisagandho, bhikkhave, itthiyā cittaṃ pariyādāya tiṭṭhatîti.

Nâhaṃ, bhikkhave, aññaṃ ekarasaṃ pi samanupassāmi yaṃ evaṃ itthiyā cittaṃ pariyādāya tiṭṭhati yathayidaṃ, bhikkhave, purisaraso.
Purisaraso, bhikkhave, itthiyā cittaṃ pariyādāya tiṭṭhatîti.

Nâhaṃ, bhikkhave, aññaṃ ekaphoṭṭhabbaṃ pi samanupassāmi yaṃ evaṃ itthiyā cittaṃ pariyādāya tiṭṭhati yathayidaṃ, bhikkhave, purisaphoṭṭhabbaṃ.
Purisaphoṭṭhabbaṃ, bhikkhave, itthiyā cittaṃ pariyādāya tiṭṭhatîti.

(A.N.)

GLOSSARY

anuyogo	application, practice, employment
antaradhānaṃ	disappearance

---

[5] Note that though the relative pronoun generally takes the case proper to its function in its own clause, as stated in this Grammar 4.2, it is sometimes "attracted" to the case of the noun to which it refers in the main clause. Thus here yaṃ is accusative, agreeing with the accusative (masculine) noun -saddaṃ although it is subject of its own clause, and therefore should be nominative.

appamādo	diligence, earnestness
itthi	woman
itthirūpaṃ	woman as an object of visual perception, female beauty
itthisaddo	the sound of a woman, the word "woman"
kosajjaṃ	idleness, indolence,
gandho	odor, scent, smell
tiṭṭhati	stands, exists, is; remains
pamādo	indolence, sloth
pariyādāya	having overpowered, taking up
puriso	man, male
phoṭṭhabbaṃ	touch, contact
raso	taste, savor
rūpaṃ	form, object of visual perception
viriyârambho	taking effort
saddo	sound, word
saddhammo	true doctrine

LESSON II

1. Kiccho manussapaṭilābho
kiccham maccānaṃ jīvitaṃ
kicchaṃ saddhammasavaṇaṃ
kiccho buddhānaṃ uppādo.

Sabbapāpassa akaraṇaṃ
kusalassa upasampadā
sacittapariyodapanaṃ
etaṃ buddhāna(ṃ) sāsanaṃ.

Na hi verena verāni
sammantîdha kudācanaṃ.
averena ca sammanti.
esa dhammo sanantano.

(Dhp.)

2. Tīhi, bhikkhave, aṃgehi samannāgato pāpaṇiko abhabbo[1] anadhigataṃ vā bhogaṃ adhigantuṃ, adhigataṃ vā bhogaṃ phātiṃ kātuṃ. katamehi tīhi? Idha, bhikkhave, pāpaṇiko pubbaṇhasamayaṃ na sakkaccaṃ kammantaṃ adhiṭṭhāti, majjhaṇhikasamayaṃ na sakkaccaṃ kammantaṃ adhiṭṭhāti, sāyaṇhasamayaṃ na sakkaccaṃ kammantaṃ adhiṭṭhāti. Imehi kho, bhikkhave, tīhi aṃgehi samannāgato pāpaṇiko abhabbo anadhigataṃ vā bhogaṃ adhigantuṃ, adhigataṃ vā bhogaṃ phātiṃ kātuṃ.

Evameva kho, bhikkhave, tīhi dhammehi samannāgato bhikkhu abhabbo anadhigataṃ vā kusalaṃ dhammaṃ adhigantuṃ, adhigataṃ vā kusalaṃ dhammaṃ phātiṃ kātuṃ. katamehi tīhi? Idha, bhikkhave, bhikkhu pubbaṇhasamayaṃ na sakkaccaṃ samādhinimittaṃ adhiṭṭhāti, majjhaṇhikasamayaṃ na sakkaccaṃ samādhinimittaṃ adhiṭṭhāti, sāyaṇhasamayaṃ na sakkaccaṃ samādhinimittaṃ adhiṭṭhāti. Imehi kho, bhikkhave, tīhi dhammehi samannāgato bhikkhu abhabbo anadhigataṃ vā kusalaṃ dhammaṃ adhigantuṃ, adhigataṃ vā kusalaṃ dhammaṃ phātiṃ kātuṃ.

Tīhi, bhikkhave, aṃgehi samannāgato pāpaṇiko bhabbo anadhigataṃ vā bhogaṃ adhigantuṃ, adhigataṃ vā bhogaṃ phātiṃ kātuṃ. katamehi tīhi? Idha, bhikkhave, pāpaṇiko pubbaṇhasamayaṃ sakkaccaṃ kammantaṃ adhiṭṭhāti, majjhaṇhikasamayaṃ... pe... sāyaṇhasamayaṃ sakkaccaṃ kammantaṃ adhiṭṭhāti. Imehi kho, bhikkhave, tīhi aṃgehi samannagāto pāpaṇiko bhabbo anadhigataṃ vā bhogaṃ adhigantuṃ, adhigataṃ vā bhogaṃ phātiṃ kātuṃ.

Evameva kho, bhikkhave, tīhi dhammehi samannāgato bhikkhu bhabbo anadhigataṃ vā kusalaṃ dhammaṃ adhigantuṃ, adhigataṃ vā kusalaṃ dhammaṃ

1 Read this as an equational sentence. See this grammar 5.

phātiṃ kātuṃ. katamehi tīhi? Idha, bhikkhave, bhikkhu pubbaṇhasamayaṃ sakkaccaṃ samādhinimittaṃ adhiṭṭhāti, majjhaṇhikasamayaṃ... pe ... sayāṇhasamayaṃ sakkaccaṃ samādhinimittaṃ adhiṭṭhāti. Imehi kho, bhikkhave, tīhi dhammehi samannāgato bhikkhu bhabbo anadhigataṃ vā kusalaṃ dhammaṃ adhigantuṃ, adhigataṃ vā kusalaṃ dhammaṃ phātiṃ kātuṃ'ti.

(-A.N.)

3.. . . Evameva kho, bhikkhave, appakā te sattā ye manussesu paccājāyanti; atha kho ete'va sattā bahutarā ye aññatra manussehi paccājāyanti. Evameva kho, bhikkhave, appakā te sattā ye majjhimesu janapadesu paccājāyanti; atha kho ete'va sattā bahutarā ye paccantimesu janapadesu paccājāyanti...

. . . Evameva kho, bhikkhave, appakā te sattā ye paññavanto, ajalā, aneḷamūgā, paṭibalā subhāsitadubbhāsitassa atthamaññātuṃ; atha kho ete'va sattā bahutarā ye duppaññā jaḷā eḷamūgā na paṭibalā subhāsitadubbhāsitassa atthamaññātuṃ.

. . . Evameva kho, bhikkhave, appakā te sattā ye ariyena paññācakkhunā samannāgatā; atha kho ete'va sattā bahutarā ye avijjāgatā sammūḷhā.

. . . Evameva kho, bhikkhave, appakā te sattā ye labhanti tathāgataṃ dassanāya; atha kho ete'va sattā bahutarā ye na labhanti tathāgataṃ dassanāya.

. . . Evameva kho, bhikkhave, appakā te sattā ye labhanti tathāgata-ppaveditaṃ dhammavinayaṃ savaṇāya; atha kho ete'va sattā bahutarā ye na labhanti tathāgatappaveditaṃ dhammavinayaṃ savaṇāya.

(-A.N.)

GLOSSARY

akaraṇaṃ	non-doing
aṃgaṃ	component, constituent part, limb, member
aññatra	outside
aññāti	comprehends, discriminates
atthamaññāti	= atthaṃ+aññāti
attho (-aṃ)	meaning, usage, use, welfare, gain, purpose
atha	now, then
atha kho	now, but, however
adhigacchati	finds, acquires, attains, comes into possession of
adhigata	obtained, acquired
adhigantuṃ	infinitive of adhigacchati (see this grammar 4)
adhiṭṭhāti	attends to
appaka	little, few
ariya	noble, distinguished
avijjāgata	ignorant
idha	here, in this world
imehi	by these: Instr-Abl Pl. of ayaṃ/ima

	(see this grammar 2)
upasampadā	acquisition, attainment, higher ordination of a monk
uppādo	arising, birth
etaṃ	this, this thing (see this grammar 2)
ete	these,those (ones) (see this grammar 2)
eva	verily, indeed
evameva	even so, thus, similarly, in like manner
esa	that (see this grammar 2)
eḷamūga	not receptive to that doctrine, stupid
katama	which, what (see this grammar 3)
kammantaṃ	business, activity
karoti	does
kātuṃ	infinitive of karoṭi (see this grammar 4)
kiccha	difficult, rare, painful
kudācanaṃ	any day, ever
kusalaṃ	virtue, good (action), merit
kho	emphatic particle
cakkhuṃ	eye
janapado	province, locality, the countryside
jaḷa	slow, stupid
jaḷo	a stupid person
jīvitaṃ	life
tathāgato	"Tathagata", a term of reference for a Buddha, literally, " The thus gone one"
tathāgatappavedita	expounded by the Tathāgata
tīhi	instrumental plural of ti, three
te	they (see this grammar 2)
dassanaṃ	sight, seeing, insight
duppañña	not wise, foolish, stupid
duppañño	foolish one, an ignorant person
dubbhāsita	ill-spoken
dhammavinayo	teachings of the Buddha: Dhamma and Vinaya
dhammo	factor, quality (see also Lesson I)
paccantima	bordering, adjoining (near), countryside
paccājāyati	is (re)born
paññavanto	wise ones, insightful persons (nominative plural of paññavant)
paññā	wisdom, knowledge, insight
paññācakkhuṃ	eye of wisdom; eye of insight
paṭibala	competent, capable

paṭilābho	attainment
manussa-	being born as a human, attaining human status
pariyodapanaṃ/-a	purification
pavedita	pointed out, expounded, declared, made known
pāpaṃ	sin, evil, bad deed, wrong action
pāpaṇiko	merchant, shopkeeper
pubbaṇhasamayaṃ	in the forenoon, in the morning
pe	signal of repetition (see this grammar 8)
phāti	increase, development
bahutara	many, more
bhabba	competent, able
bhogo	wealth, possession, item for enjoyment
macco	mortal, human being
majjhaṇhikasamayaṃ	during midday
majjhima	central, middle
maññati	thinks, deems, conceives
manusso	man, human being
ye	which ones (nominative plural masculine relative pronoun (see this grammar 2)
labhati	gets, receives; gets a chance to
veraṃ	enmity, ill-will
sa-	ones own (see this grammar 9)
sakkaccaṃ	properly, well, carefully, thoroughly
sacittaṃ	sa- plus cittaṃ (Compounding stem sacitta-)
satto	being, living being
sanantana	eternal, old, ancient
sabba	all, every
samannāgata	endowed with, possessed of (with instrumental)
samādhinimittaṃ	object of meditation, object of concentration
sammati	is pacified, ceases
sammūḷha	confused, confounded, stupid
savaṇaṃ	hearing, listening
sāyaṇhasamayaṃ	in the evening
sāsanaṃ	teaching, message, doctrine
subhāsita	well spoken
subhāsitadubbhāsitaṃ	things well and badly spoken, things proper to say and not proper to say
hi	indeed, verily (emphatic particle)

GRAMMAR II

1. NOUN FORMS

1.1. Feminine -ā stems will be entered in the glossaries in the nominative singular (which is also the stem) in -ā. (The Dative form bhāvanāya that occurred in Reading 1 was an example of this class).

EXAMPLE: sālā 'hall'

	Singular	Plural
Nom:	sālā	sālāyo (sālā)
Acc:	sālaṃ	
Gen:	sālāya	sālānaṃ
Dat:		
Inst:		sālāhi (-bhi)
Abl:		
Loc:	sālāyaṃ	sālāsu
Voc:	sāle	sālāyo (sālā)

Note the similarity of these endings to those of the -i and -ī stems (I, 1.23) [2]. Note, however, that the Singular Dative-Locative has -ya rather than yā, and that the vocative singular is -e. Note also the shortening of the final -a- of the stem in the Accusative singular.

1.2. Masculine -u Stems will be entered in the glossaries in the nominative singular (which is also the stem) in -u.

EXAMPLE: bhikkhu '(Buddhist) monk'

	Singular	Plural
Nom:	bhikkhu	bhikkhū / bhikkhavo
Acc:	bhikkhuṃ	
Gen:	bhikkhuno (-ussa)	bhikkhūnaṃ
Dat:		
Inst:	bhikkhunā (-usmā, umhā)	bhikkhūhi (-ūbhi)
Abl:		
Loc:	bhikkhumhi (-usmiṃ)	bhikkhūsu
Voc:	bhikkhu	bhikkhū / bhikkhave/-o

---

2 References to grammars of other readings will be made in this form. The Roman numeral will give the reading, and the Arabic numeral the appropriate section.

NOTE: The vocative plural in -ave is a characteristic of this particular stem, and is very frequent, as the readings have already shown. The usual vocative plural for nouns of this class will be -ū.

1.3. Neuter -u Stems will be entered in the glossaries in their alternate nominative singular in -uṃ.

EXAMPLE : cakkhu 'eye'

	Singular	Plural
Nom:	cakkhu / cakkhuṃ	cakkhū / cakkhūni
Acc:		
Gen:	cakkhuno (-ussa)	cakkhūnaṃ
Dat:		
Inst:	cakkhunā(-usmā, -umhā)	cakkhūhi (-ūbhi)
Abl:		
Loc:	cakkhumhi (-usmiṃ)	cakkhūsu
Voc:	cakkhu	cakkhū / cakkhūni

Note that these are the same as the masculine -u stems, except for the alternate nominative singular in -uṃ and the alternate plural ending -ūni.

2.PRONOUNS

2.1. Third Person Pronoun Forms:

2.11 sa/taṃ 'he, she, it' has the following gender forms in the Nominative Singular:

Masculine	so	'he'
Feminine	sā	'she'
Neuter	taṃ	'it'

The case and Number forms are as follows:

SINGULAR			
	Masculine	Neuter	Feminine
Nom:	so / sa	taṃ / tad	sā
Acc:	taṃ		taṃ
Gen:	tassa		tassā(-ya) tissā(-ya)
Dat:			
Inst:	tena		tāya
Abl:	tamhā (tasmā)		
Loc:	tamhi (tasmiṃ)		tāsaṃ/tāyaṃ/ tissaṃ/tassaṃ

PLURAL			
	Masculine	Neuter	Feminine
Nom:	te	tāni	tā / tāyo
Acc:			
Gen:	tesaṃ / tesānaṃ		tāsaṃ/tāsānaṃ
Dat:			
Inst:	tehi (tebhi)		tāhi (tābhi)
Abl:			
Loc:	tesu		tāsu

2.12. etaṃ 'this' has much the same sense as sa/taṃ, but is more definite. The forms are the same as for sa/taṃ, but with e- prefixed.

SINGULAR			
	Masculine	Neuter	Feminine
Nom:	eso/esa	etam / etad	esā
Acc:	etaṃ		etaṃ
etc.			

2.13. The relative pronoun ya/yaṃ has virtually the same forms as taṃ, except for the initial y-. Hence:

SINGULAR			
	Masculine	Neuter	Feminine
Nom:	yo	yaṃ / yad	yā
Acc:	yaṃ		yaṃ
Gen:	yassa		yassā(-ya)
Dat:			
Inst:	yena		yāya
Abl:	yamhā (yasmā)		
Loc:	yamhi (yasmiṃ)		yassaṃ/yāyaṃ

PLURAL			
	Masculine	Neuter	Feminine
Nom: Acc:	ye	yāni	yā / yāyo
Gen: Dat:	yesaṃ / yesānaṃ		yāsaṃ/yāsānaṃ
Inst: Abl:	yehi (yebhi)		yāhi (yābhi)
Loc:	yesu		yāsu

2.14. The instrumental-ablative form of the demonstrative pronoun ayaṃ/ima 'this' (imehi) occurs in this reading. ayaṃ/ima has nominative and accusative forms as follows. The remaining forms will be given later, but in general, they are much like those for the other pronouns and are thus easily recognizable.

SINGULAR			
	Masculine	Neuter	Feminine
Nom:	ayaṃ	imaṃ / idaṃ	ayaṃ
Acc:	imaṃ		imaṃ

PLURAL			
	Masculine	Neuter	Feminine
Nom: Acc:	ime	imāni	imā /imāyo

2.2. All of the pronouns given in 2.11-2.14 can be used either alone (i.e., as pronouns), or modifying following nouns (i.e., as demonstrative adjectives):

eso gacchati 'That one comes'
eso dhammo 'that doctrine'

3. THE INTERROGATIVE katama 'which, what' takes the same endings as the pronouns in 2 above. Thus (next page):

SINGULAR			
	Masculine	Neuter	Feminine
Nom:	katamo	katamaṃ	katamā
Acc:	katamaṃ		katamaṃ
etc.			

4. VERB FORMS: THE INFINITIVE IN -tuṃ

4.1. Form of the infinitive

4.11. For verbs with a present tense stem in -a, add -itum, replacing the final -a:

3rd Singular		Present Stem	Infinitive
bhavati	'be, become'	bhava-	bhavituṃ
gacchati	'go,come'	gaccha-	gacchituṃ [3]
labhati	'get'	labha-	labhituṃ [3]
passati	'see'	passa-	passituṃ [3] 4.12.

For verbs in -ā, -e, -o, add -tuṃ:

3rd Singular		Present Stem	Infinitive
aññāti	'comprehend'	aññā	aññātuṃ
deseti	'teach'	dese-	desetuṃ
neti	'lead'	ne-	netuṃ
yāti	'go'	yā	yātuṃ
hoti	'be'	ho-	hotuṃ

4.13. Irregular: Some irregular formations are:

karoti 'does'	kātuṃ
gacchati 'goes'	gantuṃ
jānāti 'knows'	ñātuṃ
tiṭṭhati 'is, remains',	ṭhātuṃ
dahati (or dhīyati) 'puts'	dahituṃ
deti (or dadāti) 'gives'	dātuṃ
passati 'sees'	daṭṭhuṃ
pāpuṇāti 'attains'	pāpuṇituṃ
pivati 'drinks'	pātuṃ
mīyati 'dies'	marituṃ
labhati 'gets, obtains'	laddhuṃ
vikkiṇāti 'sells'	vikkiṇituṃ
suṇoti (or suṇāti) 'hears, listens'	sotuṃ / suṇituṃ

NOTE: The stem of passati alternates with a stem dis- in other tenses and forms, as here.

---

[3] But see alternate form below.

4.2. Use of the infinitive: The infinitive has several uses, two of which are given here:

4.21. Dependent on a main verb as an expression of purpose:

Buddhaṃ daṭṭhuṃ gacchāmi
'I am going to see the Buddha.'

4.22. Dependent on an adjective like bhabba in the appropriate meaning, generally like that of an English infinitive ("to go", etc.) in similar usage:

pāpaṇiko abhabbo anadhigataṃ bhogaṃ adhigantuṃ.
'The merchant is incompetent to acquire wealth
(that he has) not (yet) acquired.'

4.23. Noṭe that the infinitive may take the same objects, etc. with which that verb can occur in an independent sentence, and that their cases remain the same. The subject, however, is almost always the same as that of the main verb, and if so, is unexpressed.

5. EQUATIONAL SENTENCES

Equational sentences are those in which a noun or adjective expression is predicated of the subject. i.e., English sentences like "Harry is a carpenter " or " This book is excellent". In English, these have a form of "to be", as copula, but in equational sentences in Pāli do not require a copula to be expressed with either a noun or adjective. Thus:

5.1 With Adjective as Predicate:

eso dhammo sanantano 'This doctrine is eternal.'
ayaṃ pāpaṇiko abhabbo (bhogaṃ adhigantuṃ)
This merchant is incompetent (to acquire wealth)'.
kicchaṃ jīvitaṃ 'life is difficult (to obtain)',
(or) 'difficult (indeed) is life.'

Note that the adjective agrees with the subject; in this case nominative singular, masculine for the first two examples, neuter in the last.
As with other kinds of sentences, the order of elements may be varied for emphasis. Thus the predicate may come first, as in the last example above, or in:

appakā te sattā 'few are those beings'
As the examples show, the agreement will be the same regardless of the order.

5.2 With Noun as Predicate:

etaṃ sāsanaṃ 'This is the teaching.'

6. THE CORRELATIVE CONSTRUCTION:

Relative clauses were discussed in I, 4. Most commonly, however, Pāli forms such expressions by using a correlative (sometimes called "co-relative") construction. This has the following characteristics: In this construction, the relative clause is introduced by a relative pronoun or other relative form, as in the construction met earlier. However, the relative clause is not placed within the main clause, but the two clauses are kept intact and placed in sequence. The relative clause still modifies a noun or pronoun in the main clause. This modified form is commonly placed at the beginning of its clause also, and if a noun, is generally modified by a demonstrative form, commonly one of the pronominal forms given in Section 2 above which links it to the relative. That is, it is as if in English, one said "Which book I read, that book is good" instead of "The book that I read is good."

Thus:

yaṃ jānāmi *taṃ* bhaṇāmi 'I say what I know.'

yo dhammo saddhammo *so dhammo* sanantano.
'That doctrine which is the true doctrine is eternal.'

The relative clause is usually first, as in these examples. However, the other order is possible, as in some sentences in this reading [4]

ete'va sattā bahutarā *ye* na labhanti tathāgataṃ dassanāya
'Many are those beings who do not get to see the Tathāgata.'

7. PREPOSITIONS AND POSTPOSITIONS

In addition to prepositions, which precede the noun (as in English "*outside* the garden") Pāli also has postpositions, which follow the noun but have the same function. Some forms can occur as either. One of these is aññatra . With a dependent noun in the Instrumental, it means 'outside', but with a dependent noun in the Locative it means 'among':

aññatra manussesu or manussesu aññatra
'among men (mankind)'

aññatra manussehi or manussehi aññatra
'outside men (mankind)'

8. THE DISCOURSE SUBSTITUTE pe(yyālaṃ)

The form peyyālaṃ, or its shortened form pe, is used to shorten a written text by substituting for a stretch of it that is identical with some part of the preceding section. When the text is read aloud, the section is replaced and read out in full.

---

[4] Note that such examples could be seen as instances of a relative clause placed at the end of a sentence, but the effect is the same.

9. THE REFLEXIVE PREFIX sa-

sa- prefixed to a noun adds the sense 'one's own' Thus sa+cittaṃ gives sacittaṃ 'one's own mind'.

10. THE ACCUSATIVE OF TIME:

The Accusative case of a word referring to some element of time makes it a time adverb. Thus pubbaṇsamayaṃ 'in the forenoon'.

11. COMPOUNDS:

11.1. Co-ordinate Compounds: Two or more Items may be co-ordinated in a compound so as to refer to their combination (In Pāli, these are technically referred to as dvanda compounds (Sanskrit dvandva). Co-ordinate compounds are generally inflected in the neuter singular. The first element(s), as usual, are in the stem form.

dhammmavinayaṃ 'the Dhamma and Vinaya'
subhāsitadubbhāsitaṃ 'Things well spoken and things badly spoken'

11.2. Compounds with -gata: When gata, the perfect participle form of gacchati 'go' is used as the last member of a compound, it may have the special senses 'having reached, being endowed with' or 'following'.:

avijjā 'ignorance' + gata ---> avijjāgata 'ignorant'

12. SANDHI

Some forms in Pāli that begin with a consonant double that consonant when a form ending with a vowel precedes it in a single word (i.e., with prefixes or in compounds). Thus

tathāgata +pavedita---> tathāgatappavedita
a+pamādo---> appamādo

Note that this doubling occurs only with certain words. Thus putto 'son' does not have this property:

sa+putto------->saputto

One must thus learn which words behave in this way as they occur.[5]

---

[5] Unless one knows the Sanskrit equivalents, which will begin with consonant clusters, as in pramāda, pravedita.

FURTHER READINGS II

1. Tīṇi'māni,[6] bhikkhave, nidānāni kammānaṃ samudayāya.

Katamāni tīṇi?

Lobho nidānaṃ kammānaṃ samudayāya, doso nidānaṃ kammānaṃ samudayāya, moho nidānaṃ kammānaṃ samudayāya.

Yaṃ, bhikkhave, lobhapakataṃ kammaṃ lobhajaṃ lobhanidānaṃ lobhasamudayaṃ[7], taṃ kammaṃ akusalaṃ, taṃ kammaṃ sāvajjaṃ, taṃ kammaṃ dukkhavipākaṃ, taṃ kammaṃ kammasamudayāya[8] saṃvattati; na taṃ kammaṃ kammanirodhāya saṃvattati.

Yaṃ, bhikkhave, dosapakataṃ kammaṃ dosajaṃ dosanidānaṃ dosasamudayaṃ, taṃ kammaṃ akusalaṃ, taṃ kammaṃ sāvajjaṃ, taṃ kammaṃ dukkhavipākaṃ, taṃ kammaṃ kammasamudayāya saṃvattati; na taṃ kammaṃ kammanirodhāya saṃvattati.

Yaṃ, bhikkhave, mohapakataṃ kammaṃ mohajaṃ mohanidānaṃ, mohasamudayaṃ, taṃ kammaṃ akusalaṃ, taṃ kammaṃ sāvajjaṃ, taṃ kammaṃ dukkhavipākaṃ, taṃ kammaṃ kammasamudayāya saṃvattati; na taṃ kammaṃ kammanirodhāya saṃvattati.

Imāni kho, bhikkhave, tīṇi nidānāni kammānaṃ samudayāya.

Tīṇi'mani, bhikkhave, nidānāni kammānaṃ samudayāya.

Katamāni tīṇi?

Alobho nidānaṃ kammānaṃ samudayāya, adoso nidānaṃ kammānaṃ samudayāya, amoho nidānaṃ kammānaṃ samudayāya.

Yaṃ, bhikkhave, alobhapakataṃ kammaṃ alobhajaṃ, alobhanidānaṃ, alobhasamudayaṃ, taṃ kammaṃ kusalaṃ, taṃ kammaṃ anavajjaṃ, taṃ kammaṃ sukhavipākaṃ,taṃ kammaṃ kammanirodhāya saṃvattati; na taṃ kammaṃ kammasamudayāya saṃvattati.

---

[6] tīṇi'māni = tīṇi imāni/ imāni tīṇi.

[7] As stated in I,7, adjectives may precede or follow the noun they modify. Where several adjectives modify the same noun, it is not uncommon for one to precede and the rest to follow.

[8] Here, kammaṃ implies 'further or subsequent action.

Yaṃ, bhikkhave, adosapakataṃ kammaṃ, adosajaṃ, adosanidānaṃ, adosasamudayaṃ, taṃ kammaṃ kusalaṃ, taṃ kammaṃ anavajjaṃ, taṃ kammaṃ sukhavipākaṃ, taṃ kammaṃ kammanirodhāya saṃvattati; na taṃ kammaṃ kammasamudayāya saṃvattati.

Yaṃ, bhikkhave, amohapakataṃ kammaṃ, amohajaṃ, amohanidānaṃ, amohasamudayaṃ, taṃ kammaṃ kusalaṃ, taṃ kammaṃ anavajjaṃ, taṃ kammaṃ sukhavipākaṃ, taṃ kammaṃ kammanirodhāya saṃvattati; na taṃ kammaṃ kammasamudayāya saṃvattati.

Imāni kho, bhikkhave, tīṇi nidānāni kammānaṃ samudayāyâti.

(-A.N.)

2 Pañcahi, bhikkhave, dhammehi samannāgato bhikkhu cavati, nappatiṭṭhāti saddhamme.

Katamehi pañcahi?

Assaddho, bhikkhave, bhikkhu cavati, nappatiṭṭhāti saddhamme.

Ahiriko, bhikkhave, bhikkhu cavati, nappatiṭṭhāti saddhamme.

Anottappī, bhikkhave, bhikkhu cavati, nappatiṭṭhāti saddhamme.

Kusīto, bhikkhave, bhikkhu cavati, nappatiṭṭhāti saddhamme.

Duppañño, bhikkhave, bhikkhu cavati, nappatiṭṭhāti saddhamme.

Imehi kho, bhikkhave, pañcahi dhammehi samannāgato bhikkhu cavati, nappatiṭṭhāti saddhamme.

Pañcahi, bhikkhave, dhammehi sammannāgato bhikkhu na cavati, patiṭṭhāti saddhamme.

Katamehi pañcahi?

Saddho, bhikkhave, bhikkhu na cavati, patiṭṭhāti saddhamme. hirimā, bhikkhave, bhikkhu na cavati, patiṭṭhāti saddhamme. Ottappī, bhikkave, bhikkhu na cavati, patiṭṭhāti saddhamme. akusīto, bhikkhave, bhikkhu na cavati, patiṭṭhāti saddhamme. paññavā, bhikkhave, bhikkhu na cavati, patiṭṭhāti saddhamme.

Imehi kho, bhikkhave, pañcahi dhammehi samannāgato bhikkhu na cavati, patiṭṭhāti saddhamme.

(AN)

GLOSSARY

akusīta	diligent, non-lazy
adoso	non-ill-will, etc. (a+doso)
anavajja	not blameable, not at fault
anottappī	reckless, not afraid of sin, remorseless (nominative singular masculine of anotappin (also occurs as anottāpī;)
amoho	non-confusion, etc. (a+moho)
alobho	non-avarice, etc (a+lobho)
assaddha	non-determined, etc (a+saddha)
ahirika	shameless, without modesty
imāni	nominative plural neuter of ima 'this'
ottappī	not reckless, afraid of sin, scrupulous (nominative singular masculine of ottappin (also occurs as ottāpī))
kammaṃ	action, deed, action as related to rebirth
kusīta	indolent, lazy
cavati	falls (away)
-ja	born of, be born:
X-ja	be born of X
tīṇi	three (neuter nominative plural)
dukkho	sorrow, suffering
doso	anger, ill will, malice, hatred
nidānaṃ	source, cause, origin:
X-nidāna	having X as source or origin
nirodho	cessation, emancipation, calming down
pakata	done, made:
X-pakata	done out of X
pañcahi	five(instrumental masculine plural of pañca)
paññavā	wise (masculine nominative singular of paññavant)
patiṭṭhāti	stands firmly, is established
moho	delusion, ignorance, confusion
lobho	avarice, greed, covetousness
vipāko	result, fruition:
X-vipāka	having X as fruit or result
saddha	determined, faithful
samudayo	rise, origin:
X-samudaya	having X as origin, arising from X, or the origin of X
sāvajja	blameable, faulty
sukhaṃ	happiness, comfort, well-being, ease
hirimā	modest(masculine nominative singular of hirimant)

LESSON III

1. "Bhante Nāgasena, atthi koci satto, yo imamhā kāyā aññaṃ kāyaṃ saṃkamatî?" ti.

"Na hi, mahārājâ" ti.

"Yadi, bhante Nāgasena, imamhā kāyā aññaṃ kāyaṃ saṃkamanto natthi, na nu mutto bhavissati pāpakehi kammehî?" ti.

"Āma, mahārāja, yadi na paṭisandaheyya, mutto bhavissati pāpakehi kammehi; yasmā ca kho, mahārāja, paṭisandahati, tasmā na parimutto pāpakehi kammehî"ti.

"Bhante Nāgasena, na ca saṃkamati, paṭisandahati câ?" ti.

"Āma, mahārāja; na ca saṃkamati paṭisandahati câ" ti.

"Kathaṃ, bhante Nāgasena, na ca saṃkamati paṭisandahati ca? Opammaṃ karohî" ti.

"Yathā, mahārāja, kocideva puriso padīpato padīpaṃ padīpeyya, kinnu kho so, mahārāja, padīpo padīpamhā saṃkamanto?" ti.

"Na hi bhante" ti.

"Evameva kho, mahārāja, na ca saṃkamati paṭisandahati câ" ti.

(-M.P.)

2. "Taṃ kiṃ maññatha, Sāḷhā, atthi lobho" ti?

"Evaṃ, bhante."

"Abhijjhā ti kho ahaṃ, Sāḷhā, etamatthaṃ[1] vadāmi. Luddho kho ayaṃ, Sāḷhā, abhijjhālu pāṇaṃ pi hanati, adinnaṃ pi ādiyati, paradāraṃ pi gacchati, musā pi bhaṇati...yaṃ'sa hoti [2] dīgharattaṃ ahitāya dukkhāyâ" ti.

"Evaṃ, bhante."

"Taṃ kiṃ maññatha, Sāḷhā, atthi doso" ti?

"Evaṃ, bhante."

"Byāpādo ti kho ahaṃ, etamatthaṃ vadāmi. Duṭṭho kho ayaṃ, Sāḷhā, byāpannacitto pāṇaṃ pi hanati, adinnaṃ pi ādiyati, paradāraṃ pi gacchati, musā pi bhaṇati ... yaṃ'sa hoti dīgharattaṃ ahitāya dukkhāyâ" ti.

"Evaṃ, bhante."

"Taṃ kiṃ maññatha, Sāḷhā, atthi moho" ti?

"Evaṃ, bhante."

"Avijjā ti kho ahaṃ, Sāḷhā, etamatthaṃ vadāmi. Mūḷho kho ayaṃ, Sāḷhā, avijjāgato pāṇaṃ pi hanati, adinnaṃ pi ādiyati, paradāraṃ pi gacchati, musā pi bhaṇati ... yaṃ'sa hoti dīgharattaṃ ahitāya dukkhāyâ" ti.

"Evaṃ, bhante."

"Taṃ kiṃ maññatha, Sāḷhā, ime dhammā kusalā vā akusalā vā" ti?

"Akusalā, bhante."

"Sāvajjā vā anavajjā vā " ti?

"Sāvajjā, bhante."

"Viññugarahitā vā viññuppasatthā vā" ti?

"Viññugarahitā, bhante."

(-A.N.)

---

[1] etam + atthaṃ See this grammar 13 and 17.

[2] yaṃ'sa = yaṃ + assa (Dative of ayaṃ/idaṃ) It thus means 'which to him.'

3. "Yasmā ca kho, bhikkhave, sakkā akusalaṃ pajahituṃ tasmâhaṃ evaṃ vadāmi - "akusalaṃ, bhikkhave, pajahathâ" ti. Akusalaṃ ca hi'daṃ, bhikkhave, pahīnaṃ ahitāya, dukkhāya saṃvatteyya, nâhaṃ evaṃ vadeyyaṃ -"akusalaṃ bhikkhave, pajahathâ" ti. Yasmā ca kho, bhikkhave, akusalaṃ pahīnaṃ hitāya sukhāya saṃvattati tasmâhaṃ evaṃ vadāmi - "akusalaṃ, bhikkhave, pajahathâ" ti.

Kusalaṃ, bhikkhave, bhāvetha. Sakkā, bhikkhave, kusalaṃ bhāvetuṃ... Yasmā ca kho, bhikkhave, sakkā kusalaṃ bhāvetuṃ tasmâhaṃ evaṃ vadāmi - "kusalaṃ, bhikkhave, bhāvethâ" ti. Kusalaṃ ca hi'daṃ, bhikkhave, bhāvitaṃ ahitāya, dukkhāya saṃvatteyya, nâhaṃ evaṃ vadeyyaṃ - "kusalaṃ, bhikkhave bhāvethâ" ti. Yasmā ca kho, bhikkhave, kusalaṃ bhāvitaṃ hitāya, sukhāya saṃvattati tasmâhaṃ evaṃ vadāmi - "kusalaṃ, bhikkhave, bhāvethâ" ti.

(-A.N.)

GLOSSARY

añño	another (one)
atthaṃ vadati	characterizes, gives the meaning to (see this grammar 13)
atthi	(there) is (see this grammar 2)
adinnaṃ	ungiven thing
abhijjhā	covetousness
abhijjhālu	covetous one
ayaṃ	this one (also anaphoric; *i.e.*, may refer back to something that has been said)
avijjā	ignorance
avijjāgata	he who is ignorant
ahitaṃ	harm
ādiyati	takes up, takes upon
āma	yes
imamhā	ablative singular of idaṃ 'this'
evaṃ	thus
evameva	even so, just so, in similar manner, in the same manner, similarly
opammaṃ	simile, example
kathaṃ	how
karohi	do, make (2nd person imperative singular form of karoti, do)
kāyo	body
kinnu	is it (that), how is it that , (but) why (kiṃ + nu)
kiṃ	what , (or 'how' - see this grammar 8)
ko	who whichever person (see this grammar 1)
koci	any (one), some (one) (ko + ci)
kocideva	some (one) or other (ko + ci + eva with -d- inserted)
garahita	despised, condemned, not approved
ci	indefinite particle (see this grammar 10)
tasmā	therefore, hence, from that (ablative singular of so/taṃ)

dīgha	long
dīgharattaṃ	for a long time, for long
dukkhaṃ	suffering, sorrow, ill
duṭṭho	he who is wicked
doso	anger, ill will
nanu	isn't it (the case that) (na + nu see this grammar 10)
Nāgaseno	proper name; vocative singular, Nāgasena
nu	interrogative particle (see this grammar 10)
pajahati	gives up, abandons
pajahatha	2nd pl. optative or imperative of pajahati (see this grammar 5)
pajahituṃ	infinitive of pajahati
paṭisandahati	is connected, is reunited, is reborn
padīpato	-to ablative of padīpo (see this grammar 15)
padīpeyya	optative of padīpeti (see this grammar 4)
padīpeti	lights, kindles
padīpo	lamp
paradāro	someone elses wife
parimutto	one who is completely freed, a fully freed one
pasattha/pasaṭṭha	praised, extolled, commended
pahīna	given up, abandoned, calmed down
pāṇo	breath, life, living being
puriso	individual, person (as well as 'male' - cf. Lesson I glossary)
byāpannacitto	he whose mind is malevolent
byāpādo	ill will, malevolence, revengefulness
bhaṇati	says, speaks
bhante	reverend sir, sire, sir, venerable one
bhavati	is, becomes (see this grammar 2) of bhavati be)
bhāvita	begotten, increased, developed, practiced, cultured
bhāveti	begets, produces, increases, cultivates, develops (see this grammar 7)
mahārājo	great king (vocative mahārāja)
mutto	one who is released, one who is freed, released one, freed one
musā	falsely
mūḷho	fool, confused one, ignorant person
yathā	just as, like
yadi	if (see this grammar 9)
yasmā	because, since, just as (ablative singular of yam- see this grammar 12)
yo	who (relative pronoun, nominative singular masculine (see II, 2. 13)

luddho	greedy person, covetous person
vadati	says, speaks
viññū	wise man
viññugarahita	despised by the wise ones
viññupasattha	extolled, praised by the wise ones
sakkā	it is possible (see this grammar 11)
saṃkanta	crossed over, passed over
saṃkamati	crosses over, transmigrates
saṃkamanto	one who crosses over, one who transmigrates (present participle, see this grammar 6)
Sāḷho	a proper name, Sāḷha
hanati, hanti	kills, strikes
hitaṃ	benefit, welfare, good
hoti	is, becomes

GRAMMAR III

1. INTERROGATIVE PRONOUN ka (ko/ kiṃ/ kā)

The interrogative pronoun has the stem ka-. Its forms are like those of the relative pronoun (2, 3.3) except for the neuter kiṃ and some alternate forms in ki-:

SINGULAR			
	Masculine	Neuter	Feminine
Nom:	ko	kiṃ	kā
Acc:	kaṃ		kaṃ
Gen:	kassa (kissa)		kassā
Dat:			
Inst:	kena		kāya
Abl:	kamhā (kasmā)		
Loc:	kamhi (kasmiṃ, kimhi, kismiṃ)		kassaṃ /kāyaṃ / kassā/ kāya

PLURAL			
	Masculine	Neuter	Feminine
Nom:	ke	kāni	kā /kāyo
Acc:			
Gen:	kesaṃ / kesānaṃ		kāsaṃ/ kāsānaṃ
Dat:			
Inst:	kehi(kebhi)		kāhi(kābhi)
Abl:			
Loc:	kesu		kāsu

2. VERBS 'to be' and 'become'

2.1. atthi ' is, exists' has the following present tense forms:

	Singular	Plural
1 Pers:	asmi/ amhi	asma/amha
2 Pers:	asi	attha
3 Pers:	atthi	santi

As a main verb, atthi generally asserts the existence of something, i.e., 'there is, there are':

atthi satto 'there is a being'

2.2. hoti 'is, becomes" has the following present tense forms:

	Singular	Plural
1 Pers:	homi	homa
2 Pers:	hosi	hotha
3 Pers:	hoti	honti

hoti may assert existence, but it may also have the sense 'become", and unlike atthi, may be used in equational; sentences (i.e., "X is Y"):

idha bhikkhu sīlavā hoti. 'herein a monk is virtuous'
(sīlavā 'virtuous')

2.3. bhavati: There is another 'be/ become' verb bhavati, which has the usual regular present tense forms (I, 2.2). In the present tense, bhavati is commonly used in the 'become' sense, but in other tenses and moods, it usually replaces hoti.

3.natthi

natthi is the negative of atthi and thus means 'is not', 'does not exist':

natthi satto yo evaṃ saṃkamati
'There is no being who thus transmigrates.'

4. THE OPTATIVE MOOD

4.1. Form of the Optative: The optative form of the verb in Pāli has several sets of endings. One set , with some alternate endings in the singular is as follows (the others will be given later). These endings are added to the present stem, and the final vowel of the stem is lost:

	Singular	Plural
1 Pers:	-eyyāmi/-eyyaṃ	-eyyāma
2 Pers:	-eyyāsi (eyya)	-eyyātha
3 Pers:	-eyya (-eyyāti)	-eyyuṃ

Thus, for labhati 'gets', stem labha-:

Optative of labhati 'gets'

	Singular	Plural
1 Pers:	labheyyāmi/labheyyaṃ	labheyyāma
2 Pers:	labheyyāsi (labheyya)	labheyyātha
3 Pers:	labheyya (labheyyāti)	labheyyuṃ

The optative of hoti, like its other non-present-tense forms, is formed from the bhava- stem (2.3 above) . The forms are as follows:

	Singular	Plural
1 Pers:	bhaveyyāmi/bhaveyyaṃ	bhaveyyāma
2 Pers:	bhaveyyāsi(bhaveyya)	bhaveyyātha
3 Pers:	bhaveyya (bhaveyyāti)	bhaveyyuṃ

The optative of atthi is also irregular, and will be given later, as will other irregular forms as they occur.

4.2. Uses of the Optative: The optative generally indicates that the situation described is hypothetical, i.e., 'might be true or might come about.' The sense is often future, and there may be an implication that it would be good if such-and such were the case:

yadā tumhe...attanā'va jāneyyātha
'When you know this really by yourself'

The optative by itself, that is, without any special form meaning 'if' may also have a simple 'if' sense:

kusalaṃ dukkhāya saṃvatteyya.. nâham evaṃ vadeyyaṃ
'If merit led to sorrow, I would not speak thus.'

Note that the second optative in the example is not '"if" but signifies something contingent on hypothetical situation described by the first; in this casegiving a "contrary to fact" reading. (see also section 9 below)

The optative can also be used as a polite imperative (i.e., 'It would be good if you....''):

atha tumhe...vihareyyātha 'Then you (should) abide'

5. THE IMPERATIVE

The second person Imperative endings are:

	Singular	Plural
2 Pers:	-:hi	-tha

These endings are added to the present stem, with lengthening of the final stem vowel in the singular if not already long:

PRESENT TENSE STEM	IMPERATIVE SINGULAR	IMPERATIVE PLURAL
labha-	labhāhi	labhatha 'get!'
gaccha-	gacchāhi	gacchatha 'go!'
jānā-	jānāhi	jānātha 'know!'
pajaha	pajahāhi	pajahatha 'give up!'

Note that the plural imperative is the same as the ordinary (i.e., indicative) present tense form.

If the present stem ends in -a-, the stem alone may be used as a second person singular imperative:

labha '(you) get!'

6. PRESENT PARTICIPLE

6.1. Form of the Present Participle:

6.11. The Present Participle Stem is formed by adding -nt- to the present tense stem of the verb:

PRESENT TENSE	PRESENT TENSE STEM	PRESENT PARTICIPLE STEM
gacchati 'goes'	gaccha-	gacchant-
labhati 'gets'	labha-	labhant-

6.12. The full participle is formed by adding case-number-gender affixes to the stem. One such set of endings resembles those of an -a- stem masculine noun (I, 1.21), for which the nominative and accusative forms are as follows (others will be given later):

	Singular	Plural
Nom:	-anto/aṃ	-antā
Acc:	-antaṃ	-ante

EXAMPLE: gacchati 'go':

	Singular	Plural
Nom:	gacchanto/gaccham̤	gacchantā
Acc:	gacchantam̤	gacchante

6.2. Use of the Participle: One use of the present participle is as an actor verbal noun denoting the doer of the action. In this use it takes the masculine endings given above, if the doer is masculine, or if gender is unspecified:

evam desento (bhabbo)
'One who thus preaches (is competent).'

aññam kāyaṃ saṃkamanto (natthi)
'(There is no) one who transmigrates to another body.'

Another use of the present participle is to modify a noun, like the English -ing participle in "The running man'", or "The man (who is) running away." In this usage, it takes endings that agree with the noun in person, number and gender:

buddhaṃ gacchantaṃ passāmi
'(I see)the Buddha going (masc.sg. acc.).'

dhạmmaṃ desento Tathāgato evaṃ eva vadati
'The Tathagata who is preaching the Doctrine says thus.'

Note that the participle may take the objects, adverbs, etc with which it can occur in a full sentence and that the modifying expression with the participle may precede or follow the noun modified.

7. -e- and -o- STEM VERBS:
7.1. -e- Stems: There are numerous verbs in Pāli with a present stem ending in -e-. They take the same endings as the verbs above with -a, but do not lengthen the vowel in any of the forms (since the long vs. short distinction does not apply to e). Thus, for bhāveti 'increases, develops':

	Singular	Plural
1 Pers:	bhāvemi	bhāvema
2 Pers:	bhāvesi	bhāvetha
3 Pers:	bhāveti	bhāventi

Verbs in -e- commonly have a transitive or causative sense. They often have related verbs which are intransitive (if the -e- verb is transitive) or transitive (if the -e- verb is causative). The vowels within the -e- stem will usually be longer or otherwise different from those within the related verb, which will also have a stem ending in some other vowel. Compare, for example, bhavati 'becomes, exists' with bhāveti 'causes to exist, develops, increases', and other similar sets will appear as we proceed.

7.2. Verbs with -o- Stems: There are also a few verbs in Pāli with stems ending in -o-. Like those in -e-, they do not lengthen the final vowel when affixes are added (since o also does not show a long vs. short distinction)). Thus with karoti 'does, makes', the present tense is:

	Singular	Plural
1 Pers:	karomi	karoma
2 Pers:	karosi	karotha
3 Pers:	karoti	karonti

7.3. For verbs with present tense stems in -e- or -o- also, the present participle affix is -nt- added to the present stem:

PRESENT TENSE		PRESENT TENSE STEM	PRESENT PARTICIPLE STEM
karoti	'does,makes'	karo-	karont-[3]
deseti	'preaches'	dese-	desent-

8. ACCUSATIVE OF MANNER:

The accusative form of pronouns may be used as adverbs of manner: taṃ 'thus' or 'so', kiṃ 'how:

taṃ kiṃ maññatha 'So what/how do you (pl) think?'

evaṃ in addition to meaning 'thus'. has a special use as a polite "yes", i.e., " It is (just) so:"

evaṃ, bhante

'Yes, sir (It is so).'

9. yadi 'IF'

yadi 'if' may occur with the optative if the situation described is assumed to be hypothetical, i.e., not to be in fact the case:

yadi na paṭisandaheyya

'If there were no connection (but there is)'

Compare the following, without the optative:

yadi... saṃkamanto natthi

'If there is no transmigration (but there might be (i.e., accepting it at least as a premise)'

---

3 This verb also has the alternate form karant-.

10. PARTICLES

As noted in Lesson I, 3, Pāli has a number of particles or "clitics" Some others are:

10.1. Indefinite ci may be added to interrogative pronouns to form indefinite pronouns:

kiñci (<kiṃ+ci) 'anything'
koci 'anyone'
kassaci 'to/ of anyone'

10.2. Emphatics hi, kho, eva and nu all add emphasis, but they have somewhat different but sometimes overlapping senses which are difficult to render into English.

10.21. kho adds a sense like "precisely, indeed, just' or 'as for...':

evameva kho, mahārāja, na ca saṃkamati
'It is just thus, Great King, that (it) does not transmigrate.'
(i.e., 'there is no transmigration')

10.22. hi adds a sense like 'verily, forsooth, this very', or sometimes 'because':

kusalaṃ ca hi'daṃ... bhāvitam ahitāya dukkhāya saṃvatteya...
'And if this very merit (when) increased led to non well being and sorrow...'

10.23. eva adds a sense like 'only, just, surely, in fact':

evameva 'just so, just this'

10.24. nu is an interrogative emphatic, which may be added to an interrogative form to strengthen it, with a sense somewhat like English " then", or to a non-interrogative form making it interrogative, often with the implication that the answer is expected to be "yes":

kinnu (< kiṃ+nu) kho so padīpo saṃkamanto?
'Is it then that this lamp is transmigrating?'

nanu (< na+nu) 'is it not (that...)'

11. sakkā

sakkā means 'it is possible that...' or 'one can...'. It may be used with a dependent infinitive:

sakkā...gantuṃ 'One can go, <u>or</u> it is possible to go.'

12. yasmā

yasmā, the ablative form of yaṃ (II 2.13) by itself can mean 'hence, therefore'. It can also be linked with tasmā in a correlative construction with the sense 'since.....therefore".

13. etamatthaṃ (vadāmi)

etamatthaṃ is from etaṃ+attho 'that meaning' in the accusative.The construction X (i)ti etamatthaṃ vadāmi has the sense "I call (it) (of the manner of) X'.

14. COMPOUNDS

The first member of a compound, though in the stem form, can stand in various case relations to the second:

viññugarahita 'despised by the wise ones'
avijjāgato 'ignorant one, one who "goes" with ignorance'
vijānanalakkhaṇaṃ 'of the nature of vijānanaṃ'

15. Ablative case -to

The affix -to added to a noun stem forms an alternate to the ablative singular in the sense '(away) from', . This alternant is very common:

dukkhato 'from sorrow'
padīpato 'from the lamp'

16. FUTURE TENSE

Pāli has a future tense, and one form, bhavissati 'will be, will become', occurs in this lesson. The formation of the future will be given later.

17. SANDHI

When a form ending in a nasal (usually ṃ) is followed closely by one beginning in a different consonant, the nasal is often changed (i.e., "assimilated") so as to be produced in the same position as that consonant (See the Introduction, Part II, Alphabet and Pronunciation.):

viññāṇaṃ+ti ---> viññāṇanti
yaṃ+ca ⟶ yañca

ṃ never appears between vowels. Thus when a form ending in ṃ is followed by one beginning in a vowel, and the two come together in sandhi, ṃ will generally appear as m. Thus etaṃ+attham (13 above) gives etamatthaṃ.

FURTHER READINGS III

1. "Taṃ kiṃ maññatha, Sāḷhā, atthi alobho" ti?

"Evam, bhante."

"Anabhijjhā'ti kho ahaṃ, Sāḷhā, etamatthaṃ vadāmi. Aluddho kho ayaṃ, Sālhā, anabhijjhālu n'eva pāṇaṃ hanati, na adinnaṃ ādiyati, na paradāraṃ gacchati, na musā bhaṇati, paraṃ pi na tathattāya samādapeti, yaṃ'sa hoti dīgharattaṃ hitāya sukhāyâ' ti.

"Evaṃ bhante."

"Taṃ kiṃ maññatha, Sāḷhā, atthi adoso" ti?

"Evaṃ, bhante."

"abyāpādo'ti kho ahaṃ, Sāḷhā, etamatthaṃ vadāmi. Aduṭṭho kho ayaṃ, Sāḷhā, abyāpannacitto n'eva pāṇaṃ hanati, na adinnaṃ ādiyati,na paradāraṃ gacchati, na musā bhaṇati, paraṃ pi na tathattāya samādapeti, yaṃ'sa hoti dīgharattaṃ hitāya sukhāyâ" ti.

"Evam, bhante."

"Taṃ kiṃ maññatha, Sāḷhā, atthi amoho" ti?

"Evaṃ, bhante."

"Vijjā'ti kho ahaṃ, Sāḷhā, etamatthaṃ vadāmi. Amūḷho kho ayaṃ,Sāḷhā, vijjāgato n'eva pāṇaṃ hanati, na adinnaṃ ādiyati, na paradāraṃ gacchati, na musā bhaṇati, paraṃ pi na tathattāya samādapeti, yaṃ'sa hoti dīgharattaṃ hitāya sukhāyâ" ti.

"Evaṃ, bhante."

Taṃ kiṃ maññatha, Sāḷhā, ime dhammā kusalā vā akusalā vā" ti?

"Kusalā, bhante."

"Sāvajjā vā anavajjā vā" ti?

"Anavajjā, bhante."

"Viññugarahitā vā viññuppasatthā vā" ti?

"Viññuppasatthā, bhante."

"Samattā samādinnā hitāya sukhāya saṃvattanti, no vā?"

"Samattā, bhante, samādinnā hitāya sukhāya saṃvattantî" ti.

"Yadā tumhe Sāḷhā attanā'va jāneyyātha 'ime dhammā kusalā, 'ime dhammā anavajjā, ime dhammā viññuppasatthā, ime dhammā samattā, samādinnā dīgharattaṃ hitāya, sukhāya saṃvattantî'ti." atha tumhe, Sāḷhā upasampajja vihareyyāthâ" ti.

(A.N.)

2. "Nâhaṃ, bhikkhave, aññaṃ ekadhammaṃ pi samanupassāmi yaṃ evaṃ abhāvitaṃ, akammaniyaṃ hoti yathayidaṃ, bhikkhave, cittaṃ.

Cittaṃ, bhikkhave, abhāvitaṃ, akammaniyaṃ hotî" ti.

"Nâhaṃ, bhikkhave, aññaṃ ekadhammaṃ pi samanupassāmi yaṃ evaṃ bhāvitaṃ kammaniyaṃ hoti yathayidaṃ, bhikkhave, cittaṃ.

Cittaṃ, bhikkhave, bhāvitaṃ kammaniyaṃ hotî" ti.

"Nâhaṃ, bhikkhave, aññaṃ ekadhammaṃ pi samanupassāmi yaṃ evaṃ abhāvitaṃ mahato anatthāya saṃvattati yathayidaṃ, bhikkhave, cittaṃ.

Cittaṃ, bhikkhave, abhāvitaṃ mahato anatthāya saṃvattatī" ti.

"Nâhaṃ, bhikkhave, aññaṃ ekadhammaṃ pi samanupassāmi yaṃ evam bhāvitaṃ mahato atthāya saṃvattati yathayidaṃ, bhikkhave, cittaṃ.

Cittaṃ, bhikkhave, bhāvitaṃ mahato atthāya. saṃvattatī" ti.

Nâhaṃ, bhikkhave, aññaṃ ekadhammaṃ pi samanupassāmi yaṃ evaṃ abhāvitaṃ apātubhūtaṃ mahato anatthāya saṃvattati yathayidaṃ, bhikkhave, cittaṃ.

Cittaṃ, bhikkhave, abhāvitaṃ apātubhūtaṃ mahato anatthāya saṃvattatī" ti.

"Nâhaṃ, bhikkhave, aññaṃ ekadhammaṃ pi samanupassāmi yaṃ evaṃ bhāvitaṃ pātubhūtaṃ mahato atthāya saṃvattati yathayidaṃ, bhikkhave, cittaṃ.

Cittaṃ, bhikkhave, bhāvitaṃ pātubhūtaṃ mahato atthāya saṃvattatī"ti.

"Nâhaṃ, bhikkhave, aññaṃ ekadhammaṃ pi samanupassāmi yaṃ evam abhāvitaṃ abahulīkataṃ mahato anatthāya saṃvattati yathayidaṃ bhikkhave, cittaṃ.

Cittaṃ, bhikkhave, abhāvitaṃ abahulīkataṃ mahato anatthāya saṃvattatī" ti.

"Nâhaṃ, bhikkhave, aññaṃ ekadhammaṃ pi samanupassāmi yaṃ evaṃ bhāvitaṃ bahulīkataṃ mahato atthāya saṃvattati yathayidaṃ bhikkhave,cittaṃ.

Cittaṃ, bhikkhave, bhāvitaṃ bahulīkataṃ mahato atthāya saṃvattatī"ti.

"Nâhaṃ, bhikkhave, aññaṃ ekadhammaṃ pi samanupassāmi yaṃ evaṃ abhāvitaṃ abahulīkataṃ dukkhâdhivāhaṃ hoti yathayidaṃ, bhikkhave, cittaṃ.

Cittaṃ, bhikkhave, abhāvitaṃ, abahulīkataṃ dukkhâdhivāhaṃ hotī"ti.

(A.N.)

3. "Idaṃ kho pana bhikkhave dukkhaṃ ariyasaccaṃ:

Jāti pi dukkhā, jarā pi dukkhā, vyādhi pi dukkhā, maraṇaṃ pi dukkhaṃ, appiyehi sampayogo dukkho, piyehi vippayogo dukkho, yaṃ p'icchaṃ na labhati taṃ pi dukkhaṃ. Saṃkhittena pañc'upādānakkhandhā pi dukkhā."

(D.N.)

4. "Bhante Nāgasena, kiṃlakkhaṇaṃ viññāṇan" ti?

"Vijānanalakkhaṇaṃ, mahārāja, viññāṇan" ti.

"Opammaṃ karohī" ti.

"Yathā, mahārāja, nagaraguttiko majjhe nagare siṃghāṭake nisinno passeyya puratthimadisato purisaṃ āgacchantaṃ, passeyya dakkhiṇadisato purisaṃ āgacchantaṃ, passeyya pacchimadisato purisaṃ āgacchantaṃ, passeyya uttaradisato purisaṃ āgacchantaṃ, evameva kho, mahārāja, yañca puriso cakkhunā rūpaṃ passati taṃ viññāṇena vijānāti, yañca sotena saddaṃ suṇāti taṃ viññāṇena vijānāti, yañca ghānena gandhaṃ ghāyati taṃ viññāṇena vijānāti, yañca jivhāya rasaṃ sāyati taṃ viññāṇena vijānāti, yañca kāyena phoṭṭhabbaṃ phusati taṃ viññāṇena vijānāti, yañca manasā dhammaṃ vijānāti taṃ viññāṇena vijānāti.

"Evaṃ kho, mahārāja, vijānanalakkhaṇaṃ viññāṇan" ti.

"Kallo'si[4] bhante Nāgasenâ" ti. (M.P)

GLOSSARY

akammaniya	inactive, sluggish, slothful, lazy
attanā	by oneself (instrumental singular of attan, 'self')
aduṭṭha	free from malice or ill-will, not wicked
aduṭṭho	one who is characterized by aduṭṭha
adhivāha	bringing, entailing
X-adhivāha	entailing X
anabhijjhā	absence of covetousness or desire
anabhijjhālū	one characterized by anabhijjhā
appiyo	that which is disagreeable or unpleasant (person or thing)
abyāpannacitto	one whose mind is free from malice or ill-will
abyāpādo	non-ill-will, benevolence, non-anger
amūḷho	one who is not confused
aluddho	non-covetous person
āgacchanta	coming
icchā	desire
uttara	northern
upasampajja	having stepped onto, having arrived at, having taken upon oneself
kammaniya	ready, active, functional
kalla	dextrous, smart, clever
kiṃlakkhaṇaṃ	of what nature, of what characteristic (from kiṃ 'what' +lakkhaṇaṃ (see below))
ghānaṃ	nose
ghāyati	smells
jarā	old age, decrepitude, decay
jāti	birth, rebirth, possibility of rebirth
jānāti	knows, realizes, comprehends, understands
jivhā	tongue
tathattaṃ	that state
tumhe	you (nominative plural of tvaṃ, 'you')
dakkhiṇa	southern
disā	direction
dukkha	painful, of suffering

[4] **kallo**, Nominative Singular Masc. of **kalla** plus **asi** (see this grammar 2.1).

nagaraguttiko	superintendent of a city
nagaraṃ	city, town
nisinna	seated
no	not verily (na + u ; negative emphatic)
pacchima	western
pañca	five
pañcupādānakkhandhā	the factors of the "fivefold clinging to existence," the five aggregates, the elements or substrata of sensory existence
pana	verily, but
paro	another (person)
passati	sees, realizes
pātubhūta	manifested, become manifest, appeared
piyo	pleasant one, agreeable one, dear one
puratthima	eastern
phusati	touches, feels
bahulīkata	practiced frequently, exercised, expanded
majjha(aṃ)	middle, midst
manasā	by/with the mind (instrumental singular of mana(s) 'mind')
maraṇaṃ	death
yadā	when
lakkhaṇaṃ	feature, mark, characteristic, discriminating mark
X lakkhaṇaṃ	characterized or marked by X
vijānanaṃ	act of cognizing, discriminating
vijānāti	perceives, understands with discrimination, discriminates
vijjā	discriminative knowledge, wisdom, insight
vijjāgato	one who has attained wisdom
viññāṇaṃ	consciousness
vippayogo	separation, dissociation
viharati	lives, resides, abides, leads a life
vyādhi	sickness, malady, illness, disease
saṃkhittena	in short
saccaṃ	truth
samatta	completed, grasped, accomplished
samādapeti	encourages, incites, rouses
samādinna	taken upon oneself, accepted
sampayogo	union, association
sāyati	tastes
siṃghāṭako	cross, cross-roads (or siṃghāṭakaṃ)
suṇāti	hears, listens
sotaṃ	ear

LESSON IV

1 Evameva kho, bhikkhave, cattāro'me[1] samaṇabrāhmaṇānaṃ upakkilesā, yehi upakkilesehi upakkiliṭṭhā eke samaṇabrāhmaṇā na tapanti, na bhāsanti, na virocanti.

Katame cattāro?

Santi, bhikkhave, eke samaṇabrāhmaṇā suraṃ pivanti merayaṃ, surāmerayapānā appaṭiviratā. Ayaṃ, bhikkhave, paṭhamo samaṇabrāhmaṇānaṃ upakkileso, yena upakkilesena upakkiliṭṭhā eke samaṇabrāhmaṇā na tapanti, na bhāsanti, na virocanti.

Santi, bhikkhave, eke samaṇabrāhmaṇā methunaṃ dhammaṃ paṭisevanti, methunasmā dhammā appaṭiviratā. Ayaṃ, bhikkhave, dutiyo samaṇabrāhmaṇānaṃ upakkileso, yena upakkilesena upakkiliṭṭhā eke samaṇabrāhmaṇā na tapanti, na bhāsanti, na virocanti.

Santi, bhikkhave, eke samaṇabrāhmaṇā jātarūparajataṃ sādiyanti, jātarūparajatapaṭiggahaṇā appaṭiviratā. Ayaṃ, bhikkhave, tatiyo samaṇabrāhmaṇānaṃ upakkileso, yena upakkilesena upakkiliṭṭhā eke samaṇabrāhmaṇā na tapanti, na bhāsanti, na virocanti.

Santi, bhikkhave, eke samaṇabrāhmaṇā micchājīvena jīvanti, micchājīvā appaṭiviratā. Ayaṃ, bhikkhave, catuttho samaṇabrāhmaṇānaṃ upakkileso, yena upakkilesena upakkiliṭṭhā eke samaṇabrāhmaṇā na tapanti, na bhāsanti, na virocanti.

Ime kho, bhikkhave, cattāro samaṇabrāhmaṇānaṃ upakkilesā, yehi upakkilesehi upakkiliṭṭhā eke samaṇabrāhmaṇā na tapanti, na bhāsanti, na virocantîti.

Suraṃ pivanti merayaṃ
paṭisevanti methunaṃ
rajataṃ jātarūpaṃ ca
sādiyanti aviddasū
micchājīvena jīvanti
eke samaṇabrāhmaṇā.
(-A.N.)

2 Bhojanaṃ, Suppavāse, dentī ariyasāvikā paṭiggāhakānaṃ cattāri ṭhānāni deti.
Katamāni cattāri?
Āyuṃ deti, vaṇṇaṃ deti, sukhaṃ deti, balaṃ deti.

---

[1] cattāro + ime

Āyuṃ kho pana datvā, āyussa bhāginī hoti dibbassa vā mānusassa vā. Vaṇṇaṃ datvā, vaṇṇassa bhāginī hoti dibbassa vā mānusassa vā. Sukhaṃ datvā, sukhassa bhāginī hoti dibbassa vā mānusassa vā. Balaṃ datvā, balassa bhāginī hoti dibbassa vā mānusassa vā.

Bhojanaṃ, Suppavāse, dentī ariyasāvikā paṭiggāhakānaṃ imāni cattāri ṭhānāni detīti.

(-A.N.)

3. Na bhaje pāpake mitte - na bhaje purisâdhame.
Bhajetha mitte kalyāṇe - bhajetha purisuttame.

Sabbe tasanti daṇḍassa - sabbe bhāyanti maccuno.
Attānaṃ upamaṃ katvā - na haneyya na ghātaye

Sabbe tasanti daṇḍassa - sabbesaṃ jīvitaṃ piyaṃ.
Attānaṃ upamaṃ katvā - na haneyya na ghātaye

Bahuṃ pi ce sahitaṃ bhāsamāno -na takkaro hoti naro pamatto
gopo'va[2] gāvo gaṇayaṃ paresaṃ -na bhāgavā sāmaññassa hoti.

Appaṃ pi ce sahitaṃ bhāsamāno -dhammassa hoti anudhammacārī
rāgañ ca dosañ ca pahāya mohaṃ -sammappajāno suvimuttacitto
anupādiyāno idha vā huraṃ vā -sa bhāgavā sāmaññassa hoti.

Piyato jāyatī [3] soko - piyato jāyatī bhayaṃ.
Piyato vippamuttassa - n'atthi soko. kuto bhayaṃ?

Pemato jāyatī soko - pemato jāyatī bhayaṃ.
Pemato vippamuttassa - n'atthi soko. kuto bhayaṃ?

Ratiyā jāyatī soko - ratiyā jāyatī bhayaṃ.
Ratiyā vippamuttassa - n'atthi soko. kuto bhayaṃ?
Kāmato jāyatī soko - kāmato jāyatī bhayaṃ.
Kāmato vippamuttassa - n'atthi soko. kuto bhayaṃ?

Taṇhāya jāyatī soko - taṇhāya jāyatī bhayaṃ.
Taṇhāya vippamuttassa - n'atthi soko. kuto bhayaṃ?

(-Dhp.)

---

[2] gopo+ iva see Glossary and this grammar 10.

[3] Rhythmic length (*i.e.*, lengthened to suit the poetic meter).

GLOSSARY

attānaṃ	self, soul (accusative singular of attan)
adhama	low, base, wicked
-puriso	base, wicked person
anudhammacārī	nominative singular of anudhammacārin 'one who acts in accordance with the Dhamma'
anupādiyāno	freed from clinging (present participle of anupādiyati 'does not cling (to earthly things)'
appaṃ	(a) little, not much
ariyasāvikā	a noble female devotee, a female disciple or devotee of the noble ones
aviddasu	ignorant, foolish (one)
ājīva	life, living, livelihood
āyuṃ	long life, vitality, longevity
ime	these (masculine plural of ima/ayaṃ (see this grammar 1)
iva	like, as (see this grammar 10)
uttama	noble, best, highest
purisa-	noble, best person
upakkiliṭṭha	defiled (with instrumental of the defilement)
upakkileso	defilement, taint, mental impurity
upamā	analogy, simile, example
eke	some, a few(see this grammar 7 under eka)
kalyāṇa	sincere, noble, good
kāmo (-aṃ)	(sense) desire
kuto	whence, from where
gaṇayaṃ	counting (Nominative singular present participle of gaṇeti 'counts, reckons')
gāvo	accusative pl. (irreg.) of go
go	cow
gopo	cowherd
ghātayati	causes to kill
cattāri	(see this grammar 7 under catu)
cattāro	(see this grammar 7 under catu)
catu	four
catuttha	fourth
ce	if (see this grammar 11)
jātarūpaṃ	gold
jāyati	arises, is born
jīvati	lives
jīvo	life

ṭhānaṃ	place, locality, condition, cause
takkara	doing thus, acting accordingly
takkaro	a doer therof
taṇhā	craving, thirst
tatiya	third
tapati	shines, is bright, lustrous
tasati	fears (with Genitive: see this grammar 9)
daṇḍa	staff, rod, punishment
datvā	having given (see this grammar 3)
dibba	divine
dutiya	second
deti	gives, donates
dentī	one who gives (feminine -see this grammar 5)
naro	man, individual
paṭiggahaṇaṃ	acceptance, receiving
paṭiggāhako	recipient, he who receives
paṭivirata	restrained from, abstained from (with ablative)
paṭisevati	follows, pursues, indulges in, experiences
paṭhama	first
pamatto	one who is lazy, not diligent
para	other
paresaṃ	(of) others(genitive/dative plural of para 'other' -see this grammar 8)
pahāya	having given up, forsaking
pānaṃ	drink, drinking
piyaṃ	pleasant thing, dear thing, pleasure
pivati	drinks
puriso	man, person
pemaṃ	love, affection
balaṃ	strength, power, force
bahuṃ	much, a lot
brāhmaṇo	Brahmin; in Buddhist texts, sometimes one who lives a noble life, irrespective of caste
bhajati	associates with (with accusative)
bhayaṃ	fear, apprehension
bhāgavā	sharer, participant in (nominative singular of bhāgavant)
bhāginī	participant, sharer (feminine, with genitive of the thing shared)
bhāyati	fears
bhāsati	shines forth, is bright
bhāsamāno	(one who is) reciting. (Present participle of bhāsati 'says, recites', see this grammar 4)
bhojanaṃ	meal, nourishment

maccu	death, the god of death
mānusa	human
micchā	wrong, incorrect
mitto	friend
methuna	sexual
-dhammo	sexual intercourse
merayaṃ	fermented liquor
rajataṃ	silver, any non-gold coin
rati	love, attachment
rāgo	attachment, lust
loko	world, people in general
vaṇṇo	color, complexion
vippamutto	one who is freed
virocati	shines forth, is brilliant
santi	3rd Pers. Pl of atthi 'is' (see III. 2.1)
sabbesaṃ	Dative-Genitive of sabbe 'all' (see this grammar 8)
samaṇo	recluse, mendicant
sammappajāno	fully comprehending one
sahitaṃ	texts, scriptures taken as a whole
sādiyati	appropriates, takes on oneself, enjoys
sāmaññaṃ	state of an ascetic or monk, the holy life
Suppavāsā	proper name (feminine)
Suppavāse	Vocative form
surā	liquor
suvimuttacitto	one with a well-freed mind
soko	sorrow, grief
huraṃ	in the other world, in another existence

GRAMMAR IV

1. FORMS OF ima 'THIS, THAT'

Some forms of ima (ayaṃ) were given in II, 2.14. The entire set is as follows:

SINGULAR			
	Masculine	Neuter	Feminine
Nom:	ayaṃ	imaṃ	ayaṃ
Acc:	imaṃ	idaṃ	imaṃ
Gen:	imassa / assa		imissā(ya) imāya / assā(ya)
Dat:			
Inst:	iminā / anena		imāya
Abl:	imamhā / imasmā / asmā		
Loc:	imasmiṃ / imamhi asmiṃ		imissaṃ /imissā imāyaṃ / assaṃ

PLURAL			
	Masculine	Neuter	Feminine
Nom:	ime	imāni	imā(yo)
Acc:			
Gen:	imesaṃ / imesānaṃ esaṃ / esānaṃ		imāsaṃ / imāsānaṃ
Dat:			
Inst:	imebhi/ imehi ebhi / ehi		imābhi / imāhi
Abl:			
Loc:	imesu/esu		imāsu

2. THE NOUN go 'COW'

The noun go 'cow' is masculine, and unlike English 'cow' does not imply female, but indicates the singular of "cattle". This noun is irregular in Pāli and has a number of variant forms. Most of them, however, resemble the forms of other nouns sufficiently to be easily recognizable. they are given here for reference:

(Paradigm of forms on following page)

go 'cow'

	Singular	Plural
Nom:	go	gāvo / gavo
Acc:	gāvaṃ/gavaṃ/gāvuṃ	
Gen:	gāvassa /gavassa	gavaṃ / gunnaṃ
Dat:		gonaṃ
Inst:	gāvena / gavena	gohi / gcbhi
Abl:	gāvā / gāvamha / (-smā) gavā / gavamha / (-smā)	
Loc:	gāve / gāvamhi / (-smiṃ) gave / gavamhi / (-smiṃ)	gāvesu / gavesu / gosu
Voc:	go	gāvo / gavo

3. THE GERUND

3.1. Form of the Gerund:

3.11. tvā(na) Gerunds: The most common affix for the gerund is tvā or tvāna. For verbs with a present stem ending in -a, that -a- is usually replaced by -i- when tvā(na) is added, so the stem is the same as for the infinitive (II, 4). Thus:

PRES 3RD SINGULAR	INFINITIVE	GERUND
bhavati 'is, becomes'	bhavituṃ	bhavitvā(na)
labhati 'gets, obtains'	labhituṃ	labhitvā(na)
garahati 'despises'	garahituṃ	garahitvā(na)

For verbs with a present stem in -e, -tvā(na) is added directly, like the infinitive ending:

neti 'leads'	netuṃ	netvā(na)
deseti 'preaches'	desetuṃ	desetvā(na)

For other verbs, the affix -tvā(na) is added directly to the verb root rather than to the present or infinitive stem, but the root may undergo changes in shape, and there are many irregularities. Some forms are given below. Others will be given as they appear in readings.

Pres 3rd Singular	Gerund
karoti 'does'	katvā(na)
gacchati 'goes'	gantvā(na)
suṇoti / suṇāti 'hears'	sutvā(na)

pivati 'drinks'	pitvā(na)
passati 'sees'	disvā(na)
deti / dadāti 'gives'	datvā(na)
jānāti 'knows'	ñatvā(na) /jānitvā(na)
labhati 'gets'	laddhā(na)

3.12. -ya Gerunds: There are also gerunds formed by adding -ya. These are particularly common with verbs which have a prefix or prefixes added to the root. The form pariyādāya 'having taken over (completely)' which occurred in Further Reading I is an example, since it is the gerund of pariyādāti 'takes, grasps' (< pari + ā + the verb root dā).

3.2. Use of the Gerund: The gerund usually expresses action prior to that of the main verb, and the two actions may be more or less closely linked. The sense is often like that of English "go and see." Thus:

gantvā deseti 'having gone, preaches' or 'goes and preaches'

cittaṃ pariyādāya tiṭṭhati
'having taken over the mind, remains'
or 'takes over the mind and remains.'

Note that as in the last example, the gerund may have its own objects, etc., but the subject is generally the same as that of the main verb.

4. PRESENT PARTICIPLE IN -māna

4.1 In addition to the -ant- present participle (III, 6.1), there is a form in -māna. The affix -māna is usually added directly to the present stem:

PRESENT 3RD SINGULAR	PRESENT PARTICIPLE
gacchati 'goes'	gacchamāna
uppajjati 'is born'	uppajjamāna

Verbs with a present stem in -e change -e- to -aya- before -māna:

deseti 'preaches'	desayamāna

The -māna participle is commonly called the "middle" present participle, on the basis of its origin in Sanskrit, in which it generally occurred on verbs with a passive or reflexive sense. While there are echoes of this in Pāli, so that this affix is often encountered on verb roots having such a sense, the distinction has been largely lost. Thus for the most part the māna affix is simply an alternative for -ant-, and many verbs appear in both forms: gacchanta or gacchamāna; desenta or desayamāna.

4.2. Some verbs also have present participles of this type in -āna rather than -māna. The form anupādiyāno in this reading, is such a participle from anupādiyati 'does not cling (to earthly things).'

The form sammappajāno, which occurs in this lesson, is also actually an irregular middle present participle of sammappajānāti 'fully understands, comprehends.'

4.3. Note that these participles, like others, can occur either adjectivally or as nouns. Thus sammappajāno can either be used by itself as a noun; i.e., 'one who fully comprehends', or be used adjectivally, modifying a (masculine singular) noun, as in sammappajāno puriso ' a person who fully comprehends.'

5. FEMININE PRESENT PARTICIPLE IN -ī and ā

The present participle in -ant- may form a feminine verbal noun by taking the affixes of an -ī stem feminine noun (I, 1.23). The usual sense is 'she who does the action of the verb' Thus:

denti 'she who gives'
karontī 'she who does', etc.

The -māna present participle, however, takes the endings of a feminine -ā stem (II, 1.1) when it is used as a noun; thus gacchamānā 'she who goes', etc.

6. MORE OPTATIVES

In addition to the optative endings given in connection with Lesson III, there are alternate endings in some of the person-number categories as follows:

	Singular		Plural
1 Pers:	-e		-ema (-eyyāmhe)
2 Pers:	-e	(-etho)	-etha (-eyyavho)
3 Pers:	-e	(-etha)	(-eraṃ)

The endings in parentheses are sometimes referred to as the "middle" ones on the basis of their Sanskrit origin. However, as with the participles (Section 4 above), this distinction is largely lost in Pāli.

7. NUMERALS

7.1. Stem Forms

The stem forms of the first five numerals are:

eka	'one'
dvi	'two'
ti	'three'
catu	'four'
pañca	'five'

7.2. eka 'One' has both singular and plural forms. In the singular, it is commonly used as a pronoun. The plural is used both as a pronoun and as an adjective, and it has the sense 'some'. In both numbers, eka inflects like sa/taṃ (II, 2.11). The forms are as follows:

eka 'one'

<table>
<tr><th colspan="4">SINGULAR</th></tr>
<tr><th></th><th>Masculine</th><th>Neuter</th><th>Feminine</th></tr>
<tr><td>Nom:</td><td>eko</td><td rowspan="2">ekaṃ</td><td>ekā</td></tr>
<tr><td>Acc::</td><td>ekaṃ</td><td>ekaṃ</td></tr>
<tr><td>Gen:</td><td colspan="2" rowspan="2">ekassa</td><td rowspan="2">ekissā(ya)
ekissaṃ
(ekāya)</td></tr>
<tr><td>Dat:</td></tr>
<tr><td>Inst:</td><td colspan="2">ekena</td><td rowspan="2">ekāya</td></tr>
<tr><td>Abl:</td><td colspan="2">ekamhā (ekasmā)</td></tr>
<tr><td>Loc::</td><td colspan="2">ekamhi (ekasmiṃ)</td><td>ekissaṃ(ekāyaṃ)</td></tr>
</table>

<table>
<tr><th colspan="4">PLURAL</th></tr>
<tr><th></th><th>Masculine</th><th>Neuter</th><th>Feminine</th></tr>
<tr><td>Nom:</td><td rowspan="2">eke</td><td rowspan="2">ekāni</td><td rowspan="2">ekā(yo)</td></tr>
<tr><td>Acc:</td></tr>
<tr><td>Gen:</td><td colspan="2" rowspan="2">ekesaṃ (ekesānaṃ)</td><td rowspan="2">ekāsaṃ
(ekāsānaṃ)</td></tr>
<tr><td>Dat:</td></tr>
<tr><td>Inst:</td><td colspan="2" rowspan="2">ekehi (ekebhi)</td><td rowspan="2">ekāhi
(ekābhi)</td></tr>
<tr><td>Abl:</td></tr>
<tr><td>Loc:</td><td colspan="2">ekesu</td><td>ekāsu</td></tr>
</table>

7.3. ti 'Three' and catu 'Four' are like eka in that they distinguish gender.
ti 'three'

<table>
<tr><th></th><th>Masculine</th><th>Neuter</th><th>Feminine</th></tr>
<tr><td>Nom-Acc:</td><td>tayo</td><td>tīṇi</td><td>tisso</td></tr>
<tr><td>Dat-Gen:</td><td colspan="2">tiṇṇaṃ / tiṇṇannaṃ</td><td>tissannaṃ</td></tr>
<tr><td>Inst-Abl:</td><td colspan="3">tīhi / tībhi</td></tr>
<tr><td>Loc:</td><td colspan="3">tīsu</td></tr>
</table>

catu 'four'

	Masculine	Neuter	Feminine
Nom-Acc:	cattāro caturo	cattāri	catasso
Dat-Gen:	catunnaṃ		catassannaṃ
Inst-Abl:	catūhi / catūbhi / catubbhi		
Loc:	catūsu		

7.4 dvi 'Two' does not distinguish gender. It has the following case forms:

dvi 'two'

	All Genders
Nom-Acc:	dve / duve
Dat-Gen:	dvinnaṃ / duvinnaṃ
Inst-Abl:	dvīhi / dvībhi (dīhi)
Loc:	dvīsu (duvesu)

7.5. Other Numerals: The remaining numerals, like dvi, do not have different gender forms. They take case endings like pañca 'five', given below:

pañca 'five'

	All Genders
Nom-Acc:	pañca
Dat-Gen:	pañcannaṃ
Inst-Abl:	pañcahi
Loc:	pañcasu

8. sabba 'ALL' and para 'OTHER'

When sabba 'all' is used by itself as a pronoun (rather than modifying a noun) it takes the plural endings of a pronoun like sa/tam (II, 2.11). Thus Nominative Singular Masculine sabbe, Neuter sabbāni, Feminine sabbā, Masculine-Neuter Genitive-Dative sabbesaṃ, etc.

para 'other' takes the pronominal endings in the same way; thus genitive (or dative) plural paresaṃ 'of others' in this lesson's reading.

9. GENITIVE OF FEAR

Verbs of fearing, such as tasati and bhāyati take the genitive of the thing feared:

tasanti daṇḍassa '(They) fear the rod'.

10. iva 'LIKE, AS'

The form iva 'like, as' most commonly appears in sandhi as a clitic -va. It is used in forming similes or comparisons, and is added to the form with which something is being compared. Thus the example in this reading:

gopo'va gāvo gaṇayaṃ paresaṃ
'like a cowherd counting the cattle of others'

11. ce 'IF'

ce is another form with the sense 'If'. It is a clitic,(see Lesson IGrammar 3) and thus cannot begin a sentence, but must follow some other form, usually the first word in its own ('if) sentence:

ahañce eva kho pana musāvadī assaṃ...
'If I were to lie (Literally 'be a liar (musāvadin= 'liar'))

In the example just given assaṃ is the optative of atthi 'be', and thus the sense here is hypothetical, contrary to fact, as in the examples in Lesson III, Grammar 4.2 and 9.

FURTHER READING IV

1. Dve'mā, bhikkhave, parisā.
Katamā dve?
Uttānā ca parisā gambhīrāca parisā.

Katamā ca, bhikkhave, uttānā parisā?
Idha, bhikkhave, yassaṃ parisāyaṃ bhikkhū uddhatā honti unnalā capalā mukharā vikiṇṇavācā... asampajānā asamāhitā vibbhantacittā pākat'indriyā.
Ayaṃ vuccati, bhikkhave, uttānā parisā.

Katamā ca, bhikkhave, gambhīrā parisā?
Idha, bhikkhave, yassaṃ parisāyaṃ bhikkhū anuddhatā honti anunnalā acapalā amukharā avikiṇṇavācā...sampajānā samāhitā ekaggacittā saṃvut'indriyā.
Ayaṃ vuccati, bhikkhave, gambhīrā parisā.
Imā kho, bhikkhave, dve parisā.

Dve'mā, bhikkhave, parisā.
Katamā dve?
Vaggā ca parisā samaggā ca parisā.

Katamā ca, bhikkhave, vaggā parisā?

Idha, bhikkhave, yassaṃ parisāyaṃ bhikkhū bhaṇḍanajātā kalahajātā vivādâpannā...viharanti.

Ayaṃ vuccati, bhikkhave, vaggā parisā.

Katamā ca, bhikkhave, samaggā parisā?

Idha, bhikkhave, yassaṃ parisāyaṃ bhikkhū samaggā sammodamānā avivadamānā khīrodakībhūtā...viharanti.

Ayaṃ vuccati, bhikkhave, samaggā parisā.

Imā kho, bhikkhave, dve parisā.

Dve'mā, bhikkhave, parisā.

Katamā dve?

Visamā ca parisā samā ca parisā.

Katamā ca, bhikkhave, visamā parisā?

Idha, bhikkhave, yassaṃ parisāyaṃ adhammakammāni pavattanti dhammakammāni nappavattanti, avinayakammāni pavattanti vinayakammāni nappavattanti, adhammakammāni dippanti dhammakammāni na dippanti, avinayakammāni dippanti vinayakammāni na dippanti.

Ayaṃ vuccati, bhikkhave, visamā parisā .

Katamā ca, bhikkhave, samā parisā?

Idha, bhikkhave, yassaṃ parisāyaṃ dhammakammāni pavattanti adhammakammāni nappavattanti, vinayakammāni pavattanti avinayakammāni nappavattanti, dhammakammāni dippanti, adhammakammāni na dippanti, vinayakammāni dippanti avinayakammāni na dippanti.

Ayaṃ vuccati, bhikkhave, samā parisā.

Imā kho, bhikkhave, dve parisā.

(-A.N.)

2. Appamādo amatapadaṃ - pamādo maccuno padaṃ
appamattā na mīyanti - ye pamattā yathā matā

Etaṃ visesato ñatvā - appamādamhi paṇḍitā
appamāde pamodanti - ariyānaṃ gocare ratā

Yathā pi rahado gambhīro - vippasanno anāvilo
evaṃ dhammāni sutvāna - vippasīdanti paṇḍitā

Selo yathā ekaghano - vātena na samīrati
evaṃ nindāpasaṃsāsu - na samiñjanti paṇḍitā.

Andhabhūto ayaṃ loko - tanuk'ettha vipassati
sakunto jālamutto'va - appo saggāya gacchati.

Udakaṃ hi nayanti nettikā – usukārā namayanti tejanaṃ
dāruṃ namayanti tacchakā – attānaṃ damayanti paṇḍitā
(-Dhp.)

3. Dve'māni, bhikkhave, sukhāni.
Katamāni dve?
Gihisukhaṃ ca pabbajitasukhaṃ ca.
Imāni kho, bhikkave, dve sukhāni.
Etadaggaṃ, bhikkhave, imesaṃ dvinnaṃ sukhānaṃ yadidaṃ pabbajitasukhaṃ ti.

Dve'māni, bhikkhave, sukhāni.
Katamāni dve?
Kāmasukhaṃ ca nekkhammasukhaṃ ca.
Imāni kho, bhikkhave, dve sukhāni.
Etadaggaṃ, bhikkhave, imesaṃ dvinnaṃ sukhānaṃ yadidaṃ nekkhammasukhaṃ ti.

Dve'māni, bhikkhave, sukhāni.
Katamāni dve?
Upadhisukhaṃ ca nirupadhisukhaṃ ca.
Imāni kho, bhikkhave, dve sukhāni.
Etadaggaṃ, bhikkhave, imesaṃ dvinnaṃ sukhānaṃ yadidaṃ nirupadhisukhaṃ ti.

Dve'māni, bhikkhave, sukhāni.
Katamāni dve?
Sâmisaṃ ca sukhaṃ nirāmisaṃ ca sukhaṃ.
Imāni kho, bhikkhave, dve sukhāni.
Etadaggaṃ, bhikkhave, imesaṃ dvinnaṃ sukhānaṃ yadidaṃ nirāmisaṃ sukhaṃ ti.

Dve'māni, bhikkhave, sukhāni.
Katamāni dve?
Ariyasukhaṃ ca anariyasukhaṃ ca.
Imāni kho, bhikkhave, dve sukhāni.
Etadaggaṃ, bhikkhave, imesaṃ dvinnaṃ sukhānaṃ yadidaṃ ariyasukhaṃ ti.

Dve'māni, bhikkhave, sukhāni.
Katamāni dve?
Kāyikaṃ ca sukhaṃ cetasikaṃ ca sukhaṃ.
Imāni kho, bhikkhave, dve sukhāni.
Etadaggaṃ, bhikkhave, imesaṃ dvinnaṃ sukhānaṃ yadidaṃ cetasikaṃ sukhaṃ ti.
(-A.N.)

4. Pañcahi, bhikkhave, aṃgehi samannāgato rājā cakkavattī dhammen'eva cakkaṃ pavatteti, taṃ hoti cakkaṃ appaṭivattiyaṃ kenaci[4] manussabhūtena paccatthikena pāṇinā.

Katamehi pañcahi?

---

[4] Instrumental of ko (Grammar III,1) plus indefinite -ci. Thus 'by any(one at all)'.

Idha, bhikkhave, rājā cakkavattī atthaññū ca hoti, dhammaññū ca mattaññū ca, kālaññū ca, parisaññū ca.

Imehi kho, bhikkhave, pañcahi aṃgehi samannāgato rājā cakkavattī dhammen'eva cakkaṃ pavatteti, taṃ hoti cakkaṃ appaṭivattiyaṃ kenaci manussabhūtena paccatthikena pāṇinā.

Evameva kho, bhikkhave, pañcahi dhammehi samannāgato tathāgato arahaṃ sammāsambuddho dhammen'eva anuttaraṃ dhammacakkaṃ pavatteti, taṃ hoti cakkaṃ appaṭivattiyaṃ samaṇena vā brāhmaṇena vā devena vā mārena vā brahmunā vā kenaci vā lokasmiṃ.

Katamehi pañcahi?

Idha, bhikkhave, tathāgato arahaṃ sammāsambuddho atthaññū, dhammaññū, mattaññū, kālaññū, parisaññū.

Imehi kho, bhikkhave, pañcahi dhammehi samannāgato tathāgato arahaṃ sammāsambuddho dhammen'eva anuttaraṃ dhammacakkaṃ pavatteti, taṃ hoti cakkaṃ appaṭivattiyaṃ samaṇena vā brāhmaṇena vā devena vā mārena vā brahmunā vā kenaci vā lokasmiṃ" ti.

(-A.N.)

GLOSSARY

atthaññū	one who knows what is useful, one who knows the correct meaning or proper goal
attho (-aṃ)	interest, advantage, gain
anuttara	incomparable, excellent
andhabhūta	blinded, (mentally) blind, ignorant
appamatto	one who is diligent
appaṭivattiya	not to be turned back, irresistable (a+paṭivattiya)
appo	a few
amataṃ	ambrosia or the deathless state
amatapadaṃ	the region or place of ambrosia, the sphere of immortality, or the path to immortality (see padaṃ below)
arahaṃ	deserving one, one who has attained absolute emancipation (nominative singular of arahant)
ariyo	noble one
āmisaṃ	material substance, food, flesh greed, sensual desire,lust
āvila	stirred up, agitated, stained, disturbed
āsavo	that which flows (out or onto), clinging,

	desire. In Buddhist philosophy, a technical term for certain ideas which intoxicate the mind.
indriyaṃ	faculty, sense
uttāna	plain, open, evident, superficial, shallow
udakaṃ	water
uddhata	unbalanced, disturbed, agitated
unnala	arrogant, proud, showing off
upadhi	substratum (of rebirth), attachment, basis for rebirth, clinging to rebirth
usukāro	arrow-maker, fletcher
ekaggacitta	of concentrated mind, of tranquil mind
ekaghana	compact, solid, hard
etadaggaṃ ... yadidaṃ...	this (or this one) is best...namely....
ettha	here
kalaho	quarrel, dispute
kalahajāta	quarrelsome, disputing
kāyika	pertaining to the body, physical
kālo	proper time
kālaññū	one who knows the proper time (for something)
kiñcana	worldly attachment, a trifle
khīraṃ	milk
khīrodakībhūta	like milk and water i.e.,at harmony as milk and water blend
gambhīra	deep
gihi	compounding stem of gihin
gihin	a householder, a layman
gocara	sphere, range
cakkaṃ	wheel, wheel as a symbol of efficacy in conquering
cakkavattī	Nominative singular of cakkavattin, 'universal monarch'
capala	unsteady, fickle, vain
cetasika	belonging to the mind, mental
jālaṃ	net
ñatvā	having known, having understood
tacchako	carpenter
tanuko	a few
tejanaṃ	point or shaft of an arrow, arrow
damayati	restrains,controls
dāruṃ	wood
dippati	shines, shines forth
dhammaññū	one who knows that which is proper, one who knows the doctrine
dhammo	that which is proper, just, righteous,true

dhammakammaṃ	righteous deed or activity, activity pertaining to the doctrine
namayati	bends, fashions
nayati	leads, takes
nindā	blame
nirāmisa	not characterized by or not comprising āmisaṃ
nirupadhi	free from passions, or attachment, desireless
nekkhammaṃ	renunciation of worldliness, freedom from lust, craving and desires
nettiko	irrigator
paccatthika(o)	opponent, opposing
paṭivattiya	to be turned back, resistible
paṇḍito	wise one
padaṃ	place, foot, footstep, path
pabbajito	one who has renounced household life, a recluse
pamodati	rejoices, enjoys, finds pleasure in
pamatto	one who is lazy, not diligent
parisaññū	knowing or knower of the assembly
parisā	assembly, group, gathering, retinue
pavattati	proceeds, goes on
pavatteti	set in motion, keeps going (transitive)
pasaṃsā	praise
pākata	common, vulgar, uncontrolled
pākatindriya	of uncontrolled mind
pāṇin	a living being (instrumental singular = pāṇinā)
buddha	enlightened, awakened
brahmā	Brahma, Supreme God (instrumental singular = brahmunā)
bhaṇḍanaṃ	quarrel, quarreling, strife
bhaṇḍanajāta	quarrelsome
mata	dead
mattā	measure, quantity, right measure
mattaññū	knowing the right measure, moderate
manussabhūta	human (being), (one) in human form
māro	death, god of death, tempter
mīyati	dies
mukhara	garrulous, noisy, scurrilous
mutta	freed
yassaṃ	in which one (feminine) - (locative singular of yā 'which (feminine)' (See II. 2.13)
rata	delighting in, intent on, devoted to, attached to
rahado	lake

loko	world, universe
vagga	dissociated, dissentious
vāto	wind
vikkiṇṇavāca	of loose talk
vinayakammaṃ	ethical activity, activities pertaining to monastic discipline
vipassati	sees clearly, insightfully, have spiritual insight.
vippasanna	clear
vippasīdati	is serene, tranquil, becomes calm
vibbhantacitta	with wandering or confused mind
vivadati	disputes, quarrels
vivadamāna	disputing, quarreling(-māna participle of vivadati)
vivādo	dispute, quarrel, contention
-āpanna	disputing, quarreling
visama	unequal, disharmonious
visesato	specially, particularly
vuccati	is called
sakunto	bird
saggo	heaven, celestial world, happy place
sama	even, equal, harmonious, level
samagga	being in unity
samāhita	collected, composed, settled, attentive
samiñjati	is moved, shaken
samīrati	is moved, blown
sampajāna	thoughtful, mindful, attentive, deliberate
sammodamāna	in agreement, on friendly terms, rejoicing together (-māna participle of sammodati, 'rejoices')
sâmisa	with, characterized by or having āmisaṃ
sâsava	with, having, or characterized by, āsavo
sutvāna	having heard, having listened to
selo	rock

LESSON V

1. "Jāneyya nu kho, bho Gotama, asappuriso asappurisaṃ - 'asappuriso ayaṃ bhavaṃ'" ti?

"Aṭṭhānaṃ kho etaṃ, brāhmaṇa, anavakāso yaṃ asappuriso asappurisaṃ jāneyya - 'asappuriso ayaṃ bhavaṃ'" ti.

"Jāneyya pana, bho Gotama, asappuriso sappurisaṃ - 'Sappuriso ayaṃ bhavaṃ'" ti?

"Etaṃ pi kho, brāhmaṇa, aṭṭhānaṃ, anavakāso yaṃ asappuriso sappurisaṃ jāneyya - 'sappuriso ayaṃ bhavaṃ'" ti.

"Jāneyya nu kho, bho Gotama, sappuriso sappurisaṃ - "Sappuriso ayaṃ bhavaṃ'" ti?

"Ṭhānaṃ kho etaṃ, brāhmaṇa, vijjati yaṃ sappuriso sappurisaṃ jāneyya - 'sappuriso ayaṃ bhavaṃ'" ti.

"Jāneyya pana, bho Gotama, sappuriso asappurisaṃ - 'asappuriso ayaṃ bhavaṃ'" ti?

"Etaṃ pi kho, brāhmaṇa, ṭhānaṃ vijjati yaṃ sappuriso asappurisaṃ jāneyya- 'asappuriso ayaṃ bhavaṃ'" ti.

(-A.N.)

2. Yo hi koci manussesu - gorakkhaṃ upajīvati
evaṃ Vāseṭṭha, jānāhi - 'kassako' so, na brāhmaṇo.

Yo hi koci manussesu - puthusippena jīvati
evaṃ, Vāseṭṭha, jānāhi - 'sippiko' so, na brāhmaṇo.

Yo hi koci manussesu - vohāraṃ upajīvati
evaṃ, Vāseṭṭha, jānāhi - 'Vāṇijo' so, na brāhmaṇo.

Yo hi koci manussesu - parapessena jīvati
evaṃ, Vāseṭṭha, jānāhi - 'Pessiko' so, na brāhmaṇo.

Yo hi koci manussesu - adinnaṃ upajīvati
evaṃ, Vāseṭṭha, jānāhi - 'coro' eso, na brāhmaṇo.

Yo hi koci manussesu - issatthaṃ upajīvati
evaṃ, Vāseṭṭha, jānāhi - 'Yodhājīvo', na brāhmaṇo.

Yo hi koci manussesu - porohiccena jīvati
evaṃ, Vāseṭṭha, jānāhi - 'Yājako' so, na brāhmaṇo.

Yo hi koci manussesu - gāmaṃ raṭṭhañca bhuñjati
evaṃ, Vāseṭṭha, jānāhi - 'rājā' eso, na brāhmaṇo.

Na câhaṃ 'brāhmaṇaṃ' brūmi - yonijaṃ mattisambhavaṃ.
'Bhovādi' nāma so hoti - sa ve hoti sakiñcano.

akiñcanaṃ, anādānaṃ - tamahaṃ[1] brūmi ' Brāhmaṇaṃ.'

Sabbasaṃyojanaṃ chetvā - yo ve na paritassati
saṃgâtigaṃ, visaṃyuttaṃ - taṃ ahaṃ brūmi ' brāhmaṇaṃ.'
(-S.N.)

3. appamādena maghavā - devānaṃ seṭṭhataṃ gato
appamādaṃ pasaṃsanti - pamādo garahito sadā.

yathâpi ruciraṃ pupphaṃ - vaṇṇavantaṃ agandhakaṃ
evaṃ subhāsitā vācā - aphalā hoti akubbato.

yathâpi ruciraṃ pupphaṃ - vaṇṇavantaṃ sagandhakaṃ
evaṃ subhāsitā vācā - saphalā hoti sakubbato.

dīghā jāgarato ratti - dīghaṃ santassa yojanaṃ
dīgho bālānaṃ saṃsāro - saddhammaṃ avijānataṃ.
(-Dhp.)

4. asevanā ca bālānaṃ - paṇḍitānañca sevanā
pūjā ca pūjanīyānaṃ - etaṃ maṃgalamuttamaṃ.
bāhusaccaṃ ca sippañca - vinayo ca susikkhito
subhāsitā ca yā vācā - etaṃ maṃgalamuttamaṃ.
dānañca dhammacariyā ca - ñātakānaṃ ca saṃgaho
anavajjāni kammāni - etaṃ maṃgalamuttamaṃ.
ārati virati pāpā - majjapānā ca saṃyamo
appamādo ca dhammesu - etaṃ maṃgalamuttamaṃ.
gāravo ca nivāto ca - santuṭṭhī ca kattaññutā
kālena dhammasavanaṃ - etaṃ maṃgalamuttamaṃ.
khantī ca sovacassatā - samaṇānañca dassanaṃ
kālena dhammasākacchā - etaṃ maṃgalamuttamaṃ.
(-S.N.)

GLOSSARY

akiñcano	one who has nothing, one who is free from worldly attachment
aṭṭhānaṃ	not possible, no place (for it) (a + ṭhānaṃ - see this grammar 7)
anādāno	one who is free from attachment
api	even
avakāso	possibility, space, (there is a) possibility
ārati	abstention, leaving off
issatthaṃ	bow, archery
uttama	highest, best, noble

[1] tam + ahaṃ

upajīvati	lives on, depends on
kataññutā	gratitude
kassako	a husbandman, farmer, cultivator
kālena	in time, at the proper time
kubbanta	practitioner, doer, one who practices (dative kubbato - See this grammar 3)
khanti	patience, forbearance
gāmo	village
gāravo	reverence, respect, esteem
Gotama	one of the Gotama family, the family name of the Buddha (Sanskrit Gautama)
gorakkhā	cow-keeping, tending the cattle
coro	thief, robber
chetvā	having cut off, having destroyed, having removed (tvā(na) gerund of chindati, 'cuts, severs')
jāgarati	is awake, is watchful
jāgaranto	one who is wakeful (present participle masculine-See this grammar 3)
ñātako	relative, kinsman
ṭhānaṃ...(vijjati)	it is possible, it is conceivable (see this grammar 7)
dānaṃ	giving, charity
devo	god
dhammacariyā	righteous living
nāma	just, indeed, for sure
nivāto	modesty, gentleness
parapessa	serving others
paritassati	is excited, is worried, is tormented
pasaṃsati	praises
pānaṃ	drink, drinking
puthu	many, various, individual, diverse, separate(ly)
pupphaṃ	flower
pūjanīyo	respect-worthy person
pūjā	worship, offering
pessiko	a messenger, a servant
porohiccaṃ	office of a family priest
bāhusaccaṃ	learning, knowledge
brūti	says, tells, calls, shows, explains
bhavaṃ	individual, person
bhuñjati	enjoys, eats, partakes of
bho	friend, sir(polite form of address)
bhovādi	nominative singular of bhovādin, a brahmin (according to the way he addresses others)

maghavā	nominative singular of maghavant Indra, king of the gods (see this grammar 2)
maṃgalaṃ	blessing, good omen, auspices, celebration, festival
-uttamaṃ	highest, best blessing
majjaṃ	intoxicating drink, liquor
mattisambhava	born of a mother
yājako	one who sacrifices, a priest
yojanaṃ	a measure of space, a distance of about 4 to 8 miles
yodhājivo	a warrior, a soldier
yonija	born of a womb
raṭṭhaṃ	reign, kingdom, empire, country
ratti	night
rucira	agreeable, attractive
vaṇṇavanta	colorful
vācā	word, speech
vāṇijo	a merchant
Vāseṭṭho	a proper name
vijānanta	knowing clearly (pres participle.of vijānati) (see this grammar 3)
vinayo	discipline
virati	complete abstention
visaṃyutto	he who is detached
ve	verily, indeed, truly
vohāro	trade, business, merchandise
saṃyamo	control, restraint
saṃyojanaṃ	bond, fetter (that binds one to the wheel of transmigration)
saṃsaro	life cycle
sakiñcano	one who has something, one who is full of worldly attachment (sa + kiñcano)
sakubbanto	doer, one who practices
sagandhaka	fragrant, having fragrance (sa+gandhaka see this grammar 8)
saṃgaho	assistance, protection, kind disposition
saṃgâtigo	he who has gone beyond (overcome) attachment
sadā	always, forever
santuṭṭhi	contentment
santo	fatigued one, he who is tired
sappuriso	a virtuous man, a worthy man, a good man
saphala	fruitful
sākacchā	conversation, discussion
sippaṃ	craft, technical knowledge, art

sippiko	artisan, craftsman
susikkhita	well-trained, well-practiced
seṭṭhatā	excellence, foremost place
sevanā	association
sovacassatā	gentleness, obedience

GRAMMAR V

1. FIRST AND SECOND PERSON PRONOUNS:

1.1 First Person: The first person pronouns ahaṃ 'I' and mayaṃ 'we' have forms as follows:

	Singular 'I'
Nom:	ahaṃ
Acc:	maṃ (mamaṃ)
Gen:	mama/mayhaṃ (mamaṃ/amhaṃ)
Dat:	mama/mayhaṃ (mamaṃ/amhaṃ)
Inst:	mayā
Abl:	mayā
Loc:	mayi

	Plural 'we'
Nom:	mayaṃ (amhe)
Acc:	amhe (asme/amhākaṃ/asmākaṃ)
Gen:	amhākaṃ (asmākaṃ/amhaṃ)
Dat:	amhākaṃ (asmākaṃ/amhaṃ)
Inst:	amhehi (amhebhi)
Abl:	amhehi (amhebhi)
Loc:	amhesu

1.2 Second Person: The second person pronouns tvaṃ 'thou, you (Singular)' and tumhe 'you (plural)' have forms as follows:

	Singular 'thou, you'
Nom:	tvaṃ (tuvaṃ)
Acc:	taṃ (tvaṃ/tuvaṃ/tavaṃ)
Gen:	tava/tuyhaṃ (tavaṃ/tumhaṃ)
Dat:	tava/tuyhaṃ (tavaṃ/tumhaṃ)
Inst:	tayā (tvayā)
Abl:	tayā (tvayā)
Loc:	tayi (tvayi)

	Plural 'you'
Nom:	tumhe
Acc:	tumhe (tumhākaṃ)
Gen:	tumhākaṃ
Dat:	tumhākaṃ
Inst:	tumhehi (tumhebhi)
Abl:	tumhehi (tumhebhi)
Loc:	tumhesu

1.3 Enclitic Forms of the Pronouns: The first and second person pronouns also have short, or "enclitic" forms, They do not have forms for the different cases, and thus one must tell from context which case is intended in a particular usage. However, they are also not used in all cases. The forms, and the cases in which they are used, are shown in the following charts:

First Person

	Form	Cases Represented
Sg.'I'	me	Inst.,Dat.,Gen.
Pl. 'We'	no	Acc.,Dat.,Inst.,Gen.

Second Person

	Form	Cases Represented
Sg.'Thou'	te	Inst.,Dat.,Gen.
Pl. 'You'	vo	Acc.,Dat.,Inst.,Gen.

2. NOUNS AND ADJECTIVES IN -vant AND -mant

There are nouns and adjectives with a stem in -mant or -vant.They have the same endings, except for the presence of the -m- or the -v-. Their case and gender forms are shown below, using silavant- 'virtuous (one)' as an example.

2.1 Masculine

	Singular	Plural
Nom:	sīlavā / -vanto	sīlavanto /-vantā
Acc:	sīlavantaṃ (sīlavaṃ)	sīlavanto /-vante
Gen: Dat:	sīlavato / -vantassa	sīlavataṃ/-vantānaṃ
Inst: Abl:	sīlavatā / -vantena	sīlavantehi (-ebhi)
Loc:	sīlavati /-vante (-vantamhi/-vantasmiṃ)	sīlavantesu
Voc:	sīlavā,-va /-vanta	sīlavanto/-vantā

The alternants following the slash (/) are analogical ones formed from the full -vant- stem by adding the endings of -a- stem nouns (I, 1. 21). Although later formations, they are found in all stages of the language. Note that the other forms have three stems: one in -va- (or -ma- for the -mant- stems), in the Nominative-Vocative singular; one in -vant-(-mant-) in the Accusative Singular and all of the plural except for the Dative-Genitive; and one in -mat- (-vat-) for the rest of the forms.

2.2 Neuter: The neuter forms are just like the masculine, except for the Nominative , Accusative, and the plural Vocative. These forms are as follows:

	Singular	Plural
Nom: Acc:	sīlavaṃ	sīlavanti/-vantāni
Voc:	sīlava	sīlavanti/-vantāni

2.3 Feminine: The feminine is formed by adding -ī- to either the -vant-(-mant-) or the -vat- (-mat-) stem. The Nominative Singular is thus either sīlavantī or sīlavatī. This then takes the same endings as a regular feminine noun in -ī- (I, 1. 232)

3. PRESENT PARTICIPLE CASE AND NUMBER ENDINGS

Some forms of the present participle in -ant- were given in III, 6.12. The others are, for the most part, like those of a -vant- (-mant-) noun.

3.1 Masculine: The full set of masculine forms is as follows, using gacchanta 'going, the goer' as example:

<table>
<tr><th></th><th>Singular</th><th>Plural</th></tr>
<tr><td>Nom:</td><td>gacchanto/gaccham̩</td><td rowspan="2">gacchanto /gacchantā /gacchante</td></tr>
<tr><td>Acc:</td><td>gacchantam̩</td></tr>
<tr><td>Gen:</td><td rowspan="2">gacchato</td><td rowspan="2">gacchatam̩ /gacchantānam̩</td></tr>
<tr><td>Dat:</td></tr>
<tr><td>Inst:</td><td rowspan="2">gacchatā</td><td rowspan="2">gacchantehi (-ebhi)</td></tr>
<tr><td>Abl:</td></tr>
<tr><td>Loc:</td><td>gacchati</td><td>gacchantesu</td></tr>
<tr><td>Voc:</td><td>gaccham̩/gacchanta</td><td>gacchanto/ gacchantā</td></tr>
</table>

3.2 Neuter: The neuter forms are like the masculine, except fot the Nominative-accusative which are as follows:

<table>
<tr><th></th><th>Singular</th><th>Plural</th></tr>
<tr><td>Nom:</td><td rowspan="2">gacchantam̩</td><td rowspan="2">gacchantāni / gacchanti</td></tr>
<tr><td>Acc:</td></tr>
</table>

3.3 Feminine: As mentioned in IV, 5, the present participle can take the feminine -ī ending. The case forms are like those of other -ī stems, but -nt- may become -t- before the non-nominative-accusative endings.

Thus Singular Genitive-Dative-Instrumental-Ablative detiyā, Plural Genitive-Dative detīnam̩, etc.

4. arahant

The noun arahant 'Arahant, deserving one', which occurred in Further Reading IV in the nominative singular araham̩, was originally the present participle of the verb arahati 'is worthy, deserves'. However, it also has a Nominative Singular arahā, like a -vant- (-mant-) noun, and the nominative plural appears as arahā as well as arahanto. Otherwise, it takes the same endings as vant- (-mant-) nouns or the present participle.

5. PAST PARTICIPLE

5.1 Formation of the Past Participle: The past participle (sometimes called the perfect or the passive participle) is most commonly formed with one of the two affixes -ta or-na. Of these two, -ta is the most common.

5.11 -ta Participles: The -ta ending is added directly to the verb root. Some, but not all, roots that end in a consonant add -i- before the -ta. Thus:

Verb	Root	Past Participle
suṇoti/suṇāti 'hears'	su-	suta
bhavati 'is, becomes'	bhū	bhūta
gacchati 'goes'	ga(m)-	gata
labhati 'gets, obtains'	labh-	laddha (<labh+ta)
passati 'sees'	dis- [2]	diṭṭha (<dis+ta)
garahati 'despises'	garah-	garahita
patati 'falls'	pat-	patita

As the examples show, shape changes, which may be complex, often take place between the root and the present tense, and there may be others when -ta is added, commonly involving assimilation of consonants and such changes as a (regular) shift of aspiration to the end of a cluster, as in

labh+ta -->labhta-->labtha-->laddha.

Although some regularities are discernible, there are numerous irregular forms, and detailed rules for the formation of the past participle will not be given here. For the present, it is simplest to learn the forms as they occur.

5.12 -na Participles: For some verbs, the past participle affix is -na. As with -ta, there are various changes in the root and stem which will not be given here. Examples are:

Verb		Root	Past Participle
deti/dadāti	'gives'	dā-	dinna
uppajjati	'is born, arises'	uppad-	uppanna
chindati	'cuts'	chid-	chinna

5.2 Use of the Participle:

5.21 The past participle, like the present participle, may be used as an adjective modifying nouns. As the name suggests, the sense will generally be past or completed action. This use is already familiar, since many of the forms that have been introduced as adjectives so far are actually past participles. Thus, for example, danta 'tamed, subdued' from dameti 'tames, controls'; pahīna 'given

---

2 As noted earlier, the root dis- replaces the root of passati in non-present forms.

up, abandoned' from pajahati 'gives up, renounces, abandons', etc. As stated earlier, these forms agree with the noun in number, gender, and case:

cittaṃ dantaṃ 'the mind (when) tamed, the tamed mind'
(Neuter Singular Nominative/Accusative)
akusalaṃ pahīnaṃ bad action, (when) given up
(Neuter Singular Nominative/Accusative)

They may either precede or follow the noun they modify. Thus we could also find dantaṃ cittaṃ 'the tamed mind' or pahinaṃ akusalaṃ 'abandoned bad action, bad action refrained from'.

As we have also seen, past participles (although they were not identified as such) may occur as predicates in equational sentences, and again, there is agreement:

ime dhammā (viññu)garahitā.
'These actions are despised (by the wise)'

5.2 Past participles may also, like the present participle, take gender-number endings to form nouns. In the case of the past participle, the noun will generally refer to the performer of the action (i.e., the subject of the verb)if the verb from which it is formed is intransitive, or the one who has undergone the action, i.e., the object of the verb) if the verb is transitive.

The gender number endings, and their case forms, are those of -a stem masculine and neuter (I, 1.21-2) and -ā stem feminine (II, 1.1) nouns The form Tathāgato 'the thus-gone one', used for the Buddha is an example, being formed from gata, the participle of gacchati. Similarly,the form mutto 'freed one' is formed from the past participle of muñcati 'to release' and can have a feminine form muttā 'she who is released'. Similarly, the form adinnaṃ' that which is not given' is the a- negative of the past participle of deti (or dadāti) 'gives, with a neuter singular ending. These formations are very common in Pāli, and many more examples will occur as we proceed.

6. yohi koci

yohi koci (yo 'relative'+ hi 'emphatic' plus ko 'who' + ci 'indefinite') has the sense 'who (so) ever' The locative case on a plural dependent noun following such an expression has the sense "among'. Thus:

yohi koci manussesu 'whoever among men'.

7. ṭhānaṃ AND aṭṭhānaṃ

7.1 ṭhānaṃ ' place, space', often followed by vijjati 'be found, exist' has the sense that whatever follows is possible',(literally 'there is a place for X'):

ṭhānaṃ...vijjati yaṃ sappuriso sappurisaṃ jāneyya...
'It is possible that a good man might recognize a good man'

7.2 aṭthānaṃ, as the opposite of ṭhānaṃ means 'impossible, cannot be.'

Note that avakāso 'space, possibility' and the negative anavakāso are also used with the same general import as ṭhānaṃ and aṭṭhānaṃ. Note also the following construction, in which both aṭṭhānaṃ and anavakāso are used, as equational predicates of etaṃ introducing an impossibility:

etaṃ...aṭṭhānaṃ, anavakāso yaṃ..
'That is impossible, it cannot be that...'

8. PREFIX sa- 'with'

In addition to the prefix sa- 'ones own' (II, 9), there is a homonymous prefix sa- meaning 'with, accompanied by' or 'having'. Thus sakiñcano '(one) having worldly attachment' from sa- + kiñcano 'worldly attachment.' Compare akiñcano '(one) without worldly attachment'. other examples of this prefix have occurred in earlier readings, though they were not noted as such. Thus sâsava 'with, having or characterized by āsavo ('clinging, desire') and sâmisa 'with, characterized by or having āmisaṃ (' material substance, food, flesh, sensual desire, lust') in Further Reading IV.

9 'THIS, NOT THAT'

'This, not that', i.e., 'X not Y' can be expressed in Pāli by X na Y:

rājā eso, na brāhmaṇo
'That one (is a) "king", not a brahmin.'

10. 'LIVE BY'

'Live by (means of)' can be expressed in two ways:
upajīvati 'lives on, depends on' plus the accusative, or
jīvati 'lives' plus the instrumental.

FURTHER READINGS V

1. "Chahi, bhikkhave, dhammehi samannāgato bhikkhu āhuneyyo hoti pāhuneyyo dakkhiṇeyyo añjalikaraṇīyo, anuttaraṃ puññakkhettaṃ lokassa.

Katamehi chahi?

Idha, bhikkhave, bhikkhu cakkhunā rūpaṃ disvā n'eva sumano hoti na dummano, upekkhako viharati sato sampajāno.
Sotena saddaṃ sutvā ...pe...
ghānena gandhaṃ ghāyitvā ...pe...
jivhāya rasaṃ sāyitvā ...pe...
kāyena phoṭṭhabbaṃ phusitvā ...pe...
manasā dhammaṃ viññāya n'eva sumano hoti na dummano, upekkhako viharati sato sampajāno.

Imehi kho, bhikkhave, chahi dhammehi samannāgato bhikkhu āhuneyyo hoti pāhuṇeyyo dakkhiṇeyyo añjalikaraṇīyo anuttaraṃ puññakkhettaṃ lokassâ" ti.

(-A.N.)

2. "Tena hi, Sīvaka, taññev'ettha paṭipucchāmi. Yathā te khameyya tathā naṃ byākareyyāsi.

Taṃ kiṃ maññasi, Sīvaka, santaṃ vā ajjhattaṃ lobhaṃ "atthi me ajjhattaṃ lobho" ti pajānāsi, asantaṃ vā ajjhattaṃ lobhaṃ "n'atthi me ajjhattaṃ lobho" ti pajānāsî" ti?

"Evaṃ bhante."

"Yaṃ kho tvaṃ, Sīvaka, santaṃ vā ajjhattaṃ lobhaṃ 'atthi me ajjhattaṃ lobho' ti pajānāsi, asantaṃ vā ajjhattaṃ lobhaṃ 'n'atthi me ajjhattaṃ lobho' ti pajānāsi - evaṃ pi kho, Sīvaka, sandiṭṭhiko dhammo hoti...

"Taṃ kiṃ maññasi, Sīvaka, santaṃ vā ajjhattaṃ dosaṃ...pe...
santaṃ vā ajjhattaṃ mohaṃ...pe...
santaṃ vā ajjhattaṃ lobhadhammaṃ...pe...
santaṃ vā ajjhattaṃ dosadhammaṃ...pe...
santaṃ vā ajjhattaṃ mohadhammaṃ "atthi me ajjhattaṃ mohadhammo" ti pajānāsi, asantaṃ vā ajjhattaṃ mohadhammaṃ "n'atthi me ajjhattaṃ mohadhammo" ti pajānāsî"ti?

"Evaṃ bhante."

Yaṃ kho tvaṃ, Sīvaka, santaṃ vā ajjhattaṃ mohadhammaṃ "atthi me ajjhattaṃ mohadhammo" ti pajānāsi, asantaṃ vā ajjhattaṃ mohadhammaṃ "n'atthi me ajjhattaṃ mohadhammo" ti pajānāsi - evaṃ kho, Sīvaka, sandiṭṭhiko dhammo hoti."

"Abhikkantaṃ, bhante, abhikkantaṃ, bhante...upāsakaṃ maṃ, bhante, bhagavā dhāretu ajjatagge pāṇ'upetaṃ saranaṃ gataṃ" ti.

(-A.N.)

3. Rājā āha: "Bhante Nāgasena, yo jānanto pāpakammaṃ karoti yo ca ajānanto pāpakammaṃ karoti, kassa bahutaraṃ apuññan" ti?

Thero āha: "yo kho mahārāja ajānanto pāpakammaṃ karoti tassa bahutaraṃ apuññan" ti.

Tena hi, bhante Nāgasena, yo amhākaṃ[3] rājaputto vā rājamahāmatto vā ajānanto pāpakammaṃ karoti taṃ mayaṃ diguṇaṃ daṇḍemâ" ti.

"Taṃ kiṃ maññasi mahārāja: tattaṃ ayoguḷaṃ ādittaṃ sampajjalitaṃ, eko ajānanto gaṇheyya, eko jānanto gaṇheyya, katamo balikataraṃ ḍayheyyâ"ti?

"Yo kho bhante ajānanto gaṇheyya so balikataraṃ ḍayheyyâ" ti.

"Evameva kho mahārāja yo ajānanto pāpakammaṃ karoti tassa bahutaraṃ apuññan" ti.

"Kallo'si bhante Nāgasenâ" ti. (-M.P.)

---

3 Honorific (royal) plural.

4. "Taṃ kiṃ maññatha, bhikkhave, 'rūpaṃ niccaṃ vā aniccaṃ vā'?" ti.
"Aniccaṃ bhante."
"Yaṃ panâniccaṃ, dukkhaṃ vā taṃ sukhaṃ vā?" ti.
"Dukkhaṃ bhante."
"Yaṃ panâniccaṃ dukkhaṃ vipariṇāmadhammaṃ, kallannu[4] taṃ samanupassituṃ, 'etaṃ mama, eso'hamasmi, eso me attā'?" ti.
"No h'etaṃ, bhante."
Vedanā...pe...sañña...pe...saṃkhārā...pe...viññāṇaṃ niccaṃ vā aniccaṃ vā?" ti.
"Aniccaṃ, bhante."
"Yaṃ panâniccaṃ,dukkhaṃ vā taṃ sukhaṃ vā?' ti.
"Dukkhaṃ, bhante."
"Yaṃ panâniccaṃ, dukkhaṃ, vipariṇāmadhammaṃ, kallannu taṃ samanupassituṃ, 'etaṃ mama, eso'hamasmi, eso me attā'?" ti.
"No h'etaṃ bhante." (-S.N.)

GLOSSARY

ajjatagge	from today on (= ajjato + agge)
ajjhattaṃ	inwardly, internally, subjective(ly)
añjalikaraṇīya	worthy of respectful salutation
aññatara	some, a certain
abhikkantaṃ	excellent, superb, wonderful, (literally, gone-beyond-ly)
ayoguḷo	iron ball
avoca	third singular past of vatti, 'says.speaks'
āditta	burning, blazing
āha	said
āhuneyya	venerable, worthy of offerings'
upasaṃkami	third singular past of upasaṃkamati 'approaches'
upāsako	lay-devotee, practicing Buddhist
upekkhaka	indifferent, disinterested
upeti	approaches, attains, comes to, reaches (the past participle upeta has the sense 'endowed with')
etadavoca	etad (=etam) + avoca
khamati	is fitting, seems good"
khettaṃ	field, sphere
gaṇhāti	picks up, takes
chahi	instrumental-ablative of cha- 'six'
ḍayhati	gets burned
(X) dhamma	of the nature of X
taññeva	= taṃ+ eva

---

[4] kallaṃ (Neuter of kalla) + nu (interrogative) i.e. 'so then is it smart...?'

tatta	heated, hot
tathā	thus, so
tena hi	if so, in that case
thero	elder, senior (bhikkhu)
dakkhiṇeyya	worthy of offerings or gifts
daṇḍeti	punishes
diguṇaṃ	doubly, twofold
disvā	having seen
dummana	unhappy, downcast
dhāreti	holds, bears, accepts, contains
dhāretu	third singular imperative of dhāreti (i.e., 'let him, her, it'...)
naṃ	alternate form of the pronoun taṃ
nicca	permanent, non-transitory
no	negative 'not'; more emphatic than na
pajānāti	realizes, understands well
paṭipucchati	asks in response, inquires
paṭipucchissāmi	First Person Future of paṭipucchati
pāṇupetaṃ	for life (literally 'possessed-with-breath-ly' ‹pāṇa(ṃ) 'breath' +upetaṃ neuter past participle of upeti (see above)
pāpakammaṃ	evil, sinful act
pāhuṇeyya	worthy of hospitality
puññaṃ	merit, righteousness
balikataraṃ	more, more greatly
byākaroti	explains, answers, brings to light
bhagavant	fortunate one (used as an epithet for the Buddha)
mahāmatto	chief minister
yaṃ	that, since, for (adverbial use of the neuter accusative of ya-)
rājaputto	prince
viññāya	having perceived or known
vipariṇāma	change
vedanā	feeling, sensation
saṃkhāro	essential condition, a thing conditioned, "mental coefficients"
saññā	perception, recognition
sata	mindful
santa	existing, being (present participle of atthi)
sandiṭṭhika	visible, empirical, empirically ascertainable, of advantage in this life
sampajjalita	ablaze, in flames
sammodi	past of sammodati - 'rejoices'
Sīvako	a proper name
sumana	of a happy mind, of a pleased mind

LESSON VI

1. Pañca-sikkhāpadāni:

1. Pāṇâtipātā veramaṇī sikkhāpadaṃ samādiyāmi.

2. Adinnâdānā veramaṇī sikkhāpadaṃ samādiyāmi.

3. Kāmesu micchâcārā veramaṇī sikkhāpadaṃ samādiyāmi.

4. Musāvādā veramaṇī sikkhāpadaṃ samādiyāmi.

5. Surāmerayamajja-pamādaṭṭhānā veramaṇī sikkhāpadaṃ samādiyāmi.

2. Yathâpi cando vimalo - gaccham[1] ākāsadhātuyā
sabbe tārāgaṇe loke - ābhāya atirocati,
tath'eva sīlasampanno - saddho purisapuggalo
sabbe maccharino loke - cāgena atirocati.

Yathâpi megho thanayaṃ - vijjumālī satakkaku
thalaṃ ninnaṃ ca pūreti - abhivassaṃ vasundharaṃ,
evaṃ dassanasampanno - Sammāsambuddhasāvako
maccharim adhigaṇhāti - pañcaṭhānehi paṇḍito.

Āyunā yasasā c'eva - vaṇṇena ca sukhena ca
sa ve bhogaparibyūḷho - pecca sagge pamodatî" ti.
(-A.N.)

3. Atha kho Selo brāhmaṇo tīhi māṇavakasatehi parivuto...yena Keṇiyassa jaṭilassa assamo ten'upasaṃkami. Addasā kho Selo brāhmaṇo Keṇiyassamiye jaṭile app'ekacce uddhanāni khaṇante, app'ekacce kaṭṭhāni phālente, app'ekacce bhājanāni dhovante, app'ekacce udakamaṇikaṃ patiṭṭhāpente, app'ekacce āsanāni paññāpente, Keṇiyaṃ pana jaṭilaṃ sāmaṃ yeva maṇḍalamālaṃ paṭiyādentaṃ.

Disvāna Keṇiyaṃ jaṭilaṃ etadavoca: 'Kinnukho bhoto Keṇiyassa āvāho vā bhavissati, vivāho vā bhavissati, mahāyañño vā paccupaṭṭhito, rājā vā Māgadho Seniyo Bimbisāro, nimantito svātanāya saddhiṃ balakāyenâ' ti?

"Na me, Sela, āvāho bhavissati n'api vivāho bhavissati, n'api rājā Māgadho Seniyo Bimbisāro, nimantito svātanāya saddhiṃ balakāyena. Api ca kho me mahāyañño paccupaṭṭhito atthi. Samaṇo Gotamo Sakyaputto Sakyakulā pabbajito. Aṃguttarāpesu cārikaṃ caramāno mahatā bhikkhusaṃghena...Āpaṇaṃ anuppatto. ...So me nimantito svātanāya saddhiṃ bhikkhusaṃghenâ" ti.

"'Buddho' ti, bho Keṇiya, vadesi?"

---

[1] Nominative Singular of the prtesent participle--see Grammar V,1.

"'Buddho' ti, bho Sela, vadāmi."

"'Buddho' ti, bho Keṇiya, vadesi?"
"'Buddho' ti, bho Sela, vadāmi."

"Ghoso pi kho eso dullabho lokasmiṃ yadidaṃ 'buddho' " ti.
(-S.N.)

4. "Dve'me, bhikkhave, puggalā loke uppajjamānā uppajjanti bahujanahitāya bahujanasukhāya, bahuno janassa atthāya hitāya sukhāya...

Katame dve?

Tathāgato ca arahaṃ sammāsambuddho, rājā ca cakkavattī. Ime kho, bhikkhave, dve puggalā loke uppajjamānā uppajjanti bahujanahitāya bahujanasukhāya, bahuno janassa atthāya hitāya sukhāya..." iti.

Dve'me, bhikkhave, puggalā loke uppajjamānā uppajjanti acchariyamanussā.

Katame dve?

Tathāgato ca arahaṃ sammāsambuddho, rājā ca cakkavattī. Ime kho, bhikkhave, dve puggalā loke uppajjamānā uppajjanti acchariyamanussā" ti.

"Dvinnaṃ, bhikkhave, puggalānaṃ kālakiriyā bahuno janassa anutappā hoti. Katamesaṃ dvinnaṃ?

Tathāgatassa ca arahato sammāsambuddhassa, rañño ca cakkavattissa.

Imesaṃ kho, bhikkhave, dvinnaṃ puggalānaṃ kālakiriyā bahuno janassa anutappā hotī" ti.

"Dve'me, bhikkhave, thūpârahā.

Katame dve?

Tathāgato ca arahaṃ sammāsambuddho, rājā ca cakkavattī. Ime kho, bhikkhave, dve thūpârahā" ti.
(-A.N.)

5. Tameva vācaṃ bhāseyya - yāy'attānaṃ na tāpaye
pare ca na vihiṃseyya - sā ve vācā subhāsitā.

Piyavācameva bhāseyya - yā vācā patinanditā
yaṃ anādāya pāpāni - paresaṃ bhāsate piyaṃ.

'Saccaṃ ve amatā vācā' - esa dhammo sanantano -
'sacce atthe ca dhamme ca' - āhu, 'santo patiṭṭhitā.'
(-S.N.)

GLOSSARY

Aṃguttarāpa	place name
acchariya	wonderful, marvelous
atirocati	outshine, excel
attānaṃ	accusative of attan 'self' (see this grammar 1.1)
atha	now, then
adinnâdāna(ṃ)	seizing or grasping that which is not given to one
addasā	saw (3rd singular past tense of dassati[2] (passati) 'sees')
adhigaṇhāti	excels, surpasses
anādāya	without taking or accepting
anutappa	to be regretted (from anutappati 'regrets, repents')
anuppatta	reached, one who has reached
api(ca)	but, still
app'ekacce	api + ekacce (see this grammar 17)
abhivassati	rains (down), sheds rain
arahā	alternate nom. sg. of arahant (see V.4)
ariyo	noble one
assamiya	belonging to a monastery or hermitage
assamo	monastery, hermitage, ashram
ākāsadhātu	space element, space, sky (ākāso 'sky, space' +dhātu (see this glossary)
āpaṇo	place name
ābhā	shine, luster, sheen
āyu	longevity, duration of life
āvāho	wedding, bringing a bride
āsanaṃ	seat
āhu	(they) say or said
udakaṃ	water
uddhanaṃ	fire hearth, oven
uppajjati	is born, is reborn in, arises, originates
ekacce	some, a few
etad	=etaṃ
esa	alternate form of eso (see II, 2.12)
kaṭṭhaṃ	wood, firewood
katvā	having done or made
kāmo(aṃ)	sense-desire, sense-pleasure

[2] This verb is commonly cited as such in grammars and dictionaries, but does not actually occur in that form. The actual occurring present tense form is dakkhiti, and passati is also used in the same sense.

kālo	proper time
kālakiriyā	death, passing away
kiṃ	what (see III, 1) used here as an interrogative particle
kinnukho	(=kiṃ + nu + kho); why, what for, what is it then
kuddho	angry one
kulaṃ	lineage, clan, family
Keṇiyo	proper name
khaṇanto	digging (present participle of khaṇati)
ghoso	noise, sound
cando	moon
cāgo	liberality, generosity.
cārikā	sojourn, wandering, journey
cārikaṃ caramāno	(while) going on alms-pilgrimage
jaṭilo	one who wears matted hair, an ascetic
jano	individual, person, people (collectively),
-ṭṭhānaṃ	sandhi form of ṭhānaṃ
(X) ṭṭhānaṃ	condition or state of X (see this grammar 15)
tāpayati	torments, tortures
tārāgaṇo	galaxy of stars, host of stars
thanayati	roars, thunders
thalaṃ	plateau, raised dry ground
thūpâraha	worthy of a stupa
thūpo	stupa, tope
dassanaṃ	perfect knowledge, insight
dullabha	rare, difficult to obtain
dhātu	element, relic, basis (feminine-see this grammar 6)
dhovanto	one who washes, one who cleans
nimanteti	invites
ninnaṃ	low land
nu	then, now
paccupaṭṭhāti	is present
paññāpento	one who prepares or arranges
paṭiyādeti	prepares, arranges
paṇḍito	wise one
patiṭṭhāpento	one who places, one who keeps
patiṭṭhita	established, fixed, founded upon
patinandita	rejoiced, welcomed
pabbajita	renounced, ordained, gone forth (into the holy life)
pamodati	rejoices, enjoys, finds pleasure in
paribyūḷha	provided with
parivuta	followed by, surrounded by
pare	other(ones) (see this Grammar 13)

pāṇātipāto	destruction of life, killing
pāpaṃ	sin. evil
puggalo	person, individual
putto	son
purisapuggalo	individual, man
pūreti	fills
pecca	having departed, after death
phālenta	splitting, breaking (present participle of phāleti)
balakāyo	army
bahu	many
Bimbisāro	proper name
bhavissati	will be (third future active indicative of bhavati 'be, become')
bhājanaṃ	vessel, utensil
bhāsati	says, speaks
bhāsate	is spoken, speaks (third singular present, middle voice,indicative)
bhikkhusaṃgho	community of Buddhist monks
bhogo	enjoyment, item for enjoyment, wealth, possession
bhoto	Dative-Genitive of bhavant 'venerable' (see this grammar 4)
maccharin	greedy one, selfish and avaricious one, stingy one
majjaṃ	intoxicant
maṇikaṃ	a big jar, pot
maṇḍalamāla	pavilion, a circular hall with a peaked roof
mata	dead, (one who is) dead
mahanto	great, big (one)
mahāyañño	great sacrifice, big alms-giving
Māgadha	of the Magadha (country)
māṇavako	youth, young man (especially a young Brahmin)
micchâcāro	wrong behavior
musāvādo	lying, falsehood
me	my, to me, by me (see V, 1.3)
megho	rain cloud
yañño	sacrifice, almsgiving
yadidaṃ	that is, namely
yasas	fame, repute, glory
yena...tena	where...there (see this grammar 10)
loko	world
vaṇṇo	outward appearance, complexion
vadeti	says, speaks
vasundharā	earth

vācā	word, speech
vijjumālin	wearing a garland or row of lightning (epithet for a cloud)
vimala	clear, clean, bright
vivāho	marriage, wedding, carrying or sending away of a bride
vihiṃsati	injures, hurts, oppresses
ve	indeed, verily
veramaṇī	abstinence
Sakya	family name (of the Buddha's lineage)
saccaṃ	truth
sata	hundred
satakkaku	epithet for a cloud (literally, 'the hundred-cornered one')
saddha	believing, determined
saddhiṃ	with
sanantana	eternal, old, ancient
santo	good person (declines as an -ant participle stem, see V, 3)
samādiyati	takes upon or with oneself
sammāsambuddho	perfectly enlightened one, a fully enlightened Buddha capable of teaching others
sāmaṃ	of oneself, by oneself
sāmaṃ yeva	= sāmaṃ + eva)
sāvako	disciple
sikkhāpadaṃ	precept, rule, instruction
sīlasampanno	one endowed with virtue, one who practices morality, virtuous one
Seniya	a clan name (literally 'belonging to the army')
Selo	proper name
svātanāya	for tomorrow, for the following day
hanati	kills

GRAMMAR VI

1. MASCULINE -an STEMS

1.1 -an stem nouns have a nominative singular in -ā, but will be introduced in glossaries as ending in -an, so as to distinguish them from -ā stem nouns.

EXAMPLE: attan 'self, soul'

	Singular	Plural
Nom:	**attā**	**attāno**
Acc:	**attānaṃ / attaṃ**	
Gen:	**attano**	**attānaṃ**
Dat:		
Inst:	**attanā** / **attena**	**attanehi (-ebhi)**
Abl:	**attanā**	
Loc:	**attani**	**attanesu**
Voc:	**atta / attā**	**attāno**

NOTE: attan also has alternate plural case forms with -u- or -ū-; thus Genitive-Dative attūnaṃ, Instrumental-Ablative attūhi/-bhi, Locative attusu /-ūsu.

1.2 Many -an stem nouns have irregular or alternate forms. Thus brahman '(god) Brahma' is similar to attan, but has Vocative Singular brahme, Dative-Genitive Singular brahmuno, and the following alternate forms:

Instr-Abl Sg.: brahmunā (along with brahmanā)
Dat-Gen Pl.: brahmunaṃ (along with brahmānaṃ)

NOTE: brahman also has forms with -ṇ- instead of -n-: thus brahmuṇā, brahmaṇā, brahmuṇaṃ, brahmāṇaṃ etc.

1.3 rājan 'king' has forms as follows:

	Singular	Plural
Nom:	**rājā**	**rājāno**
Acc:	**rājānaṃ / rājaṃ**	
Gen:	**rañño / rājino (rājassa)**	**raññaṃ / rājūnaṃ (rājānaṃ)**
Dat:		
Inst:	**raññā** / **rājinā**	**rājuhi (-ubhi) rājehi (-ebhi)**
Abl:	**raññā**	
Loc:	**rājini / raññe**	**rājūsu (rājesu)**
Voc:	**rāja / rājā**	**rājāno**

2. -in STEM NOUNS

Nouns with a stem in -in have a Nominative Singular in -ī, but will be listed in glossaries ending in -in to distinguish them from -ī stem nouns. They inflect as follows (bhovādin, which occurred in Reading V, is another example of this class):

EXAMPLE: maccharin 'greedy person, miser'

<table>
<tr><th></th><th>Singular</th><th>Plural</th></tr>
<tr><td>Nom:</td><td>maccharī</td><td rowspan="2">maccharino/ maccharī</td></tr>
<tr><td>Acc:</td><td>maccharinaṃ/maccharim</td></tr>
<tr><td>Gen:</td><td rowspan="2">maccharino / maccharissa</td><td rowspan="2">maccharīnaṃ</td></tr>
<tr><td>Dat:</td></tr>
<tr><td>Inst:</td><td rowspan="2">maccharinā/ maccharimhā/-ismā</td><td rowspan="2">maccharīhi (-ībhi)</td></tr>
<tr><td>Abl:</td></tr>
<tr><td>Loc:</td><td>maccharini/-imhi(-ismiṃ)</td><td>maccharīsu</td></tr>
<tr><td>Voc:</td><td>macchari</td><td>maccharino/maccharī</td></tr>
</table>

3. mahant AND santo

3.1 mahant 'great' has endings much like the -vant/-mant stems (V, 2), but with the following nominative forms. Note that maha occurs as both singular and plural:

	Singular	Plural
Nom:	mahā	mahā / mahanto/ mahantā

3.2 santo 'virtuous person' may appear in the nominative plural as well as singular, as santo. Otherwise, it generally follows the -ant stems:

	Singular	Plural
Nom:	santo	santo / santā

Historically, sant- is the present participle of atthi, and still appears in Pāli in the sense "existing', as well as in the specialized sense of 'virtuous person' given here. Thus the meanings must be distinguished from context.

4. ADDRESS FORM bhavant

bhoto is the Genitive-Dative form of a noun bhavant 'Venerable' used as a polite form of address. The vocative address form bhante with which we are familiar is actually a related form, and appears to have been borrowed from a different dialect. Originally, these were from the present participle of the verb bhavati 'be, become', hence literally 'the existing one, being' but were specialized in this usage, and thus the case forms resemble those of a present participle. All of the case forms of bhavant do not occur, but those which may be encountered are as follows:

<table>
<tr><th></th><th>Singular</th><th>Plural</th></tr>
<tr><td>Nom:</td><td>bhavaṃ</td><td>bhavanto / bhonto</td></tr>
<tr><td>Acc:</td><td>bhavantaṃ</td><td>bhavante</td></tr>
<tr><td>Gen:</td><td rowspan="2">bhoto</td><td rowspan="2">bhavataṃ / bhavantānaṃ</td></tr>
<tr><td>Dat:</td></tr>
<tr><td>Inst:</td><td>bhotā</td><td>bhavantehi</td></tr>
<tr><td>Voc:</td><td>bhavaṃ, bho</td><td>bhonto</td></tr>
</table>

5. -as STEM NOUNS: manas

Pāli has a few Neuter nouns with a stem in -as, such as manas- 'mind., and cetas- 'thought, intention, purpose', which will be listed in that form in Glossaries here. In Sanskrit, such nouns formed a distinct class, but in Pāli, they have been converted almost completely to the Neuter -a type (I, 22), and only have distinct forms in the singular, as exemplified by the first alternants in the chart below. Note that the other alternants have the same forms as -a stem nouns. The plural forms belong completely to that type: thus Nominative Plural manāni etc.

EXAMPLE: manas 'mind'

<table>
<tr><th></th><th colspan="2">Singular</th></tr>
<tr><td>Nom:</td><td colspan="2" rowspan="2">mano / manaṃ</td></tr>
<tr><td>Acc:</td></tr>
<tr><td>Gen:</td><td colspan="2" rowspan="2">manaso / manassa</td></tr>
<tr><td>Dat:</td></tr>
<tr><td>Inst:</td><td rowspan="2">manasā/</td><td>manena</td></tr>
<tr><td>Abl:</td><td>manamhā (asmā)</td></tr>
<tr><td>Loc:</td><td colspan="2">manasi/ mane/-amhi (asmiṃ)</td></tr>
<tr><td>Voc:</td><td colspan="2">mano / manaṃ</td></tr>
</table>

6. FEMININE -u STEMS:

dhātu 'element, relic', which appears in the compound ākāsadhātu, 'sky element' in this reading represents a new type of noun with a stem ending in -u, but feminine. These nouns are relatively rare, and have endings as follows:

EXAMPLE: dhātu

	Singular	Plural
Nom:	dhātu	dhātū / dhātuyo
Acc:	dhātuṃ	
Gen:	dhātuyā	dhātūnaṃ
Dat:		
Inst:		dhātūhi/dhātūbhi
Abl:		
Loc:	dhātuyaṃ	dhātūsu
Voc:	dhātu	dhātū /dhātuyo

7. PAST TENSE ("AORIST")

Pāli has a past tense (sometimes referred to as the "Aorist", since it is largely derived from the Sanskrit aorist). There are several classes of verbs with regard to past tense formation, and forms exemplifying two of these classes appear in this lesson.

7.1 The addasā Type ("A Aorist" and "Root Aorist"). In this type, the following affixes, often accompanied by a prefix a- (called "the Augment") are added to the verb root. Other changes in the root may also take place.

	Singular	Plural
1 Pers:	-aṃ	-āma /-amha
2 Pers:	-ā	-atha / -attha
3 Pers:		uṃ / -ū

Some roots appear with the alternate endings shown above, some do not. As an example, from passati/dis- 'sees', we have the following:

	Singular	Plural
1 Pers:	addasaṃ	addasāma / addasamha
2 Pers:	addasā	addasatha / addasattha
3 Pers:		addasuṃ

One form of the past tense of gacchati 'goes' (‹gaṃ) follows this pattern (Other forms will be given later):

	Singular	Plural
1 Pers:	agamaṃ	agamāma / agamamha
2 Pers:	agamā	agamatha / agamattha
3 Pers:		agamuṃ

7.2 The upasaṃkami Type ("The -is Aorist") Another form of the past tense, the most common in Pāli, adds the following endings to the root (again, sometimes with other changes in the form of the root):

	Singular	Plural
1 Pers:	-iṃ / -isaṃ	-imha / -imhā
2 Pers:	i / ī	-ittha
3 Pers:		-iṃsu / -isuṃ

Thus, with upasaṃkamati- 'approaches' (‹upa + saṃ +kam-)

	Singular	Plural
1 Pers:	upasaṃkamiṃ	upasaṃkamimha/-imhā
2 Pers:	upasaṃkami	upasaṃkamittha
3 Pers:		upasaṃkamiṃsu

With these affixes, also, an augment a- is sometimes prefixed, particularly with shorter stems. Thus from bhāsati 'speaks', we have abhāsi 'he said', etc. When the root already has prefixes, the augment, when it appears, comes between them and the root. Thus from pavisati 'goes in, enters' (from pa + vis) we have pāvisi from pa + a + vis , where the -a- is the augment, as well as the form pavisi, without the augment.

atthi 'be, exist' also belongs to this class. Note the lengthening of the first vowel in the singular:

	Singular	Plural
1 Pers:	āsiṃ	asimha
2 Pers:	āsi	asittha
3 Pers:		asiṃsu

gacchati appears with these "-is Aorist" endings as well as those of the addasā type, and many verbs in Pāli occur in both types of past. Thus for gacchati, in addition to the forms in 7.1, we find (note the augment):

	Singular	Plural
1 Pers:	agamisaṃ / agamiṃ	agamimha
2 Pers:	agami	agamittha
3 Pers:		agamiṃsu / agamisuṃ

8. PAST OF vac- 'SAY. SPEAK'

The root vac- is defective, since it does not have present tense forms in actual use, though present tense forms vatti or vacati are sometimes cited. In Pāli, it has been supplanted in the present tense by forms of the root vad- as in vadati. However vac- does have forms in other tenses, including the past, in which it can take the endings of the addasā type, It also has alternate endings. One of these is the form avoca,'said' that occurred in the further readings of lesson five. Other forms will be given in a later lesson (VIII,4) .

9. PAST PARTICIPIAL SENTENCES WITH INSTRUMENTAL SUBJECTS

There is a very frequent type of sentence in Pāli with transitive verbs[3] in which the verb is in the past participial form -ta or -na (V, 5). The participle agrees in number and gender with the object, which is in the Nominative case, and the Subject will be in the Instrumental case. Thus the form is like English "X has been done by Y". (Word order, as usual, is variable).The usual sense is "past" or "perfect", although these sentences are sometimes referred to as "passive":

so me nimantito
'I have invited him'. or, 'He has been invited by me'

desito Ānanda mayā dhammo
'I have preached the doctrine, Ananda.'

If there is no direct object expressed, the participle will be in the Neuter Singular:

evaṃ me sutaṃ
'Thus have I heard.'

Note that the participle may also be accompanied by an auxiliary like atthi:
me mahāyañño paccupaṭṭhito atthi
'I have prepared a great sacrifice.'

[3] That is, verbs that take an object.

10. yena...tena

The correlative pair yena...tena is very commonly used in an idiom yena-X...tena-Y, where Y includes a verb of motion and X, in the Nominative case, expresses the destination:

Yena assamo ten'upasaṃkami '(He) came to the ashram.'

11. āha, āhu

āha and āhu are isolated forms, the remnant of a Sanskrit Perfect formation that has otherwise virtually disappeared in Pāli (though some later commentarial works have other Sanskrit-based Perfect forms). āha 'he (has) said' has already appeared in the readings (VI, Further Readings) and is singular. āhu is originally plural, but is also found with a singular sense: 'he, they (has/have) said'. The plural sometimes also appears as āhaṃsu. āhu is often used without an expressed subject and an indefinite sense, i.e., They say/have said' or 'It has been said.'

12. 'HUNDREDS'

One way in which things are enumerated by the hundreds in Pāli is for the noun which is counted to be compounded with sataṃ 'hundred', with the number of hundreds specified by a preceding numeral, which agrees in number and case. That is, it is if in English one said "three youth-hundreds" for "three hundred youths":

tīni mānavasatāni 'three hundred youths'

tīhi mānavasatehi 'three hundred youths (Instrumental)'

Note that the entire compound takes the Neuter gender of sataṃ even though that which is counted is animate, and that sataṃ appears in the plural.

13. para 'OTHER (ONE'S)' and añña '(AN)OTHER'

para 'other (one's) and añña '(an)other' take the endings of pronouns, like sabbe (IV, 8). Thus the plural nominative forms are pare and aññe, the plural Genitive-Dative forms are paresaṃ and aññesaṃ, etc.

14. saddhiṃ AND parivuta

saddhiṃ and parivuta both mean 'with, accompanied by', and they take dependent nouns in the instrumental case. parivuta is actually a -ta participle ('being accompanied'), and thus agrees in gender, number and case with the one accompanied:

brāhmaṇo cattāri mānavakasatehi parivuto...'
'The Brahmin, with ('accompanied by') four hundred youths...'
bhikkhusaṃghena saddhiṃ 'with a group of bhikkhus'

15. -ṭhānaṃ AND -dhamma COMPOUNDS

The forms ṭhānaṃ and dhamma commonly serve as the second members of compounds with the senses 'state of' and '(of the)nature of' respectively. An example of a -dhamma compound appeared in Further Reading V: vipariṇāmadhamma 'having change as it's nature'. ṭhānaṃ is one of those forms with a first consonant that doubles when a vowel precedes (II, 12), hence pamādaṭṭhānaṃ from pamāda+(ṭ)thānaṃ.

16. LOCATIVE 'AMONG' OR 'IN'

The plural locative of the name of a place or a group of people is commonly used to signify 'in that place., or 'among those people:'

aṃguttarāpesu — 'In the Anguttara country', or 'among the Anguttaras'

17. SANDHI

Sometimes, when a word ending in a stop consonant plus -i is followed closely by a word beginning in a vowel, the consonant doubles and the -i is lost (Ci+V --> CCV). Thus:

api+ekacca --> appekacca

As with similar sandhi phenomena in Pāli, this is particularly common in certain set phrases.

FURTHER READINGS VI

1. "Nanu te, Soṇa, rahogatassa paṭisallīnassa evaṃ cetaso parivitakko udapādi - 'ye kho keci bhagavato sāvakā āraddhaviriyā viharanti, ahaṃ tesaṃ aññataro. Atha ca pana me na anupādāya āsavehi cittaṃ vimuccati; saṃvijjanti kho pana me kule bhogā, sakkā bhoge ca bhuñjituṃ puññāni ca kātuṃ. Yannūnâhaṃ sikkhaṃ paccakkhāya hīnāyâvattitvā bhoge ca bhuñjeyyaṃ puññāni ca kareyyaṃ' " ti?

"Evaṃ, bhante."

"Taṃ kiṃ maññasi, Soṇa, kusalo tvaṃ pubbe agāriyabhūto vīṇāya tantissare" ti?

"Evaṃ, bhante."

"Taṃ kiṃ maññasi, Soṇa, yadā te vīṇāya tantiyo accāyatā honti, api nu te vīṇā tasmiṃ samaye saravatī vā hoti kammaññā vā" ti?

"No h'etaṃ, bhante."

"Taṃ kiṃ maññasi, Soṇa, yadā te vīṇāya tantiyo atisithilā honti, api nu te vīṇā tasmiṃ samaye saravatī vā hoti kammaññā vā" ti?

No h'etaṃ, bhante."

"Yadā pana te, Soṇa, vīṇāya tantiyo na accāyatā honti nâtisithilā same guṇe paṭṭhitā, api nu te vīṇā tasmiṃ samaye saravatī vā hoti kammaññā vā" ti?

"Evaṃ, bhante."

Evameva kho, Soṇa, accāraddhaviriyaṃ uddhaccāya saṃvattati, atisithilaviriyaṃ kosajjāya saṃvattati. Tasmātiha[4] tvaṃ, Soṇa, viriyasamataṃ adhiṭṭhaha, indriyānaṃ ca samataṃ paṭivijjha, tattha ca nimittaṃ gaṇhāhî" ti.

(-A.N.)

2. "Kodhano dubbaṇṇo hoti - atho dukkhaṃ pi seti so
atho atthaṃ gahetvāna - anatthaṃ adhipajjati.

Tato kāyena vācāya - vadhaṃ katvāna kodhano
Kodhâbhibhūto puriso - dhanajāniṃ nigacchati.

Kodhasammadasammatto - āyasakyaṃ nigacchati
ñātimittā suhajjā ca - parivajjanti kodhanaṃ.

anatthajanano kodho - kodho cittappakopano
bhayamantarato jātaṃ - taṃ jano nâvabujjhati.

Kuddho atthaṃ na jānāti - kuddho dhammaṃ na passati
andhatamaṃ tadā hoti - yaṃ kodho sahate naraṃ

nâssa[5] hirī na ottappaṃ - na vāco hoti gāravo
kodhena abhibhūtassa - na dīpaṃ hoti kiñcanaṃ.

(-A.N.)

3. Rājā āha: "Kiṃlakkhaṇo bhante manasikāro, kiṃlakkhaṇā paññā?" ti.

"Ūhanalakkhaṇo kho mahārāja manasikāro, chedanalakkhaṇā paññā"ti.

"Kathaṃ ūhanalakkhaṇo manasikāro, kathaṃ chedanalakkhaṇā paññā?; opammaṃ karohî" ti.

Jānāsi tvaṃ mahārāja yavalāvake?" ti.

---

[4] tasmā + iha with -t- inserted in sandhi.
[5] na+assa Genitive/Dative of ayaṃ

"Ama bhante, jānāmī" ti.

"Kathaṃ mahārāja yavalāvakā yavaṃ lunantī?" ti.

"Vāmena bhante hatthena yavakalāpaṃ gahetvā dakkhiṇena hatthena dāttaṃ gahetvā dāttena chindantī" ti.

"Yathā mahārāja yavalāvako vāmena hatthena yavakalāpaṃ gahetvā dakkhiṇena hatthena dāttaṃ gahetvā dāttena chindati, evam'eva kho mahārāja yogâvacaro manasikārena mānasaṃ gahetvā paññāya kilese chindati. Evaṃ kho mahārāja ūhanalakkhaṇo manasikāro, evaṃ chedanalakkhaṇā paññā" ti.

"Kallo'si bhante Nāgasenâ" ti.

(-M.P.)

4. Atha kho aññataro brāhmaṇo yena bhagavā ten'upasaṃkami, upasaṃkamitvā bhagavatā saddhiṃ sammodi...ekamantaṃ nisīdi. Ekamantaṃ nisinno kho so brāhmaṇo bhagavantaṃ etadavoca:

"Sandiṭṭhiko dhammo, sandiṭṭhiko dhammo'ti, bho Gotama, vuccati. Kittāvatā nu kho bho Gotama, sandiṭṭhiko dhammo hoti..." iti.

"Tena hi brāhmaṇa, taññev'ettha[6] paṭipucchissāmi. Yathā te khameyya tathā naṃ byākareyyāsi. Taṃ kiṃ maññasi, brāhmaṇa, santaṃ vā ajjhattaṃ rāgaṃ "atthi me ajjhattaṃ rāgo" ti pajānāsi, asantaṃ vā ajjhattaṃ rāgaṃ "n'atthi me ajjhattaṃ rāgo" ti pajānāsī" ti?

"Evaṃ, bho."

"Yaṃ kho tvaṃ, brāhmaṇa, santaṃ vā ajjhattaṃ rāgaṃ "atthi me ajjhattaṃ rāgo" ti pajānāsi, asantaṃ vā ajjhattaṃ rāgaṃ "n'atthi me ajjhattaṃ rāgo" ti pajānāsi - evaṃ pi kho brāhmaṇa sandiṭṭhiko dhammo hoti..."

"Taṃ kiṃ maññasi, brāhmaṇa, santaṃ vā ajjhattaṃ dosaṃ...pe...
santaṃ vā ajjhattaṃ mohaṃ...pe.
santaṃ vā ajjhattaṃ kāyasandosaṃ...pe...
santaṃ vā ajjhattaṃ vacīsandosaṃ...pe...
santaṃ vā ajjhattaṃ manosandosaṃ "atthi me ajjhattaṃ manosandoso"ti pajānāsi, asantaṃ vā ajjhattaṃ manosandosaṃ "n'atthi me ajjhattaṃ manosandoso" ti pajānāsī" ti?

"Evaṃ, bhante."

---

6 taṃ + eva + ettha

"Yaṃ kho tvaṃ, brāhmaṇa, santaṃ vā ajjhattaṃ manosandosaṃ "atthi me ajjhattaṃ manosandoso" ti pajānāsi, asantaṃ vā ajjhattaṃ manosandosaṃ "n'atthi me ajjhattaṃ manosandoso" ti pajānāsi - evaṃ kho brāhmaṇa, sandiṭṭhiko dhammo hoti" ...iti.

"Abhikkantaṃ, bho Gotama, abhikkantaṃ, bho Gotama, ...upāsakaṃ maṃ bhavaṃ Gotamo dhāretu ajjatagge pāṇ'upetaṃ saraṇaṃ gataṃ" ti.

5. "Manujassa pamatta cārino - taṇhā vaḍḍhati māluvā viya
so palavati hurāhuraṃ - phalamicchaṃ'va vanasmiṃ vānaro

Yaṃ esā sahatī[7] jammī - taṇhā loke visattikā
sokā tassa pavaḍḍhanti - abhivaḍḍhaṃ'va bīraṇaṃ

Yo c'etaṃ sahatī jammiṃ taṇhaṃ loke duraccayaṃ
sokā taṃhā papatanti - udabindu'va pokkharā"

(Dhp.)

GLOSSARY

agāriyabhūta	being a householder
accāyata	too long, too much stretched, too taut
accāraddhaviriyaṃ	over-exertion, too much exertion
aññatara	one, someone, one of a certain number
atisithila	too loose, lax, slack
atthaṃ gahetvāna	having held back, or given up, profit or advantage
atho	= atha
adhiṭṭhaha	concentrate, fix one's attention on, undertake, practice (imperative)
adhipajjati	attains, reaches, comes to
anattha(aṃ)	unprofitable situation or condition, harm, misery, misfortune
anupādāya	without taking hold of, without clinging to, away from (<an + gerund of upādāti 'grasp')
antarato	from within (ablative of antara 'within')
andhatamaṃ	deep darkness
abhibhūta	overcome, overwhelmed by
abhivaḍḍhati	grow, increase, outgrow
avabujjhati	realize, understand
āyasakyaṃ	dishonor, disgrace, bad repute
āraddhaviriya	energetic, resolute
icchati	desires, wishes (for), likes

[7] sahatī for sahati (Lengthened for the meter).

indriyaṃ	faculty (of experience or perception)
iha	here, now, in this world
udapādi	arose, (past of uppajjati 'arises')
udabindu	drop of water
uddhaccaṃ	over-balancing, agitation, excitement, distraction, flurry
ūhanaṃ	reasoning, consideration, examination, lifting up
ekamantaṃ	aside, on one side
ettha	in this case/context, here
ottappaṃ	shrinking back from doing wrong, remorse
kammañña	fit for work, ready for playing
kalāpa	a bundle, a bunch, a sheaf, a row
kiñcanaṃ	any
kittāvatā	in what respect, in what sense
kileso	defilement, impurity(in a moral sense)
kodhana	having anger, angry (one), uncontrolled (one)
kodho	anger, ill will
gahetvāna	ger. of gaṇhāti
guṇa	quality, nature, component
cārin	doer, behaver
cetas	mind
chindati	cuts, breaks, plucks, pierces
chedanaṃ	cutting, severing, destroying
janana	causing, bringing, producing
jammī	wretched, contemptible
jāta	born, arisen
jāni	deprivation, loss
ñāti	a relation, relative
tato	thereupon, further
tattha	there, in that
tanti	string or cord (here of a musical instrument)
tantissara	string music
tārā	star
dakkhiṇa	right (side) (also 'southern' as in F.R.III)
dāttaṃ	sickle
dīpaṃ	solid foundation, shelter, refuge
dukkhaṃ	unhappily, painfully (adverbial accusative-see III, 8)
dubbaṇṇa	of bad color, ugly, of changed color
duraccaya	hard to remove, difficult to overcome
dhanaṃ	wealth, riches, treasures
naro	man, individual
nigacchati	goes down to, enters, comes to, suffers

nimittaṃ	object of a thought
nisinna	past participle of nisīdati
nisīdati	sits (down)
nisīdi	third singular past of nisīdati
pakopana	upsetting, shaking, making turbulent
paccakkhāya	having given up, having abandoned
paññā	wisdom, insight, knowledge
paṭipucchati	questions in return. Future 1 Sg. paṭipucchissāmi
paṭivijjha	having penetrated, intuited, acquired, comprehended
paṭisallīna	secluded, retired, gone into solitude
paṭṭhita	having been set, established
papatati	drops, falls down or off
parivajjati	avoids, shuns, gives up
parivitakko	reflection, thought, consideration
palavati	floats, swims, jumps
pavaḍḍhati	grows (up), increases
passati	see, realize
puññaṃ	meritorious act
pubbe	previously, before
puriso	man, individual
pokkharaṃ	lotus leaf
phalaṃ	fruit, result
bīraṇaṃ	name of a plant
bhuñjati	enjoys, eats
manasikāro	attention, pondering, fixed thought
manujo	man
mānasaṃ	intention, purpose of mind, mental action
māluvā	(long) vine (kind of)
mitto	friend
yaṃ	when
yadā	when
yannūna	well, now rather, let (me) (used in an exhortative sense)
yannūnâhaṃ	now then, let me
yavo	barley, grain (in general);
yogâvacaro	one at home in endeavor or spiritual exercises, an earnest student, one who has applied himself to spiritual exercises (yoga)
rahogata	being alone, being in private
rāgo	attachment, lust
lāvako	cutter, reaper
lunāti	cuts, reaps
vaco	speech, word (also appears as vacā)

vacī	compounding stem of vaco
vaḍḍhati	grows, increases
vadho	harm, killing, destruction
vanaṃ	forest
vānaro	monkey
vāma	left (side)
vimuccati	be freed
viya	like, as (particle of comparison)
viriyaṃ	exertion, energy
visattikā	clinging to, adhering to. lust, desire
viharati	live, reside
vīṇā	lute
saṃvijjati	seems to be, appears, exists
sakkā	it is possible (+ inf)
saddhiṃ	with
sandosaṃ	defilement, pollution
sama	equal, even, level
samatā	equality, evenness, normal state
samayo	time, period
sammatta	intoxicated (by/with), overpowered by
sammada	drowsiness, intoxication
sammodati	exchanges friendly greetings, rejoices, delights, (past sammodi)
saravatī	having resonance or melodiousness
sahati	conquers, overcomes
sikkhā	study, training, discipline
suhajjo	friend, good-hearted one
seti	sleeps, dwells, lives
Soṇo	a proper name
hattho	hand
hirī	sense of shame, bashfulness
hīna	low, base, inferior
hīnāya āvattati	turns to the lower, gives up orders, returns to secular life
hurāhuraṃ	from existence to existence

LESSON VII

1. "Etha tumhe, Kālāmā, mā anussavena, mā paramparāya, mā itikirāya, mā piṭakasampadānena ,...mā samaṇo no[1] garûti. Yadā tumhe, Kālāmā, attanā'va jāneyyātha 'ime dhammā akusalā, ime dhammā sāvajjā, ime dhammā viññugarahitā, ime dhammā samattā samādinnā ahitāya dukkhāya saṃvattantî'ti; atha tumhe, Kālāmā, pajaheyyātha."

Taṃ kiṃ maññatha, Kālāmā, lobho purisassa ajjhattaṃ uppajjamāno uppajjati hitāya vā ahitāya vā" ti?

"Ahitāya, bhante."

"Luddho panâyaṃ, Kālāmā, purisapuggalo lobhena abhibhūto, pariyādinnacitto, pāṇaṃ pi hanati, adinnaṃ pi ādiyati, paradāraṃ pi gacchati, musā pi bhaṇati, paraṃ pi tathattāya samādapeti, yaṃ'sa[2] hoti dīgharattaṃ ahitāya dukkhāyâ" ti.

"Evaṃ, bhante."

"Taṃ kiṃ maññatha, Kālāmā, doso purisassa ajjhattaṃ uppajjamāno uppajjati hitāya vā ahitāya vâ" ti?

"Ahitāya, bhante."

"Duṭṭho panâyaṃ, Kālāmā, purisapuggalo dosena abhibhūto, pariyādinnacitto, pāṇaṃ pi hanati, adinnaṃ pi ādiyati, paradāraṃ pi gacchati, musā pi bhaṇati, paraṃ pi tathattāya samādapeti, yaṃ'sa hoti dīgharattaṃ ahitāya dukkhāyâ" ti.

Evaṃ, bhante."

"Taṃ kiṃ maññatha, Kālāmā, moho purisassa ajjhattaṃ uppajjamāno uppajjati hitāya vā ahitāya vâ" ti?

"Ahitāya, bhante."

"Mūḷho panâyaṃ, Kālāmā, purisapuggalo mohena abhibhūto, pariyādinnacitto, pāṇaṃ pi hanati, adinnaṃ pi ādiyati, paradāraṃ pi gacchati, musā pi bhaṇati, paraṃ pi tathattāya samādapeti, yaṃ sa hoti dīgharattaṃ ahitāya, dukkhāyâ" ti.

"Evaṃ, bhante."

"Taṃ kiṃ maññatha, Kālāmā, ime dhammā kusalā vā akusalā vā" ti?

"Akusalā, bhante."

"Sāvajjā vā anavajjā" ti?

"Sāvajjā bhante."

"Viññugarahitā vā viññuppasatthā vā" ti?

"Viññugarahitā, bhante."

"Samattā, samādinnā ahitāya dukkhāya saṃvattanti, no vā? Kathaṃ vā ettha hotî" ti?

"Samattā, bhante, samādinnā ahitāya dukkhāya saṃvattantî ti. Evaṃ no ettha hotî" ti.

(A.N.)

---

1 Note that this no is not the negative, but the clitic form of a pronoun (Grammar V,1.3).

2 yaṃ + assa

2. "Nâhaṃ, brāhmaṇa, sabbaṃ diṭṭhaṃ bhāsitabbaṃ ti vadāmi; na panâhaṃ, brāhmaṇa, sabbaṃ diṭṭhaṃ na bhāsitabbaṃ ti vadāmi; nâhaṃ, brāhmaṇa, sabbaṃ sutaṃ bhāsitabbaṃ ti vadāmi; na panâhaṃ, brāhmaṇa, sabbaṃ sutaṃ na bhāsitabbaṃ ti vadāmi; nâhaṃ, brāhmaṇa, sabbaṃ mutaṃ bhāsitabbaṃ ti vadāmi; na panâhaṃ, brāhmaṇa, sabbaṃ mutaṃ na bhāsitabbaṃ ti vadāmi; nâhaṃ, brāhmaṇa, sabbaṃ viññātaṃ bhāsitabbaṃ ti vadāmi; na panâhaṃ, brāhmaṇa, sabbaṃ viññātaṃ na bhāsitabbaṃ ti vadāmi"

"Yaṃ hi, brāhmaṇa, diṭṭhaṃ bhāsato akusalā dhammā abhivaḍḍhanti, kusalā dhammā parihāyanti, evarūpaṃ diṭṭhaṃ na bhāsitabbaṃ ti vadāmi. Yaṃ khv'assa[3] ca, brāhmaṇa, diṭṭhaṃ abhāsato kusalā dhammā parihāyanti, akusalā dhammā abhivaḍḍhanti, evarūpaṃ diṭṭhaṃ bhāsitabbaṃ ti vadāmi."

"Yaṃ hi, brāhmaṇa, sutaṃ bhāsato akusalā dhammā abhivaḍḍhanti, kusalā dhammā parihāyanti, evarūpaṃ sutaṃ na bhāsitabbaṃ ti vadāmi. Yaṃ ca khv'assa, brāhmaṇa, sutaṃ abhāsato kusalā dhammā parihāyanti, akusalā dhammā abhivaḍḍhanti, evarūpaṃ sutaṃ bhāsitabbaṃ ti vadāmi."

"Yaṃ hi, brāhmaṇa, mutaṃ bhāsato akusalā dhammā abhivaḍḍhanti, kusalā dhammā parihāyanti, evarūpaṃ mutaṃ na bhāsitabbaṃ ti vadāmi. Yaṃ ca khv'assa, brāhmaṇa, mutaṃ abhāsato kusalā dhammā parihāyanti, akusalā dhammā abhivaḍḍhanti, evarūpaṃ mutaṃ bhāsitabbaṃ ti vadāmi."

"Yaṃ hi, brāhmaṇa, viññātaṃ bhāsato akusalā dhammā abhivaḍḍhanti, kusalā dhammā parihāyanti, evarūpaṃ viññātaṃ na bhāsitabbaṃ ti vadāmi. Yaṃ ca khv'assa, brāhmaṇa, viññātaṃ abhāsato kusalā dhammā parihāyanti, akusalā dhammā abhivaḍḍhanti, evarūpaṃ viññātaṃ bhāsitabbaṃ ti vadāmi."

(-A.N.)

3. Saccaṃ bhaṇe na kujjheyya - dajjā'ppasmiṃ[4] pi yācito
etehi tīhi ṭhānehi - gacche devāna[5] santike.

Kāyappakopaṃ rakkheyya - kāyena saṃvuto siyā
kāyaduccaritaṃ hitvā - kāyena sucaritaṃ care.

Vacīpakopaṃ rakkheyya - vācāya saṃvuto siyā
vacīduccaritaṃ hitvā - vācāya sucaritaṃ care.

Yo pāṇamatipāteti - musāvādaṃ ca bhāsati
loke adinnaṃ ādiyati - paradāraṃ ca gacchati

---

[3] kho + assa, with the sense 'on the other hand, still, furthermore'
[4] dajjā + appasmiṃ. See this grammar 7.
[5] =devānaṃ

Surāmerayapānaṃca - yo naro anuyuñjati
idh'evameso[6] lokasmiṃ - mūlaṃ khaṇati attano.

(Dhp.)

4. Sace labhetha nipakaṃ sahāyaṃ
Saddhiṃcaraṃ sādhuvihāridhīraṃ
abhibhuyya sabbāni parissayāni
careyya tena'ttamano satīmā

No ce labhetha nipakaṃ sahāyaṃ
Saddhiṃcaraṃ sādhuvihāridhīraṃ
Rājā'va raṭṭhaṃ vijitaṃ pahāya
Eko care mātaṃg'araññe'va nāgo

(Dhp.)

GLOSSARY

atipāteti	kills, fells
attano	self's (see VI, 1.1)
attamano	delighted, pleased, happy
anuyuñjati	practises, gives oneself up to (with Acc.), attends, pursues
anussavaṃ	tradition, hearsay
appa	little
appasmiṃ dadāti	see this grammar 7
abhibhavati	overcomes ger. abhibhuyya; ppl. abhibhūta
araññaṃ	forest, woods
assa	gen. sg. of ayaṃ (IV, 1)
itikirā	hearsay, mere guesswork
eko	alone
etha	come (Second person plural of eti)
evarūpa	(of this form), such, of this type
Kālāmā	Kalamas, a proper name
kujjhati	is angry (with), is rritated
khaṇati	digs, uproots
garu	venerable (person), teacher
carati	moves (about) behaves, conducts, leads, carries out
jānāti	knows, understands, realizes
tathattaṃ	thatness, the state of being so
tumhe	you (Pl.) (V, 1.2)
dajjā	Optative of deti (or dadati) (see this grammar I)
dadāti	gives

6 idha+eva+m+eso. evạ here is the emphatic eva, and the -m- is intrusive.

diṭṭha	seen, witnessed diṭṭhaṃ a vision, that which is seen
duccaritaṃ	bad behavior, incorrect behavior
duṭṭha	wicked, malicious
nāgo	elephant
nipaka	intelligent, mature
pakopo	agitation, anger
paramparā	tradition, lineage (of scholars or teachers), series
pariyādinnacitta	with the mind completely overpowered by, with the mind completely taken over by
parissayaṃ	obstacle
parihāyati	decreases, dwindles, deteriorates
paro	other (person)
pahāya	ger. of pajahati
piṭaka	basket, a term used for the three main divisions of the Pāli canon
piṭakasampadāna	Piṭaka tradition, authority of the scriptures
purisapuggalo	individual
bhāsitabba	Future passive participle of bhāsati (see this grammar 2)
mā	prohibitive particle (see this grammar 4)
mātaṃgo	elephant, type of elephant
muta	thought, what is thought, that which is thought
mūlaṃ	root, origin
yācita	being requested, being begged for
rakkhati	guards, protects, takes care of, controls
luddha	greedy, covetous
vijita	conquered
viññāta	known, what is known, that which is known, what is perceived /recognized /understood
sace	if (see this grammar 6)
saccaṃ	truth
satimā	mindful one (nom. sg. of satimant The -i- in the reading is lengthened for the meter)
saddhiṃ caro	constant companion, one who accompanies
santike	in (to) the vicinity, near
sabba	all, every
samādinna	accepted, taken upon oneself
sahāyo	friend
sādhuvihāridhīro	one who is of noble behavior, one who is steadfast
siyā	see this grammar I
sucaritaṃ	good behavior

suta	heard, that which is heard (ppl. of suṇāti)
hitvā	give up, abandon gerund of jahāti (from root hā -see this grammar 8)

GRAMMAR VII

1. OPTATIVE

1.1. -ya Optatives: A few verbs, including deti 'gives', jānāti 'knows' and karoti 'does' sometimes appear with an optative formed with the suffix -yā. Thus, beside the third person forms dadeyya, jāneyya, and kareyya, we find dajjā (<dad + yā), jaññā (<jan + yā) or janiyā, and kariyā or kayirā (< kariyā). Some first person forms, such as dajjaṃ or dajjāmi are also found, but in general, such forms are rare.

1.2 Optative of atthi 'is': The optative of atthi 'is' is as follows:

	Singular	Plural
1 Pers:	assaṃ / siyaṃ	assāma
2 Pers:	assa	assatha
3 Pers:	assa / siyā	assu / siyuṃ

The third singular siyā form is commonly used in setting up a hypothetical situation; i.e., ' suppose there were...' or 'let it be that...'

siyā..Bhagavato...bhāsitaṃ jano aññathā pi paccāgaccheyya
'It might be (or 'suppose') that people (jano) might understand (paccāgaccheyya[7]) differently (aññathā) what the Blessed one said.'

2. FUTURE PASSIVE PARTICIPLE

2.1. The future passive participle is formed with the suffixes -(i)tabba, and -anīya, (this may be -ṇīya after a stem with -r-). The ending also appears sometimes as -aneyya, or for a few verbs, -ya. The stem used for this participle commonly, but not always, resembles the present stem. Thus:

Present	Future Passive Participle
gacchati 'goes'	gantabba
suṇāti 'hears'	sotabba
karoti 'does'	kattabba /kātabba /karaṇīya /kicca
bhavati 'is, becomes'	bhavitabba /bhabba[8] (<bhav + -ya)
carati 'moves, practices'	caritabba

[7] Literally 'go to meet' or 'return'.
[8] bhabba has the idiomatic sense 'capable' that we met in Lesson 2, Reading 2.

jānāti 'knows'	jānitabba /ñātabba /ñeyya
passati 'sees'	daṭṭhabba /dassanīya /dassaneyya
pūjeti 'worships, honors'	pūjanīya /pujja (<puj + -ya)
hanati 'kills'	hantabba / haññа (han + -ya)
deti 'gives'	dātabba / deyya
pivati 'drinks'	peyya / pātabba
labhati 'obtains'	laddhabba

2.2 The future passive participle does not simply have a future passive sense i.e., "will be done", but also connotes desireability, i.e., "should be done" or "worthy of being done." Several such forms have occurred in earlier readings, but have simply been glossed rather than explained:

bhikkhu...hoti añjalikaraṇīyo
'The bhikkhu is worthy of reverence' (añjali 'gesture of reverence')'
pūjā ca pūjanīyānaṃ
'...and worship of those worthy to be worshipped'

Note that, as these examples show, the future passive participle, like other participles may be used as either an adjective or a noun, and in either case, inflects like a masculine or neuter -a- stem or a feminine -ā- stem.

3.attan 'self, soul' AS A REFLEXIVE

The form attan (VI, 1) can be used as a reflexive pronoun, i.e., 'oneself, himself, herself yourself', etc. Commonly it remains in the singular in this usage when it is used adverbially, as in the example below, where it is in the instrumental case:

yadā tumhe attanā'va jāneyyātha...
'When you know (this) by yourselves...'

4.NEGATIVES no AND mā

4.1 mā is a prohibitive particle, and thus forms negative commands or prohibitives. It may be used with the past, the optative, or the imperative:

mā saddaṃ akattha 'Do not make noise'
(akattha= Second Person Plural Past of karoti)

mā saddaṃ akāsi 'Do not make noise'
(akāsi= Second person Singular past of karoti)

mā pamādaṃ anuyuñjetha
'You should not indulge in sloth'(or "Don't be indolent')
(anuyuñjetha = Second Person Plural Optative of anuyuñjati 'indulges in, engages in')

mā gaccha 'Don't go
(gaccha= Second Singular Imperative of gacchati (III. 5))

4.2. no is a negative emphatic. no vā has the sense 'or not', 'or isn't it'

eso dhammo kusalo, no vā
'Is this doctrine well suited (i.e. to attain the desired end)or not?'

5. eti 'COMES'

The verb eti'comes' adds the person-number affixes directly to the present stem e- : emi 'I come' etha 'you come' etc. Some other forms of this verb are:

Past Participle	ita
Imperative 2 Sg.	ehi
Imperative 2 Pl.	etha

6. sace AND -ce 'IF'

sace and -ce both express 'if'.

6.1 -ce was given in Grammar IV,11, and, as was stated there, it is a clitic, and thus follows some other form, usually the first word in its own ('if) sentence:

ahañce eva kho pana musāvadī assaṃ...
'If I were to lie (Literally 'be a liar (musāvadin= 'liar'))

(In the example just given, note the use of the optative of atthi that was given in 1.2 above.)

6.2 sace is, like English "if", an independent word, and usually occurs at the beginning of a sentence:

sace labhetha nipakam. sahāyaṃ...
'If you acquire a wise friend...

The form of the verb occuring with sace (and that in the 'then' clause) varies with the sense. In the example above from the Reading, it is in the optative. This is common, but present tense forms (and others) are also possible:

sace ...saccaṃ vadasi adāsī bhavasi
'If you speak the truth (2 sg. Pres.) You will not be a servant.'
(adāsi = 'non-servant (Feminine)')

7. LOCATIVE CASE

With deti (or dadāti) 'give', The locative case signifies 'from' or 'out of':

dajjāppamasmiṃ '(One) Should give from the little (one has')
(<dajjā + appasmiṃ)

Note that appa 'little (amount)' like para 'other' sabba 'all', etc. takes the pronominal affixes when used as a pronoun (see IV, 8)

8. THE ROOT hā

From the root hā 'decrease' several important verbs are formed, among them hāyati 'diminishes, wastes away', vijahati 'gives up, abandons, forsakes, leaves', pajahati 'gives up, abandons, renounces, forsakes', jahati or jahāti 'gives up, abandons, forsakes, leaves' and hāpeti 'omits, neglects, reduces (transitive)' Note that several of these verbs are synonyms or near-synonyms, and that most of them involve a stem jah(a)-. Some forms of these verbs are as follows:

Pres. 3 Sg:	hāyati	vijahati	pajahati /pajahāti	jahāti	hāpeti
Past 3 Sg:	hāyi	vijahi	pajahi	jahi	hāpesi
Pres. Pl:	hāyanta /hāyamāna	vijahanta	pajahanta	jahanta	hāpenta
Past Pl:	hīna	vijahita	pajahita	jahita	hāpita
Gerund:	hāyitvā	vijahitvā /vihāya	pajahitvā /pahāya	jahitvā /hitvā	hāpetvā
Fut Pl:	hātabba	vijahitabba	pajahitabba	jahitabba	hāpetabba

The form hīyati 'is decreased, decays, is given up or abandoned', is ultimately from the same root. Some forms of this verb are:

Pres 3 Sg:	hīyati
Past 3 Sg:	hīyi
Pres Part:	hīyamāna

LESSON VII FURTHER READINGS

1. "Tayo'me, brāhmaṇa, aggī pahātabbā parivajjetabbā, na sevitabbā. Katame tayo? Rāgaggi, dosaggi, mohaggi."

Kasmā câyaṃ, brāhmaṇa, rāgaggi pahātabbo parivajjetabbo, na sevitabbo? Ratto kho, brāhmaṇa, rāgena abhibhūto pariyādinnacitto kāyena duccaritaṃ carati, vācāya duccaritaṃ carati, manasā duccaritaṃ carati. So kāyena duccaritaṃ caritvā,vācāya duccaritaṃ caritvā, manasā duccaritaṃ caritvā, kāyassa bhedā paraṃ maraṇā apāyaṃ duggatiṃ vinipātaṃ nirayaṃ upapajjati. Tasmâyaṃ rāgaggi pahātabbo parivajjetabbo, na sevitabbo."

"Kasmā câyaṃ, brāhmaṇa, dosaggi pahātabbo parivajjetabbo, na sevitabbo? Duṭṭho kho, brāhmaṇa, dosena abhibhūto pariyādinnacitto kāyena duccaritaṃ carati, vācāya duccaritaṃ carati, manasā duccaritaṃ carati. So kāyena duccaritaṃ caritvā, vācāya duccaritaṃ caritvā, manasā duccaritaṃ caritvā kāyassa bhedā paraṃ maraṇā apāyaṃ duggatiṃ vinipātaṃ nirayaṃ upapajjati. Tasmâyaṃ dosaggi pahātabbo parivajjetabbo, na sevitabbo."

Kasmā câyaṃ, brāhmaṇa mohaggi pahātabbo parivajjetabbo, na sevitabbo? Mūḷho kho, brāhmaṇa, mohena abhibhūto pariyādinnacitto kāyena duccaritaṃ carati, vācāya duccaritaṃ carati, manasā duccaritaṃ carati. So kāyena duccaritaṃ caritvā, vācāya duccaritaṃ caritvā, manasā duccaritaṃ caritvā kāyassa bhedā paraṃ maraṇā apāyaṃ duggatiṃ vinipātaṃ nirayaṃ upapajjati. Tasmâyaṃ mohaggi pahātabbo parivajjetabbo, na sevitabbo. Ime kho tayo, brāhmaṇa, aggī pahātabbā parivajjetabbā, na sevitabbā."

(-A.N.)

2. Rājā āha: "Bhante Nāgasena, kiṃlakkhaṇā paññā?" ti.

"Pubbe kho mahārāja mayā vuttaṃ: 'chedanalakkhaṇā paññā'ti, api ca obhāsanalakkhaṇā pi paññā" ti.

"Kathaṃ, bhante, obhāsanalakkhaṇā paññā?" ti.

"Paññā, mahārāja, uppajjamānā avijjandhakāraṃ vidhameti, vijjobhāsaṃ janeti, ñāṇâlokaṃ vidaṃseti, ariyasaccāni pākaṭāni karoti; tato yogâvacaro aniccan-ti vā dukkhan-ti vā anattā-ti vā sammapaññāya passatî"ti.

"Opammaṃ karohî"ti.

"Yathā, mahārāja, puriso andhakāre gehe padīpaṃ paveseyya, paviṭṭho padīpo andhakāraṃ vidhameti, obhāsaṃ janeti, ālokaṃ vidaṃseti, rūpāni pākaṭāni karoti, evameva kho mahārāja, paññā uppajjamānā avijjandhakāraṃ vidhameti, vijjobhāsaṃ janeti, ñāṇâlokaṃ vidaṃseti, ariyasaccāni pākaṭāni karoti, tato yogâvacaro aniccanti vā dukkhanti vā anattāti vā sammapaññāya passati. Evaṃ kho mahārāja, obhāsanalakkhaṇā paññā" ti.

"Kallo'si bhante Nāgasenâ" ti.

(-M.P.)

3. "Bhante Nāgasena, nav'ime puggalā mantitaṃ guyhaṃ vivaranti na dhārentîti. Katame nava: rāgacarito, dosacarito, mohacarito, bhīruko, āmisagaruko, itthī, soṇḍo, paṇḍako, dārako" ti.

Thero āha "Tesaṃ ko doso?" ti.

"Rāgacarito, bhante Nāgasena, rāgavasena mantitaṃ guyhaṃ vivarati na dhāreti; duṭṭho dosavasena mantitaṃ guyhaṃ vivarati na dhāreti; mūḷho mohavasena mantitaṃ guyhaṃ vivarati na dhāreti; bhīruko bhayavasena mantitaṃ guyhaṃ vivarati na dhāreti; āmisagaruko āmisahetu mantitaṃ guyhaṃ vivarati na dhāreti; itthī ittaratāya mantitaṃ guyhaṃ vivarati na dhāreti; soṇḍiko surālolatāya mantitaṃ guyhaṃ vivarati na dhāreti; paṇḍako anekaṃsikatāya mantitaṃ guyhaṃ vivarati na dhāreti; dārako capalatāya mantitaṃ guyhaṃ vivarati na dhāreti.

Bhavatîha:

Ratto duṭṭho ca mūḷho ca - bhīru āmisacakkhuko
Itthī soṇḍo paṇḍako ca -navamo bhavati dārako
Nav'ete puggalā loke - ittarā calitā calā
Etehi mantitaṃ guyhaṃ - khippaṃ bhavati pākaṭan" ti.

(M.P.)

4. Middhī yadā hoti mahagghaso ca
Niddāyitā samparivattasāyī
Mahāvarāho'va nivāpapuṭṭho
punappunaṃ gabbhamupeti mando

Appamādaratā hotha - sacittamanurakkhatha
Duggā uddharath'attānaṃ - paṃke satto'va kuñjaro.
(Dhp.)

GLOSSARY

aggi	fire (plural aggī)[9]
anattā	not a soul, without a soul, non-substantial
anurakkhati	guards, protects, watches
anekaṃsikatā	uncertainty, doubtfulness
andhakāro(aṃ)	darkness
apāyo	calamity, a transient state of loss and woe after death
api	=-pi 'also' (see I, 3)
apica	(=api + ca) further, moreover, furthermore
ariyasaccaṃ	noble truth
avacaro	one at home in, conversant with
āmisaṃ	(raw) meat, food for enjoyment, material things
āmisagaruko	one who attaches importance to material things, items of enjoyment or food, a greedy person
āmisacakkhuka	one intent on or inclined to material enjoyment (literally, 'one with an eye on enjoyment')
āloko	seeing, sight, light
ittara	unsteady, fickle, changeable
ittaratā	changeableness
uddharati	raises, lifts up
upeti	comes, reaches
uppajjamāna	arising, being born
obhāsanaṃ	shining
obhāso	shine, splendour, luster, effulgence, appearance
kasmā	why (ablative of ko; cf. Lesson II,1)

9 This represents a new type of noun: masculine -i stems. Their remaining forms will be given in the grammar of lesson VIII.

kāyassa bhedā paraṃ maraṇā	after the breaking up of the body and after death
kuñjaro	elephant
khippaṃ	soon, quickly
gabbho	womb
garuka	heavy, important, bent on, attaching importance to
guyha	to be hidden, that which is hidden, secret
gehaṃ	house, dwelling, household, hut
capalatā	fickleness, unsteadiness
carati	move about, practice, lead
caritaṃ	behavior, character
carito	one who has a character
X-carita	one who has the character of X kind
cala	unsteady, fickle
calita	wavering, unsteady
ñāṇaṃ	knowledge, intelligence, insight
tato	thence, from that, thereupon, afterwards
dārako	child
duggaṃ	rough ground, wrong way
duggati	unhappy existence, realm of misery
doso	wrong, fault, defeat, blemish
navama	ninth
niddāyitā	a sleepy person
nirayo	purgatory, hell
nivāpapuṭṭha	fed on fodder
paṃko(aṃ)	mud
pajahati	gives up, discards, abandons
paṇḍako	eunuch, weakling
paraṃ	after
parivajjeti	shun, avoid
paviṭṭha	entered, gone into, procured ppl. of pavisati 'enters'
paveseti	makes enter, procures, furnishes, provides
passati	sees
pahātabba	Fut. pass. part. of pajahati gives up
pākaṭa	open, manifest, unconcealed ī
pākaṭaṃ karoti	makes manifest (pākataṃ will agree with the object)
puna	again
punappunaṃ	again and again
bhavatîha	(<bhavati iha) it is said (in this context)
bhīru	coward
bhīruko	fearful one, coward, one who is shy
bhedo	breaking, splitting, disunion, decomposition
mantitaṃ	(that which is) given as counsel, secret talk

mando	idiot, fool, stupid one
mahagghaso	(one who) eats much, greedy, gluttonous
mahā	big, great, large, huge (from mahant)
middhī	slothful (one)
yogo	application
rata	attached to, finding delight in
ratta	infatuated, impassioned (one)
rāgaggi	fire of passion
lolatā	nature of being fond of or addicted to, longing, greed
varāho	pig
vasena	because of, on account of
vijjobhāsa	=vijjā + obhāsa
vidaṃseti	shows, makes appear
vidhameti	destroys, ruins, does away with, dispels
vinipāto	great ruin, a place of suffering, state of punishment
vivarati	opens, discloses
vutta	said, spoken pp. of vadati
satta	sunk
samparivattasāyī	one who sleeps turning to and fro
sammappaññā	right knowledge, true wisdom
sevati	serves, practices, takes upon oneself
soṇḍiko	drunkard
soṇḍo	one who is addicted to drink, a drunkard
hetu	for the sake of, for the purpose of, by reason of
X hetu	by reason of X, for the purpose of X

LESSON VIII

1. Atha kho Venāgapurikā brāhmaṇagahapatikā yena Bhagavā ten'upasaṃkamiṃsu; upasaṃkamitvā app'ekacce Bhagavantaṃ abhivādetvā ekamantaṃ nisīdiṃsu; app'ekacce Bhagavatā saddhiṃ sammodiṃsu... ekamantaṃ nisīdiṃsu; app'ekacce nāmagottaṃ sāvetvā ekamantaṃ nisīdiṃsu; app'ekacce tuṇhībhūtā ekamantaṃ nisīdiṃsu. Ekamantaṃ nisinno kho Venāgapuriko Vacchagotto brāhmaṇo Bhagavantaṃ etadavoca:

"Acchariyaṃ, bho Gotama, abbhutaṃ, bho Gotama! Yāvañc'idaṃ bhoto Gotamassa vippasannāni indriyāni, parisuddho chavivaṇṇo pariyodāto. Seyyathâpi, bho Gotama, sāradaṃ badarapaṇḍuṃ parisuddhaṃ hoti pariyodātaṃ, evameva bhoto Gotamassa vippasannāni indriyāni parisuddho chavivaṇṇo pariyodāto. Seyyathâpi, bho Gotama, tālapakkaṃ sampati bandhanā pamuttaṃ, parisuddhaṃ hoti pariyodātaṃ, evameva bhoto Gotamassa vippasannāni indriyāni, parisuddho chavivaṇṇo pariyodāto."

(-A.N.)

2. Tena kho pana samayena Uggatasarīrassa brāhmaṇassa mahāyañño upakkhaṭo hoti. Pañca usabhasatāni thūṇ'ûpanītāni honti yaññatthāya; pañca vacchattarasatāni thūṇ'ûpanītāni honti yaññatthāya; pañca vacchatarīsatāni thūṇ'ûpanītāni honti yaññatthāya; pañca ajasatāni thūṇ'ûpanītāni honti yaññatthāya; pañca urabbhasatāni thūṇ'ûpanītāni honti yaññatthāya. Atha kho Uggatasarīro brāhmaṇo yena Bhagavā ten'upasaṃkami; upasaṃkamitvā Bhagavatā saddhiṃ sammodi... ekamantaṃ nisīdi. Ekamantaṃ nisinno kho Uggatasarīro brāhmaṇo Bhagavantaṃ etadavoca:

"Sutaṃ m'etaṃ, bho Gotama, aggissa ādānaṃ yūpassa ussāpanaṃ mahapphalaṃ hoti mahânisaṃsaṃ" ti.

"Mayā pi kho etaṃ, brāhmaṇa, sutaṃ aggissa ādānaṃ yūpassa ussāpanaṃ mahapphalaṃ hoti mahânisaṃsaṃ" ti. Dutiyaṃ pi kho Uggatasarīro brāhmaṇo...pe...tatiyaṃ pi kho Uggatasarīro brāhmaṇo Bhagavantaṃ etadavoca: "Sutaṃ m'etaṃ, bho Gotama, aggissa ādānaṃ yūpassa ussāpanaṃ mahapphalaṃ hoti mahânisaṃsaṃ" ti.

"Mayā pi kho etaṃ, brāhmaṇa, sutaṃ aggissa ādānaṃ yūpassa ussāpanaṃ mahapphalaṃ hoti mahânisaṃsaṃ" ti.

"Tayidaṃ, bho Gotama, sameti bhoto c'eva Gotamassa amhākaṃ ca, yadidaṃ sabbena sabbaṃ." Evaṃ vutte āyasmā Ānando Uggatasarīraṃ brāhmaṇaṃ etadavoca:

"Na kho, brāhmaṇa, tathāgatā evaṃ pucchitabbā – 'sutaṃ m'etaṃ, bho Gotama, aggissa ādānaṃ yūpassa ussāpanaṃ mahapphalaṃ hoti mahânisaṃsaṃ' ti. Evaṃ kho, brāhmaṇa, tathāgatā pucchitabbā 'Ahaṃ hi, bhante, aggiṃ ādātukāmo yūpaṃ ussāpetukāmo – Ovadatu maṃ, bhante, Bhagavā. Anusāsatu maṃ, bhante, Bhagavā yaṃ mama assa dīgharattaṃ hitāya sukhāyâ" ti. Atha kho Uggatasarīro brāhmaṇo Bhagavantaṃ etadavoca: "ahaṃ hi, bho Gotama, aggiṃ ādātukāmo yūpaṃ ussāpetukāmo. Ovadatu maṃ bhavaṃ Gotamo. Anusāsatu maṃ bhavaṃ Gotamo yaṃ mama assa dīgharattaṃ hitāya sukhāya' " ti.

(-A.N.)

3. Dunniggahassa lahuno - Yatthakāmanipātino
cittassa damatho sādhu. -cittaṃ dantaṃ sukhâvahaṃ.

Sududdasaṃ sunipuṇaṃ - Yatthakāmanipātinaṃ
cittaṃ rakkhetha medhāvī. - cittaṃ guttaṃ sukhâvahaṃ

Anavaṭṭhitacittassa - saddhammaṃ avijānato
Pariplavapasādassa - paññā na paripūrati.

Yāvajīvam pi ce bālo - paṇḍitaṃ payirupāsati
Na so dhammaṃ vijānāti - dabbī sūparasaṃ yathā.

Muhuttamapi ce viññū - paṇḍitaṃ payirupāsati
Khippaṃ dhammaṃ vijānāti - jivhā sūparasaṃ yathā.

Na taṃ kammaṃ kataṃ sādhu - yaṃ katvā anutappati
Yassa assumukho rodaṃ - vipākaṃ paṭisevati.

Taṃ ca kammaṃ kataṃ sādhu - Yaṃ katvā nânutappati
Yassa patīto sumano - vipākaṃ paṭisevati.

Attānameva paṭhamaṃ - patirūpe nivesaye
Atha'ññamanusāseyya - na kilisseyya paṇḍito.
(-Dhp.)

GLOSSARY

aggi	fire (see this grammar 1)
acchariyaṃ	a wonder, a marvel
ajo	a he-goat
añño	another, other (one)
atthāya	for the purpose of (see this grammar 8)
anavaṭṭhita	(an + ava + ṭhita) not steady, not well composed
anutappati	repents
anusāsati	advises, counsels, admonishes
abbhuta	exceptional, astonishing, marvellous, surprising
abhivādeti	salutes, greets, shows respect
avoca	said, spoke 3 sg. past tense of vatti 'says' (see this grammar 4)
assa	3 sg. ya optative of atthi. (see VII. 1)
assumukha	with a tearful face
ādātukāma	eager to/ desirous of putting together (See this grammar 8 under kāma)

ādānaṃ	grasping, putting up, placing
Ānando	Ānanda, a disciple and chief attendant of Buddha
ānisamso(aṃ)	advantage, good result/ consequence
āyasmā	Nom. sg. of āyasmant: 'venerable (one)' (used as adjective. or absolute as a respectful appellation of a Bhikkhu of some standing)
uggatasarīro	a name of a Brahmin. Literally 'with upright body'
upakkhaṭa	prepared, ready, administered (pp. of upakaroti)
upanīta	bring up to/into, offer, present (pp. of upaneti)
upasaṃkamati	approaches, goes near
urabbho	a ram
usabho	bull, ox
ussāpanaṃ	erection, putting up
ussāpeti	raises, lifts up, erects
evaṃ vutte	when it was said thus (locative absolute- See this grammar 3)
ovadati	advises, admonishes, instructs, exhorts
kilissati	is stained, does wrong
khippaṃ	quickly, instantly
gahapatika	belonging to the rank of a householder, a member of the gentry
gottaṃ	ancestry, lineage
chavi	skin
tayidaṃ	< taṃ + idaṃ 'thus this...'
tālapakkaṃ	palm fruit
tuṇhībhūta	(being) silent
thūṇo	pillar, post
dabbī	spoon, ladle
damatho	restraint, training, taming
dunniggaha	difficult to restrain
nāmaṃ	name (for recognition)
nāmagottaṃ	the name (for recognition) and the surname (for the lineage)
niveseti	establishes, arranges
nivesaye	third sing. optative of niveseti (see VII,1)
patirūpa	agreeable (status, position, state)
patīta	delighted, with delight
pamutta	ppl. of pamuñcati lets loose, liberates, sets free
payirupāsati	associates
paripūrati	be filled, attain fullness

pariplava	unsteady, wavering
pariplavapasāda	one whose tranquillity is superficial
pariyodāta	very clean, pure, cleansed
parisuddha	clear, pure, spotless, bright, perfect
pasādo	tranquility, serenity, clarity, purity
pucchati	questions, asks
badarapaṇḍuṃ	light yellow (fresh) Jujube fruit
bandhanaṃ	bond, fetter, stalk
mahā	great, big (<mahant)
muhuttaṃ	(for an) instant, moment
medhāvin	wise, wise one
yañño	sacrifice, almsgiving
yattha	wherever
yattha kāmanipātin	that which falls/clings wherever it wishes
yāva(ṃ)	to the extent of, as far as
yāvajīvaṃ	as long as one lives
yāvañcidaṃ	(yāvam + ca + idaṃ) that is, namely, as far as, in so far as (cf. yadidam)
yūpo	a sacrificial post
rodati	weeps, laments, cries
lahu	lightly, light
Vacchagotta	name of a Brahmin referred to by his surname ='of Vaccha lineage'
vacchataro	a weaned calf, a bullock
-tarī	a weaned female calf, a heifer
vaṇṇo	color, complexion
vippasanna	tranquil, calm, purified, clean, bright, happy, pure, sinless
Venāgapura	a city name
Venāgapurika	of Venagapura
sataṃ	a hundred (see VI, 12)
sabbena sabbaṃ	completely, altogether
sameti	corresponds, agrees
sampati	now, right now, just now
sādhu	good
sārada	autumnal, fresh
sāveti	announces, tells, declares
sukhâvaha	bringing happiness
sududdasa	exceedingly difficult to see/grasp
sunipuṇa	very subtle
sūpa	soup, broth, curry
seyyathā	just as, just like, as if

GRAMMAR VIII

1. MASCULINE -i STEMS

aggi in this reading represents a new type of noun: masculine nouns with stems ending in -i, with forms as follows. They will be listed in the glossaries in the nominative singular, but with the notation "masculine" to distinguish them from the feminine -i stems (I,23) :

EXAMPLE: aggi 'fire'

	Singular	Plural
Nom:	aggi	aggī / aggayo
Acc:	aggiṃ	
Gen:	aggissa / aggino	aggīnaṃ / agginaṃ
Dat:		
Inst:	agginā	aggībhi / aggīhi
Abl:	aggimhā /-smā	
Loc:	aggimhi / aggismiṃ	aggisu / aggīsu
Voc:	aggi	aggī / aggayo

2. THIRD PERSON IMPERATIVE

2.1 The second person imperative was given in III, 5. Pāli also has third person imperatives, with the following endings:

	Singular	Plural
3 Pers.	-tu	-ntu

Thus:

bhavatu	
hotu	'(May) he/it be!'
atthu	bhavantu
hontu	'(May) they be!'
santu	
labhatu	'(May) he/ it obtain!'
labhantu	'(May) they obtain!'

2.2 In Pāli, third person forms are commonly used in direct address to express great respect. In that case, the third person imperative is also used rather than the second person:

desetu bhante bhagavā dhammaṃ

'Sir, let the Blessed One (i.e., 'you') preach the Dhamma.'

etu kho bhante Bhagavā 'Please come, sir, O Blessed One.'

It may also be used to express a wish.

suvatthi hotu 'May there be happiness.'

3. LOCATIVE ABSOLUTE

An absolute construction expresses an action which is prior to or simultaneous with that of the main verb, but which has a different subject (unlike the gerund or present participle.) In Pāli, one absolute construction is formed by using a present or past participle in the locative case. If the subject is expressed it will also be in the locative, but objects, instruments, etc., will be in their usual cases. The past participle expresses a prior action and the present participle expresses a simultaneous one:

evaṃ sante 'That being so...'
purise āgacchante 'When the man was coming. . . .'
evaṃ vutte 'That having been said. . . .'
parinibbute Bhagavati
'When the Blessed one had achieved final liberation. . . .'

Note that the word order is variable, so that the subject need not precede the participle, as in the last example.

The past participle santa of as- has a locative form sante, as in the first example, used usually in impersonal ('there is/are') constructions like that one. It also has an alternate locative form sati, used in the same way:

taṇhāya sati 'There being craving. . . .'

4. FORMS of vac- 'SAY, SPEAK'

4.1. As stated in VI,8, The root vac- 'speak, say' verb 'speaks', does not have present tense forms in actual use in Pāli, but has been replaced in that tense by vadati, though it may be cited using the artificial forms vatti or vacati. It does have forms in other tenses, however.

The past forms of vac- (vatti, vacati) are:

	Singular	Plural
1 Pers.	avacaṃ, avocaṃ	avacumha, avocumha
2 Pers.	avaca, avoca, avacāsi	avacuttha, avocuttha
3 Pers.	avaca, avoca, avacāsi	avacuṃ, avocuṃ

Other forms are (next page):

Infinitive:	vattuṃ
Gerund:	vatvā(na)
Past participle:	vutta
Present participle:	vuccamāna
Future passive participle:	vattabba

4.2 There is also a verb vuccati (or vuccate) 'is said' which we have met earlier, made from the same stem, but with a passive sense.

5. ADDRESS FORM bhavant

bhoto is the Genitive-Dative form of a noun bhavant 'Venerable' used as a polite form of address. The vocative address form bhante with which we are familiar is actually a related form, and appears to have been borrowed from a different dialect. Originally, these were from the present participle of the verb bhavati 'is, becomes,, hence literally 'the existing one, being' but were specialized in this usage. All of the case forms of bhavant do not occur, but those which may be encountered are as follows:

	Singular	Plural
Nom:	bhavaṃ	bhavanto / bhonto
Acc:	bhavantaṃ	bhavante
Gen: Dat:	bhoto	bhavataṃ
Inst:	bhotā	bhavantehi
Voc:	bhavaṃ, bho	bhonto

6. ENDINGS ON -e VERBS: nivesaye

As we saw in Lesson III, many Pāli verbs have present stems ending in -e, such as niveseti 'establishes, settles". When affixes are added to this stem, the -e of the stem may appear as -ay-. Thus nivesaye in this reading. Similarly, one may encounter cintayati as well as cinteti 'he/she thinks'; pūjayati instead of pujeti 'makes offerings'; nayati instead of neti 'leads',etc. In general, the -e- forms are found more in later texts, the -aya ones in earlier. (This is because most of these verbs derive from Sanskrit verbs in -aya-, which generally became -e- in Pāli).

7. USE OF CASES

7.1 The instrumental is sometimes used to form time adverbs:

tena samayena 'at that time'

7.2 vatti /vacati 'speaks' takes the hearer in the accusative:

Bhagavantaṃ avoca 'he said to the Blessed one'

8. attho

attho 'use, meaning, purpose' may be used in the dative case to serve as the second member of a compound with the sense for the 'sake/purpose of'. The first member, as usual, will appear in the stem form:

yaññatthāya (yañña + atthāya) 'for the sacrifice'

9. kāma

kāma 'desiring' is used with a preceding infinitive in the sense 'desiring to carry out the action (of the infinitive)'. The infinitive loses the final -ṃ, and kāmo declines as an -o or -ā (fem.) noun.

ahaṃ Bhagavantaṃ dassanāya gantukāmo
(<gantuṃ + kāma Masc. Sg.)
'I am desirous of going to see the Blessed one.' (Man speaking)

ahaṃ Bhagavantaṃ dassanāya gantukāmā
(<gantuṃ + kāma Fem. Sg.)
'I am desirous of going to see the Blessed one.' (Woman speaking)

10. SANDHI

10.1 A word-final a or ā may be dropped when the following word begins with a vowel. The following vowel may then be lengthened:

thūṇa + upanīta thūṇ'ûpanita

10.2 A final -ā plus a following ā- may be reduced to -ā-:

mahā + ānisaṃsaṃ mahânisaṃsaṃ

LESSON VIII - FURTHER READINGS

1. Ekaṃ samayaṃ Bhagavā Vesāliyaṃ viharati Mahāvane Kūṭāgārasālāyaṃ. Atha kho Sīho senāpati yena Bhagavā ten'upasaṃkami; upasaṃkamitvā Bhagavantaṃ abhivādetvā ekamantaṃ nisīdi. Ekamantaṃ nisinno kho Sīho senāpati Bhagavantaṃ etadavoca - "Sakkā nu kho, bhante, Bhagavā sandiṭṭhikaṃ dānaphalaṃ paññāpetuṃ" ti?

"Sakkā Sīhâ" ti Bhagavā avoca - "dāyako Sīha, dānapati bahuno janassa piyo hoti manāpo. Yaṃ pi Sīha, dāyako dānapati bahuno janassa piyo hoti manāpo, idaṃ pi sandiṭṭhikaṃ dānaphalaṃ.

"Puna ca paraṃ, Sīha, dāyakaṃ dānapatiṃ santo sappurisā bhajanti. Yaṃ pi, Sīha, dāyakaṃ dānapatiṃ santo sappurisā bhajanti, idaṃ pi sandiṭṭhikaṃ dānaphalaṃ.

"Puna ca paraṃ, Sīha, dāyakassa dānapatino kalyāṇo kittisaddo abbhuggacchati. Yaṃ pi, Sīha, dāyakassa dānapatino kalyāṇo kittisaddo abbhuggacchati,idaṃ pi sandiṭṭhikaṃ dānaphalaṃ.

"Puna ca paraṃ, Sīha, dāyako dānapati yaṃ yadeva parisaṃ upasaṃkamati – yadi khattiyaparisaṃ yadi brāhmaṇaparisaṃ yadi gahapatiparisaṃ yadi samaṇaparisaṃ – visārado upasaṃkamati amaṃkubhūto. Yaṃ pi, Sīha, dāyako dānapati yaṃ yadevaparisaṃ upasaṃkamati...visārado upasaṃkamati amaṃkubhūto, idaṃ pi sandiṭṭhikaṃ dānaphalaṃ."

"Puna ca paraṃ, Sīha, dāyako dānapati kāyassa bhedā paraṃ maraṇā sugatiṃ saggaṃ lokaṃ upapajjati. Yaṃ pi, Sīha, dāyako dānapati kāyassa bhedā paraṃ maraṇā sugatiṃ saggaṃ lokaṃ upapajjati, idaṃ samparāyikaṃ dānaphalaṃ" ti. (-A.N.)

2. Ekaṃ samayaṃ Bhagavā Vesāliyaṃ viharati Mahāvane Kūṭāgārasālāyaṃ. Atha kho Mahāli Licchavi yena Bhagavā ten'upasaṃkami; upasaṃkamitvā Bhagavantaṃ abhivādetvā ekamantaṃ nisīdi. Ekamantaṃ nisinno kho Mahāli Licchavi Bhagavantaṃ etadavoca:

"Ko nu kho, bhante, hetu, ko paccayo pāpassa kammassa kiriyāya, pāpassa kammassa pavattiyā" ti?

"Lobho kho, Mahāli, hetu, lobho paccayo pāpassa kammassa kiriyāya, pāpassa kammassa pavattiyā. Doso kho, Mahāli, hetu, doso paccayo pāpassa kammassa kiriyāya pāpassa kammassa pavattiyā. Moho kho, Mahāli, hetu, moho paccayo pāpassa kammassa kiriyāya, pāpassa kammassa pavattiyā. Ayonisomanasikāro kho, Mahāli, hetu, ayonisomanisikāro paccayo pāpassa kammassa kiriyāya, pāpassa kammassa pavattiyā. Micchāpaṇihitaṃ kho, Mahāli, cittaṃ hetu, micchāpaṇihitaṃ cittaṃ paccayo pāpassa kammassa kiriyāya pāpassa kammassa pavattiyā ti. Ayaṃ kho, Mahāli, hetu, ayaṃ paccayo pāpassa kammassa kiriyāya pāpassa kammassa pavattiyā" ti. (-A.N.)

3. akkodhano'nupanāhī – amāyo rittapesuno
sa ve tādisako bhikkhu – evaṃ pecca na socati.

akkodhano'nupanāhī – amāyo rittapesuno
guttadvāro sadā bhikkhu – evaṃ pecca na socati.

akkodhano'nupanāhī – amāyo rittapesuno
kalyāṇasīlo so bhikkhu – evaṃ pecca na socati.

akkodhano'nupanāhī – amāyo rittapesuno
kalyāṇamitto so bhikkhu – evaṃ pecca na socati.

akkodhano'nupanāhī – amāyo rittapesuno
kalyāṇapañño so bhikkhu – evaṃ pecca na socati.
(ThG)

4. Rājā āha: "Bhante Nāgasena, yo idha kālakato brahmaloke uppajjeyya yo ca idha kālakato Kasmīre uppajjeyya, ko cirataraṃ ko sīghataranti?"

Samakaṃ mahārājâ"ti.

"Opammaṃ karohī"ti.

"Kuhiṃ pana mahārāja tava[1] jātanagaran"ti?

"Atthi bhante Kalasigāmo nāma, tatthâhaṃ jāto"ti.

"Kīva dūro mahārāja ito Kalasigāmo hotī"ti.

"Dumattāni bhante yojanasatānī"ti.

"Kīva dūraṃ mahārāja ito Kasmīraṃ hotī"ti?

"Dvādasa bhante yojanānī"ti.

"Ingha tvaṃ mahārāja Kalasigāmaṃ cintehī"ti.

"Cintito bhante"ti.

"Ingha tvaṃ mahārāja Kasmīraṃ cintehī"ti.

"Cintitaṃ bhante"ti.

"Katamannu kho mahārāja cirena cintitaṃ katamaṃ sīghataran"ti?

"Samakaṃ bhante"ti.

"Evameva kho mahārāja yo idha kālakato brahmaloke uppajjeyya yo ca idha kālakato Kasmīre uppajjeyya samakaṃ yeva uppajjantī"ti.

"Bhiyyo opammaṃ karohī"ti.

"Taṃ kiṃ maññasi mahārāja: dve sakuṇā ākāsena gaccheyyuṃ, tesu eko ucce rukkhe nisīdeyya eko nīce rukkhe nisīdeyya, tesaṃ samakaṃ patiṭṭhitānaṃ katamassa chāyā paṭhamataraṃ paṭhaviyaṃ patiṭṭhaheyya, katamassa chāyā cirena paṭhaviyaṃ patiṭṭhaheyyâ"ti?

"Samakaṃ bhante"ti.

"Evameva kho mahārāja yo idha kālakato brahmaloke uppajjeyya yo ca idha kālakato Kasmīre uppajjeyya samakaṃ yeva uppajjantī"ti.

"Kallo'si bhante Nāgasenâ"ti.

(-M.P.)

---

[1]Genitive of tvaṃ --see Grammar V.1.

GLOSSARY:

akkhodano	without anger, without ill will
anupanāhin	one without ill-will (-in stem, see VI, 2)
abbhuggacchati	go forth, go out, rise into
aṃāya	non-deceitful
ākāso(aṃ)	outer space, sky
ārāmo	park, resort for pastime, a private park given to the Buddha or the Sangha
ingha	particle of exhortation: 'come on, go on, look here, go ahead,'
ito	from here, hence
ucca	tall, high, lofty
upapajjati/ uppajjati	be born
karaṇa	making, causing, producing
X karaṇa	making X
Kalasigāmo	place name
kalyāṇasīla	of good conduct
kalyāṇamitto	good friend, good companion
Kasmīraṃ	place name: Kashmir
kālakata	dead
kitti	fame, renown, glory
kittisaddo	sound of fame, praise, renown
kiriyā	doing, action
kīva	how much, how many, how great
kuhiṃ	where
kūṭāgārasālā	gabled house, pavilion
khattiya	of the warrior (Kṣatriya) caste
gahapati	householder
guttadvāra	with guarded senses (literally, 'guarded door or entrance')
cinteti	thinks (of)
cirataraṃ	rather long, longer, delayed
cirena	after a long time
chāyā	shadow, (light) image
jāta	born
tattha	there
tādisaka	of such a quality/nature
dānapati	a liberal donor
dāyako	giver, (lay) donor
du-	two (compounding stem)
dūra	far
dvādasa	twelve
nivāseti	dress oneself
nīca	low

paggaṇhāti	stretches forth, holds out/up, takes up, makes ready
paccayo	reason, ground, cause, motive, means, condition
X-paccaya	having X as paccayo
paññāpeti	indicates, points out, makes known, declares
paṭhamataraṃ	as early as possible, (very) first
paṭhavī	earth
paṇidahati	puts forth, longs for, applies, directs, ppl. paṇihita
pavatti	manifestation, wielding, execution,happening
puna ca paraṃ	moreover, furthermore
brahmaloko	Brahma-world
bhiyyo	further, more
maṃkubhūta	discontented, troubled, confused
matta	about, only
manāpa	agreeable, pleasing, pleasant
Mahāli	a name of a person
mahāvana	a name of a park
yaṃ yadeva	whichever
yonisomanasikāro	proper attention, correct reflection
rittapesuna	free from slander (< ritta 'devoid of, having relinquished' + pesuna(ṃ) 'slander')
rukkho	tree
Licchavi	a clan name
visārado	self-possessed, confident, wise, knowing how to conduct oneself
Vesālī	a place name
sakuṇo	bird
sant	good person, true person
samakaṃ	equally, at the same time
samparāyika	belonging to the next world
sīghataraṃ	faster, sooner
Sīho	a proper name
sugati	happiness, bliss, happy fate, happy state, a realm of bliss
senāpati	a general
hetu	basis, cause

LESSON IX

1. Ekaṃ samayaṃ Bhagavā Bhoganagare viharati Ānandacetiye. Tatra kho Bhagavā bhikkhū āmantesi - "bhikkhavo" ti.

"Bhadante" ti te bhikkhū Bhagavato paccassosuṃ.

Bhagavā etadavoca - "cattāro'me, bhikkhave, mahâpadese desessāmi, taṃ suṇātha, sādhukaṃ manasikarotha; bhāsissāmi" ti.

"Evaṃ, bhante" ti kho te bhikkhū Bhagavato paccassosuṃ.

Bhagavā etadavoca:

"Katame, bhikkhave, cattāro mahāpadesā? Idha, bhikkhave, bhikkhu evaṃ vadeyya - 'Sammukhā m'etaṃ, āvuso, Bhagavato sutaṃ, sammukhā paṭiggahitaṃ - ayaṃ dhammo, ayaṃ vinayo, idaṃ satthusāsanaṃ' ti. Tassa, bhikkhave, bhikkhuno bhāsitaṃ n'eva abhinanditabbaṃ nappaṭikkositabbaṃ. Anabhinanditvā appaṭikkositvā tāni padabyañjanāni sādhukaṃ uggahetvā sutte otāretabbāni, vinaye sandassetabbāni. Tāni ce sutte otāriyamānāni vinaye sandassiyamānāni na c'eva sutte otaranti na vinaye sandissanti, niṭṭhamettha [1] gantabbaṃ: 'Addhā, idaṃ na eva tassa Bhagavato vacanaṃ Arahato Sammāsambuddhassa...' iti h'etaṃ, bhikkhave, chaḍḍeyyātha."

"Idha pana, bhikkhave, bhikkhu evaṃ vadeyya - 'sammukhā m'etaṃ, āvuso, Bhagavato sutaṃ, sammukhā paṭiggahitaṃ - ayaṃ dhammo, ayaṃ vinayo, idaṃ satthusāsanaṃ' ti. Tassa, bhikkhave, bhikkhuno bhāsitaṃ n'eva abhinanditabbaṃ nappaṭikkositabbaṃ. Anabhinanditvā appaṭikkositvā tāni padabyañjanāni sādhukaṃ uggahetvā sutte otāretabbāni, vinaye sandassetabbāni. Tāni ce sutte otāriyamānāni vinaye sandassiyamānāni sutte c'eva otaranti vinaye ca sandissanti, niṭṭhamettha gantabbaṃ: 'Addhā, idaṃ tassa Bhagavato vacanaṃ Arahato Sammāsambuddhassa. . . iti. Idaṃ, bhikkhave, paṭhamaṃ mahāpadesaṃ dhāreyyātha." (-A.N.)

2. "Ahaṃ kho, bhikkhave, ekâsanabhojanaṃ bhuñjāmi: ekâsanabhojanaṃ kho ahaṃ bhikkhave, bhuñjamāno appābādhataṃ ca sañjānāmi, appātaṃkataṃ ca lahuṭṭhānaṃ ca balaṃ ca phāsuvihāraṃ ca. Etha tumhe'pi bhikkhave, ekâsanabhojanaṃ bhuñjatha; ekāsanabhojanaṃ kho bhikkhave, tumhe'pi bhuñjamānā appābādhataṃ ca sañjānissatha appātaṃkataṃ ca lahuṭṭhānaṃ ca balaṃ ca phāsuvihārañcâ" ti. (M.N.)

3. Pāpaṃ ce puriso kayirā - na taṃ kayirā punappunaṃ
na tamhi chandaṃ kayirātha [2] - dukkho pāpassa uccayo.
Puññaṃ ce puriso kayirā - kayirāth'etaṃ punappunaṃ

---

[1] niṭṭhaṃ+ettha

[2] -tha here is third person. This ending will be given in a later lesson.

tamhi chandaṃ kayirātha - sukho puññassa uccayo.
Pāpo'pi [3] passati bhadraṃ- yāva pāpaṃ na paccati;
yadā ca paccati pāpaṃ -atha pāpo pāpāni passati.
Bhadro'pi passati pāpaṃ - yāva bhadraṃ na paccati;
yadā ca paccati bhadraṃ - atha bhadro bhadrāni passati.
Pāṇimhi ce vaṇo nâssa - hareyya pāṇinā visaṃ;
nâbbaṇaṃ [4] visamanveti - n'atthi pāpaṃ akubbato.
Gabbhaṃ eke uppajjanti - nirayaṃ pāpakammino
saggaṃ sugatino yanti - parinibbanti anâsavā.
(Dhp.)

GLOSSARY:

akubbant	non-doer
addhā	certainly, verily
anāsavo	one free from the four āsavas: i.e., kāmâsava, sensuality, bhavâsāva, craving for rebirth, diṭṭhâsava, speculation, avijjâsava, ignorance
anveti	enters, follows
apadeso	reason, cause, argument, statement
appātaṃkatā	freedom from illness
appābādhatā	good health
abbaṇa	= a + vaṇa-
abhinandati	rejoices (over), approves of, delights in
Ānandacetiyaṃ	monastery named Ānanda
āmantesi	addressed (past of āmanteti 'calls. addresses')
āvuso	friend, brother, sir (a form of polite address)
uggaheti	learns
uccayo	heaping up, accumulation
ekâsanabhojanaṃ	taking only a single meal (solid food) a day (adverbial accusative)
otarati	descends, enters into
otāriyati	is caused to descend (see this grammar 4)
otāriyamāna	that which is caused to be brought down (see this grammar 5)
otāreti	causes to descend, brings down, lowers
kammin	one who acts, doer
kāyira	optative of karoti (see this grammar 7)
chaḍḍheti	gives up, discards

3 From api 'even'.
4 na+a+vaṇa

chandaṃ	desire, delight
tatra	there
deseti	preaches, declares
niṭṭhaṃ gacchati	conclude, arrive at a conclusion
paccati	ripens
paccassosuṃ	Third Plural Past of paṭissuṇāti (see this grammar 2.3)
paṭikkosati	blames, rejects
paṭiggahita	Past ppl. of paṭigaṇhāti, 'receive, accept'
padaṃ	word, (in addition to 'place, foot' etc. given in Lesson IV)
parinibbāti	passes away without rebirth , is emancipated
pāṇi (m)	hand
pāpo	evildoer
phāsuvihāro	comfort, ease
byañjanaṃ	syllable, consonant, sign, mark
bhadante	'sir, sire' a form of address generally used in addressing the Buddha (by monks)
bhadraṃ	good
bhadro	good one, (doer of good)
Bhoganagaraṃ	the city of Bhoga
manasikaroti	reflects upon, considers well, bears in mind, recognizes
mahâpadeso	mahā + apadeso [5]
yāti	goes, proceeds, goes on
yāva	until, as long as, up to
lahuṭṭhānaṃ	lightness of body, bodily vigor, good health
vacanaṃ	utterance, word, saying, speech, remark
vaṇo	wound
vadati	says, speaks
vinayo	discipline, code of ethics, monastic discipline, principles of good behavior[6]
visaṃ	poison
sañjānāti	knows, recognizes, is aware of
satthu	genitive of satthar 'teacher, the Buddha' (see this grammar I.1)
sandassiyamāna	that which is compared with
sandasseti	compares with, shows (against)
sandissati	tallies with, agrees with
sammukha	face to face, in presence
sādhukaṃ	well (adverb)

[5] This has also been interpreted as mahā + padeso 'province, part, area. location.'

[6] The term vinayo refers to a large collection of rules governing the monastic life of the bhikkhus, as against the term dhammo, referring to the theoretical and philosophical part of the Pali canon.

sāsanaṃ	teaching, message, order
sugatin	righteous one
suttaṃ	discursive part of Buddhist scriptures (Sanskrit sūtra)
harati	take away, remove

GRAMMAR IX

1. -ar NOUNS

1.1 A new type of noun, -ar nouns, occurs in this lesson. They will be listed with -ar in the glossaries. There are two subtypes: (1.) Nouns formed with a suffix -tar, and (2.) Relationship nouns (a small set.) They have forms as follows;

1.11 Agent Nouns:

EXAMPLE: satthar 'teacher, the Buddha'

	Singular	Plural
Nom:	satthā	satthāro
Acc:	satthāraṃ (-araṃ)	/satthāre
Gen:	satthu(-ssa)/	satthūnam / satthārānaṃ/
Dat:	satthuno	satthānaṃ
Inst:	/ satthunā	satthārehi(-ebhi)/
Abl:	satthārā / sattharā	satthūhi
Loc:	satthari	satthūsu / satthāresu
Voc:	satthā/sattha/satthe	satthāro

1.12 Relationship Nouns:

EXAMPLE: pitar 'father'

	Singular	Plural
Nom:	pitā	pitaro
Acc:	pitaraṃ / pituṃ	pitare
Gen:	pitu / pituno / pitussa	pitunnaṃ(-ūnaṃ)
Dat:		pitarānaṃ / pitānaṃ
Inst:	pitunā	pitūhi (-ūbhi) /
Abl:	pitarā	pitarehi (-ebhi)
Loc:	pitari	pitūsu / pitaresu
Voc:	pita / pitā	pitaro

Note that the two subtypes are almost alike. The important differences are:

1) The relationship nouns have -ar- wherever the agent nouns have either -ār- or -ar-.

2) The Dative Plural is usually -unnaṃ for the relationship nouns but -ūnaṃ for the agent nouns.

1.2 The -ar stem nouns have a stem form in -u (satthu, pitu) which occurs in compounds. Thus:

satthusāsanaṃ 'the teaching of the Master'.
pitusantakaṃ 'father's possession'

1.3 The -ar nouns given above are masculine. There are also feminine relationship nouns like mātar 'mother' which inflect similarly:
EXAMPLE: mātar 'mother'

	Singular	Plural
Nom:	mātā	mātaro
Acc:	mātaraṃ	
Gen:	mātu / mātuyā	mātūnaṃ
Dat:		
Inst:	mātarā / mātuyā	mātūhi
Abl:		
Loc:	mātari/ mātuyā(-yaṃ)	mātusu
Voc:	māta / mātā	mātaro

2. PAST TENSE
2.1 The assosi Type Past Tense: ("the -s- Aorist")

Two forms of the past tense were given in VI, 7. Another form appears in this lesson. It is formed by adding the following suffixes (as with the other types an augment a- may sometimes be prefixed):

	Singular	Plural
1 Pers:	-siṃ	-(i)mha (-simha)
2 Pers:	-si	-(i)ttha (-sittha)
3 Pers:		-suṃ / -(i)ṃsu

Note that the first, second and third person singular forms are like those of the upasaṃkami type (VI, 7.2) with a preceding -s-. So are the alternate first and second plural forms, but they are rare. One third person form is like that of the addasa type (VI, 7.1) with a preceding -s-. The other plural forms are like the upasaṃkami type.

The verb root may undergo changes to form a past stem to go with these endings. Thus, for su- 'hear' (pres. suṇāti) and kar- 'do' (pres. karoti), we have (note the augments) (forms on next page):

su- 'hear'

	Singular	Plural
1 Pers:	assosiṃ	assumha
2 Pers:	assosi	assuttha
3 Pers:		assosuṃ

kar- 'do'

	Singular	Plural
1 Pers:	akāsiṃ	akamha
2 Pers:	akāsi	akattha
3 Pers:		akāsuṃ, akaṃsu

Note that the stem-final vowels "shorten" (ā becomes a, o becomes u) before the endings without -s-.

Verbs with present tense stems in -e-, whether causative or not, commonly take this type of past tense, and form it from the present stem. With these, e › ay before the endings without -s-, and the linking vowel -i- appears:

deseti 'preaches, tells'

	Singular	Plural
1 Pers:	desesiṃ	desayimha (desesimha)
2 Pers:	desesi	desayittha (desesittha)
3 Pers:		desesuṃ/desayiṃsu

2.2 The Past of gacchati:

The verb gacchati 'goes' may appear with past tense forms of the upasaṃkami type (compare VI, 7.1) Thus:

	Singular	Plural
1 Pers:	agamisaṃ, agamiṃ	agamimha
2 Pers:	agami	agamittha
3 Pers:		agamisuṃ, agamiṃsu

2.3 The Past of paṭissuṇāti: The verb paṭissuṇāti 'promises, assents, agrees' has a past tense of the assosi type, but a very irregular past stem paccasso-. Hence paccassosi 'he/you agreed', etc.

It also has an alternate past stem paṭisun- which takes the upasaṃkami type endings: paṭisuṇi 'he/you agreed', etc.

The gerund is paṭissuṇitvā or paṭissutvā.

3. FUTURE TENSE

3.1 The future tense in Pāli is formed by adding -(i)ss- followed by the present tense endings, to the present stem. Hence, for bhavati 'be':

	Singular	Plural
1 Pers:	bhavissāmi	bhavissāma
2 Pers:	bhavissasi	bhavissatha
3 Pers:	bhavissati	bhavissanti

Sometimes the stem used may differ from the present stem, or there may be alternate forms. Hence:

gacchati 'goes' has gamissati along with gacchissati
suṇāti 'hears' has sossati along with suṇissati

3.2 The future tense may be used to indicate probability or a general truth as well as indicating future time.

4. PASSIVE VERBS

There are are some verbs in Pāli that have a passive sense. That is, the subject of the verb is that which is effected or brought about. Thus vuccati 'is said', dassiyati 'is seen' etc. Such passive verbs are commonly related to transitive verbs. Often, the passive verb will be formed by adding -iya- or -īya- to the present stem of the transitive verb, which may undergo further changes of form. Hence deti 'gives', dīyati 'is given'; pūjeti 'worships', pūjiyati 'is worshipped', karoti 'does' kariyati or karīyati 'is done' etc. Sometimes the passive verb has a double consonant while the related transitive verb has a single one or a consonant cluster: thus hanati 'kills', haññati 'is killed'; bhindati breaks' bhijjati 'is broken; pacati 'cooks', paccati 'is cooked', etc. (these double consonants occurred because some passives were formed earlier by adding -y-, which doubled the preceding consonant, sometimes changing it, and disappeared.) In any case, in Pāli these pairings must be learned as they occur, since the relationship may be more or less transparent due to the changes that have taken place.

5. PRESENT PARTICIPLES OF PASSIVE VERBS IN -māna

The passive verbs described in 4 above often occur with the -māna participle (IV,4) . Thus pūjiyamāna 'being worshipped' vuccamāna 'being spoken', dassiyamāna 'being seen', kayiramāna 'being done' etc. Similarly desiyamāna 'being preached', related to deseti 'preaches'.

6. yāti 'GOES'

yāti 'goes, goes on, proceeds' has the following forms in the present tense:

	Singular	Plural
1 Pers:	yāmi	yāma
2 Pers:	yāsi	yātha
3 Pers:	yāti	yanti

Other forms are:.

Present participle: yanti
Infinitive: yātuṃ / (yātave)
Past Participle: yātā

7. kayirā

kayirā and kayirātha are -ya optatives of karoti (See VII, 1).

FURTHER READINGS IX

1. Evaṃ me sutaṃ. Ekaṃ samayaṃ Bhagavā Rājagahe viharati Veḷuvane Kalandakanivāpe. Tena kho pana samayena Sigālako gahapatiputto kālass'eva vuṭṭhāya Rājagahā nikkhamitvā allavattho allakeso pañjaliko puthudisā namassati: puratthimaṃ disaṃ dakkhiṇaṃ disaṃ pacchimaṃ disaṃ uttaraṃ disaṃ heṭṭimaṃ disaṃ uparimaṃ disaṃ.

Atha kho Bhagavā pubbaṇhasamayaṃ nivāsetvā pattacīvaramādāya Rājagahaṃ piṇḍāya pāvisi. Addasā kho Bhagavā Sigālakaṃ gahapatiputtaṃ kālass'eva uṭṭhāya Rājagahā nikkhamitvā allavatthaṃ allakesaṃ pañjalikaṃ puthudisā namassantaṃ: puratthimaṃ disaṃ dakkhiṇaṃ disaṃ pacchimaṃ disaṃ uttaraṃ disaṃ heṭṭhimaṃ disaṃ uparimaṃ disaṃ. Disvā Sigālakaṃ gahapatiputtaṃ etadavoca. "kinnu tvaṃ, gahapatiputta, kālass'eva vuṭṭhāya Rājagahā nikkhamitvā allavattho allakeso pañjaliko puthudisā namassasi: puratthimaṃ disaṃ dakkhiṇaṃ disaṃ pacchimaṃ disaṃ uttaraṃ disaṃ heṭṭhimaṃ disaṃ uparimaṃ disanti?"

"Pitā maṃ bhante kālaṃ karonto evaṃ avaca: 'disā tāta namasseyyāsī'ti." So kho ahaṃ bhante pitu vacanaṃ sakkaronto garukaronto mānento pūjento kālasse'va vuṭṭhāya Rājagahā nikkhamitvā allavattho allakeso pañjaliko puthudisā namassāmi: puratthimaṃ disaṃ-pe-uparimaṃ disanti."

"Na kho gahapatiputta ariyassa vinaye evaṃ chaddisā namassitabbāti."

"Yathākathaṃ pana bhante ariyassa vinaye chaddisā namassitabbā? Sādhu me bhante Bhagavā tathā dhammaṃ desetu yathā ariyassa vinaye chaddisā namassitabbāti."

"Tena hi gahapatiputta suṇohi sādhukaṃ manasikarohi, bhāsissāmī" ti.

"Evaṃ bhante" ti kho Sigālo gahapatiputto Bhagavato paccassosi.

Bhagavā etadavoca: "Yato kho, gahapatiputta, ariyasāvakassa cattāro kammakilesā pahīṇā honti, catūhi ṭhānehi pāpakammaṃ na karoti, cha ca bhogānaṃ apāyamukhāni na sevati, so evaṃ cuddasa pāpakâpagato, chaddisā paṭicchādī, ubhaya lokavijayāya paṭipanno hoti, tassa ayaṃ c'eva loko āraddho hoti paro ca loko. So kāyassa bhedā parammaraṇā sugatiṃ saggaṃ lokaṃ upapajjati.

(-D.N.)

2. Atha kho bhikkhave Vipassissa Bhagavato arahato Sammāsambuddhassa etadahosi: "Yannūnâhaṃ dhammaṃ deseyyan"ti. Atha kho bhikkhave Vipassissa Bhagavato arahato Sammāsambuddhassa etadahosi: "adhigato me ayaṃ dhammo gambhīro duddaso duranubodho santo paṇīto atakkâvacaro nipuṇo paṇḍitavedanīyo. Ālayarāmā kho panâyaṃ pajā ālayaratā ālayasamuditā. Ālāyarāmāya kho pana pajāya ālayaratāya ālayasamuditāya duddasaṃ idaṃ ṭhānaṃ yadidaṃ idappaccayatā-paṭiccasamuppādo. Idampi kho ṭhānaṃ duddasaṃ yadidaṃ sabbasaṃkhārasamatho sabbûpadhipaṭinissaggo taṇhakkhayo virāgo nirodho nibbāṇaṃ. Ahañc'eva kho pana dhammaṃ deseyyaṃ, pare ca me na ājāneyyuṃ, so mam'assa kilamatho, sā mam'assa vihesā" ti.

(-D.N.)

3. Ko imaṃ paṭhaviṃ vijessati
yamalokañca imaṃ sadevakaṃ
ko dhammapadaṃ sudesitaṃ
kusalo pupphamiva pacessati?

Sekho paṭhaviṃ vijessati
yamalokañca imaṃ sadevakaṃ
sekho dhammapadaṃ sudesitaṃ
kusalo pupphamiva pacessati.

Pheṇûpamaṃ kāyamimaṃ viditvā
marīcidhammaṃ abhisambudhāno
chetvāna mārassa papupphakāni
adassanaṃ maccurājassa gacche.

Yo bālo maññati bālyaṃ
paṇḍito'vâpi [7] tena so
bālo ca paṇḍitamānī
sa ve bālo'ti vuccati.

(-Dhp.)

[7] paṇḍito + eva + api

GLOSSARY:

atakkâvacara	beyond logic (or sophistry), beyond the sphere, of thought, profound
adassana	non-seeing, away from sight
addasā	3sg. past of passati (see VI, 6.1)
adhigata	realized, understood, highly realized
apagata	be away from, desist from
apāyamukhaṃ	cause of ruin
abhisambudhāno	one who understands
ariyassa vinaye	in the principles of behavior taught by the noble ones; normally this refers to the way of life of the noble ones. (cf. vinayo in the main reading of this lesson)
alla	wet
avaca	said
assa	3sg. optative of atthi
ahosi	was, occurred (past of hoti)
etadahosi	such a thought occurred to one
ādāya	having taken
ājānāti	grasp, understand
āraddha	begun, well begun, (well) undertaken
ālayarata	lustful, delighting in desire
ālayarāma	clinging to lust
ālayasamudita	arisen from desire, craving
idappaccayatā	having its foundation in this, causally connected
upama	like, similar
X-upama	like X, similar to X
uparima	upper, above, overhead
ubhaya	both
kammakileso	depravity of action, bad works
kalandakanivāpa	a place name (literally, 'squirrel feed')
kāyassa bhedā parammaraṇā	after complete death (literally, after the breaking up of the body and after death)
kālaṃ karoti	passes away, dies
kālo	time, morning
kālassa eva	in early morning
kilamatho	fatigue, exhaustion
kusalo	skilled one
keso	hair (normally in the plural, kesā)
khayo	cessation
garukaroti	respects, considers seriously

gahapatiputto	a man of the middle class, a nobleman, a householder
cuddasa	fourteen
cha	six
chaddisā	the six directions (North, South, East, West, Up, Down)
chindati	cuts, severs
chetvāna	having cut off, having severed
ṭhānaṃ	fact, principle, conclusion
taṇhā	craving
tāto	father, child dear one (an endearing term of address used irrespective of the age of the addressee; normally in the vocative singular as tāta)
disā	direction
duddasa	difficult to see, incomprehensible (by the ordinary person)
duranubodha	difficult to be understood
deseti	preaches, declares
dhammapadaṃ	word of righteousness
namassati	salutes, venerates, honors, pays homage to
nikkhamati	sets forth, comes out of
nipuṇa	efficient, subtle, abstruse, clever, skillful, accomplished
nibbāṇaṃ	emancipation
nirodho	cessation
nivāseti	dresses oneself, puts on clothes (robes)
pacessati	future 3 sg. of pacināti 'gathers'
paccassosi	assents, agrees (3 Sg. past of paṭi(s)suṇāti)
pacchima	west, western
pajā	people, progeny, offspring
pañjalika	with folded hands
paṭiccasamuppādo	arising on the grounds of a preceding cause, dependent origination (theory of the twelve causes)
paṭicchādin	covering, enveloping
paṭinissaggo	renunciation, giving up, rejection, forsaking
paṭipanna	stepped on to, entering on
paṇīta	exalted, excellent
paṇḍitamānin	one who thinks himself wise
paṇḍitavedanīya	to be understood by the wise
pattacīvaraṃ	bowl and robe
papupphakaṃ	flowery arrows, flower-tipped arrows (of sensual passion)
paro	other, next

pavisati	enters
pahīna	calmed, given up (past participle of pajahati)
pāpakaṃ	bad action
piṇḍo	a lump of food (usually of food as alms)
piṇḍāya	for alms (begging)
pitu	compounding stem or pitar 'father' (see this grammar I.12)
puthu	separate, individual, various
puratthima	easern
pūjeti	woships, adores, offers
pheṇaṃ	foam, froth
pheṇūpama	pheṇa + upama
bālyaṃ	folly, idiocy
maccurājā	king of death
maññati	thinks, knows
marīcidhamma	nature of a mirage
māneti	respect, honor
māro	death, Māra (death personified)
yato	since, whence, because
yathākathaṃ pana	(yathā+kathaṃ+pana) then how, how so then
yannūna	well now (yaṃ+nūna)
yamaloko	world of Yama (ruler of the kingdom of the dead)
Rājagaha	place name
vatthaṃ	cloth(es)
vijayo	victory, triumph
vijeti	wins, conquers
viditvā	knows, realizes (gerund of vindati)
Vipassin	name of a Buddha previous to Gotama
virāgo	detachment
vihesā	vexation
(v)uṭṭhahati	rise, get up (alternatively, (v)uṭṭhāti) [8]
(v)uṭṭhāya	gerund of (v)uṭṭhahati/(v)uṭṭhati
saṃkhārā	(pl) the sum of the conditions resulting in life or existence; synergies
sakkaroti	respects. (pres. participle sakkaronta)
santa	tranquil, calm
samatho	cessation, calming down
sekho	one still in training, one who has not yet achieved arahantship
heṭṭhima	lower, below

[8] The v- may appear when a form of this verb appears following a word ending in a vowel.

LESSON X

1. Ekasmiṃ samaye satthā gaṇaṃ pahāya ekako'va ekaṃ vanaṃ pāvisi. Pārileyyakanāmo eko hatthirājā'pi hatthigaṇaṃ pahāya taṃ vanaṃ pavisitvā, bhagavantaṃ ekassa rukkhassa mūle nisinnaṃ disvā, pādena paharanto rukkhamūlaṃ sodhetvā soṇḍāya sākhaṃ gahetvā sammajji. Tato paṭṭhāya divase divase soṇḍāya ghaṭaṃ gahetvā pānīya-paribhojanīya-udakaṃ āharati. Uṇhodakena atthe sati uṇhodakaṃ paṭiyādeti: kathaṃ? kaṭṭhāni ghaṃsitvā aggiṃ pāteti; tattha dārūni pakkhipanto jāletvā, tattha tattha pāsāṇe pacitvā, dārukhaṇḍakena pavaṭṭetvā, khuddakasoṇḍiyaṃ khipati. Tato hatthaṃ otāretvā, udakassa tattabhāvaṃ jānitvā, gantvā satthāraṃ vandati. Satthā tattha gantvā nahāyati. Atha nānāvidhāni phalāni āharitvā deti.

Yadā pana satthā gāmaṃ piṇḍāya pavisati, tadā satthu pattacīvaramādāya kumbhe ṭhapetvā, satthārā saddhiṃ yeva gacchati; rattiṃ vāḷamiganivāraṇatthaṃ mahantaṃ daṇḍaṃ soṇḍāya gahetvā yāva aruṇ'uggamanā vanasaṇḍe vicarati.

(Rasv.)

2. Atīte kira Bārāṇasiyaṃ sālittakasippe nipphattiṃ patto eko pīṭhasappī ahosi. So nagaradvāre ekassa vaṭarukkhassa heṭṭhā nisinno sakkharā khipitvā tassa paṇṇāni chindanto "hatthirūpakaṃ no dassehi, assarūpakaṃ no dassehi" ti gāmadārakehi vuccamāno icchit'icchitāni rūpāni dassetvā tesaṃ santikā khādanīy'ādīni labhati.

Ath'ekadivasaṃ rājā uyyānaṃ gacchanto taṃ padesaṃ pāpuṇi. Dārakā pīṭhasappiṃ pāroh'antare katvā palāyiṃsu. Rañño[1] ṭhitamajjhantike rukkhamūlaṃ paviṭṭhassa chiddacchāyā sarīraṃ phari. So '"kinnukho etaṃ" ti uddhaṃ olokento rukkhassa paṇṇesu hatthirūpakādīni disvā "kass'etaṃ kamman"ti pucchitvā, "pīṭhasappino" ti sutvā taṃ pakkosāpetvā āha: "mayhaṃ purohito atimukharo, appamattake'pi vutte bahuṃ bhaṇanto maṃ upaddavati; sakkhissasi tassa mukhe nāḷimattā ajalaṇḍikā khipitun"ti? "Sakkhissāmi, deva; ajalaṇḍikā āharāpetvā purohitena saddhiṃ tumhe antosāṇiyaṃ nisīdatha. Ahamettha kattabbaṃ jānissāmī"ti.

Rājā tathā kāresi. Itaro'pi kattariy'aggena sāṇiyaṃ chiddaṃ katvā, purohitassa raññā saddhiṃ kathentassa mukhe vivaṭamatte ek'ekaṃ ajalaṇḍikaṃ khipi. Purohito mukhaṃ paviṭṭhaṃ paviṭṭhaṃ gili. Pīṭhasappī khīṇāsu ajalaṇḍikāsu sāṇiṃ cālesi. Rājā tāya saññāya ajalaṇḍikānaṃ khīṇabhāvaṃ ñatvā āha: "ācariya, ahaṃ tumhehi saddhiṃ kathento kathaṃ nittharituṃ na sakkhissāmi. Tumhe[2] atimukharatāya nāḷimattā ajalaṇḍikā gilantā pi tunhībhāvaṃ nâpajjathâ"ti.

---

[1] Genitive of rājan. See Grammar 6.1 and this grammar 1..

[2] Honorific plural

Brāhmaṇo maṃkubhāvaṃ āpajjitvā tato paṭṭhāya mukhaṃ vivaritvā raññā saddhiṃ sallapituṃ nâsakkhi. Rājā pīṭhasappiṃ pakkosāpetvā "taṃ nissāya me sukhaṃ laddhan"ti tuṭṭho tassa sabbaṭṭhakaṃ nāma dhanaṃ datvā nagarassa catūsu disāsu cattāro varagāme adāsi.

(DhpAk.)

3. Yathâgāraṃ ducchannaṃ – vuṭṭhi samativijjhati
evaṃ abhāvitaṃ cittaṃ – rāgo samativijjhati.

Yathâgāraṃ succhannaṃ – vuṭṭhi na samativijjhati
evaṃ subhāvitaṃ cittaṃ – rāgo na samativijjhati.

Idha socati pecca socati – pāpakārī ubhayattha socati
so socati so vihaññati – disvā kammakiliṭṭhamattano.

Idha modati pecca modati – katapuñño ubhayattha modati
so modati so pamodati – disvā kammavisuddhimattano.

Idha tappati pecca tappati – pāpakārī ubhayattha tappati
"pāpaṃ me katan" ti tappati – bhiyyo tappati duggatiṃ gato.

Idha nandati pecca nandati – katapuñño ubhayattha nandati.
"puññaṃ me katan" ti nandati – bhiyyo nandati suggatiṃ gato.

(Dhp)

GLOSSARY

agāraṃ	house
aggaṃ	tip, end
ajalaṇḍikā	goat dung
ati	very, excessively
atīto	the past
attano	one's own
antare	in between, among
anto	inside, within, behind
antosāṇiyaṃ	behind the curtain
appamattakaṃ	even a little
abhāvita	uncultivated, not developed, untrained
aruṇ'uggamanaṃ	dawnlight (<aruṇa 'dawn' +uggamanaṃ 'rising, increasing'
asso	horse
ācariyo	teacher
ādī(-ni)	etcetera, and so forth (see this grammar 9)
āpajjati	arrives at, reaches, meets
āharati	brings

āharāpeti	causes to bring
icchita	past participle of icchati 'wants, desires'
icchit'icchitāni	see this grammar 8
itara	the other one
uṇha	warm, hot
uddhaṃ	up, above
upaddavati	causes trouble, troubles (someone), annoys
ubhayattha	in both places
uyyānaṃ	park
ekaka	being alone
oloketi	looks (at)
kata	past participle of karoti
katapuñño	one who has done pure deeds or good actions (see this grammar 11)
kattari	scissors
kathā	story, speech, tale, talk
katheti	speaks, talks
kāreti	causes to do
kira	it is said, truly, really (report by hearsay)
kiliṭṭhaṃ	foulness, impurity (neuter past participle of kilissati ,'become soiled, stained or impure'
kumbho	frontal lobes of an elephant
khādanīya	edible, eatable
khipati	throws, puts
khīṇa	exhausted, over, finished
khuddaka	small
gaṇo	group, multitude, crowd
gantvā	gerund. of gacchati
gahetvā	gerund. of gaṇhāti
gilati	swallows
ghaṃseti	rubs against
ghaṭo(aṃ)	pot
cāleti	shakes
chiddaṃ	hole, cut
jāleti	kindles
ṭhapeti	keeps, places, puts
ṭhitamajjhantike	at midday, at noon
tattabhāvo	hotness, the fact that it is warm/hot, warmth
tappati	suffers, is tormented
tuṭṭha	pleased, being happy/glad
tuṇhībhāvo	silence, state of being silent
daṇḍo	(walking) stick, cudgel, club
dasseti	shows
dārukhaṇḍakaṃ	a piece of (fire)wood, a stick

divaso	day
duggati	evil state
ducchanna	ill-thatched, badly covered
devo	god; also used as an epithet for king
dvāraṃ	door, gate
nandati	rejoices, is happy
nahāyati	bathes
nānāvidha	various
nāḷī	a measure of capacity , a cupful
nāḷimatta	about a nāḷī
nittharati	concludes, ends, finishes
nipphatti	conclusion, end, completion
nivāraṇatthaṃ	for the purpose of preventing, to prevent
nissāya	because of, on account of
pakkosāpeti	summons, calls
pakkhipati	throws, puts
pacati	cooks, bakes, heats
paṭiyādeti	prepares, arranges
paṭṭhāya	(starting) from (see this grammar 7)
paṇṇaṃ	leaf
patta	attained, reached
pattaṃ (-o)	(alms) bowl
paribhojanīya	to be used
palāyati	flees, runs away
pavaṭṭeti	turns, rolls
pavisitvā	gerund of pavisati
paharati	hits, strikes, beats
pahāya	gerund of pajahāti
pāteti	fells, makes fall
aggimpāteti	starts a fire, kindles
pādo	foot
pānīyaṃ	water for drinking
pāpakārin	evil-doer
pāpuṇati	reaches
Pārileyyako	a name of an elephant
pāroho	downard roots from the branch of a banyan tree, tillering
pāvisi,	past of pavisati
pāsāṇo	stone
pīṭhasappin	a cripple
purohito	the kings head-priest
pharati	spreads, pervades, falls on
bahuṃ	much
Bārāṇasī	Benares

maṃkubhāvo	downcast-ness, discontent, confusion, moral weakness
mukhaṃ	mouth, face
mukharatā	talkativeness
modati	rejoices, is happy
rūpakaṃ	image, likeness
laddha	past participle of labhati
vaṭarukkho	a banyan tree
vanasaṇḍo(aṃ)	jungle, forest
vandati	bows down at, salutes
varagāmo	hereditary village, a village given as gift
vāḷamigo	a wild beast
vicarati	moves about
vivaṭa	open
vivaṭamatta	as soon as it was open
visuddhi	purity
vihaññati	suffers
vuccamāna	being said, being addressed
vuṭṭhi	rain
sakkoti	is able, can
sakkharā	pebble
sakkhissati	future of sakkoti
saññā	sign, signal, indication
sati	locative Singular of santa, (see this grammar 2)
santikaṃ	the vicinity (of)
santikā	(ablative) from the vicinity of
sabbaṭṭhaka	a gift comprising eight of everything given
samativijjhati	pierces through
sammajjati	sweeps
sarīraṃ	body
sallapati	talks, speaks
sāṇi	curtain
sākhā	branch
sālittakasippa	art of slinging stones
suggati	=sugati (f.) 'good state'
succhanna	well-thatched, well-covered
subhāvita	well-developed/cultivated/trained
soṇḍā	elephants trunk
soṇḍī	a natural tank in a rock
sodheti	clears, cleans
hatthaṃ	hand, trunk of an elephant
hatthirājan	elephant-king, chief of elephants
hatthin (-ī)	elephant
heṭṭhā	below, beneath, underneath

GRAMMAR X

1. GENITIVE ABSOLUTE

The locative absolute was presented in VIII, 3. Absolute constructions also occur in the genitive. This construction is similar to that with the locative, except that the participle, and its subject (if present) will both be in the genitive case. As with the locative absolute, the subject of the absolute and the participle will agree in case, number and gender, and the subject will be different from that of the main sentence. With a past participle, the construction indicates an action prior to the main clause:

acira-pakkantassa Bhagavato ayaṃ... kathā udapādi
'Shortly after the Blessed one had departed, this conversation arose.'

2. sati AND sante IN LOCATIVE ABSOLUTES

atthi 'be, exist' has a present participle santa (VII,3). This has two locative forms, sati and sante. In the locative absolute, sati is most often used, but sante appears when the sense is impersonal, i.e., when the absolute has no specific subject, either expressed or implied:

mahārājassa ruciyā sati...
'at the kings command'
(Literally, 'there being the king's liking')

but:

evaṃ sante 'that being the case'

3. GERUND -tvā(na)

The gerund in tvā(na) or āya was given in IV, 3. A number of examples occur in the present reading. Note that they can be "chained" to express a sequence of actions prior to the main verb:

Ekā itthī puttaṃ ādāya mukhadhovanatthāya paṇḍitassa pokkharaniṃ gantvā puttaṃ nahāpetvā attano sāṇake nisīdāpetvā mukhaṃ dhovitvā nahātuṃ otari.

'A certain woman, taking her child, went to the pandit's lotus-pond (pokkharani) to wash (literally 'wash the face') and having bathed her son, placed him on her own garment, washed ((her?) face) and descended (into the pond) to bathe.'

A present or past participle, with its appropriate objects, adverbs, etc, may modify a preceding or a following noun. The participle and the noun will agree in number, case and gender, and the construction may have the the sense of an English relative clause, particularly when the participle follows the noun: (Reading 3).Thus

sīlasampanno puriso
'A man (who is) endowed with virtue'

cittaṃ dantaṃ mahato atthāya saṃvattati ti.
'The mind which is tamed (or 'when tamed') leads to great advantage.'

A participle may also follow the object of a verb with a meaning like "see" or "hear" to form the equivalent of an English construction like "I saw him going" or "I saw him seated there:"

Ānandaṃ gacchantaṃ addasāma.
'(We) saw Ananda going.'

Bhagavantaṃ ekaṃ rukkhassa mūle nisinnaṃ disvā
'Seeing the Blessed One seated at the base of a tree...'

The present participle may also serve to indicate contemporaneous action or sometimes the manner of an action, particularly when it refers to the subject of the (main) sentence:

dārūni pakkhipanto jālesi
'(He) threw firewood there and kindled (it)'

5. FUTURE PARTICIPLE IN -nīya

Future participles in -tabba, -ya, and -nīya were given in VII,2, and some verbs may appear with more than one of these endings. Thus karoti has the form karaṇīya as well as kātabba or kattabba. These forms, and especially -nīya, may be used as nouns with the sense 'that which should undergo the action of the verb, or which is worthy of it': Thus pūjanīya 'that which should be worshipped, that which is worthy of worship.' Often too, these forms have taken on idiomatic meaning, such as khādanīya, from khādati 'eats', which generally means 'solid food', and karaṇīya has sometimes the specific sense 'obligation.'

6. CAUSATIVE VERBS:

It will be obvious by now that many different verbs are related to each other by being derived from the same root. Thus, pairs like otarati 'descend' and otāreti 'lower' or āharati 'bring'and āharāpeti 'cause to bring' have appeared in readings. Some pairs of this kind result from the formation of causative verbs. Causative verbs are formed in three main ways:

1. By adding the suffix -e- (earlier -aya-) to a stem which commonly differs from the present stem, often by having a longer or a different vowel:

otarati 'descends'	otāreti 'causes to descend, lowers'
jalati 'burns'	jāleti 'causes to burn, lights'
pavattati 'rolls'	pavatteti 'starts something rolling, causes to roll'

2. By adding -p-and the -e- suffix to verb stems ending in -ā:

tiṭṭhati (root ṭhā) 'exists, stands	ṭhapeti 'places, puts'
deti/dadāti 'gives'	dāpeti 'induce to give'

3. By adding -āpe-(-āpaya) to the present stem:

nisīdati 'sits'	nisīdāpeti 'seats (someone)'
vadati 'speaks'	vadāpeti 'makes (someone) speak'

Often there are alternate forms of the causative. Thus there is kārāpeti in addition to kāreti from karoti 'does, makes', and in addition to vadāpeti 'makes one speak' there is vādeti, from the same root which has the specialized meaning 'plays an instrument' (i.e., in addition to the meaning 'say' given in Reading 6). Sometimes, the base verb and the causative may overlap in meaning, or even have the same meaning. Thus the causative verb uggaheti learn (well)' which appeared in Reading 9, has the same sense as uggaṇhāti, from which it is derived.

Most commonly, if the verb from which the causative is formed is intransitive, the causative verb is transitive, and if the basic verb is transitive the causative means 'to get someone to do it'. However, there are numerous exceptions. Thus pakkosāpeti can mean 'summons, calls for', but so can pakkosati, the verb from which it is formed, and many causative verbs have idiomatic meanings (like vādeti above). However, it is useful to be aware of the general pattern, since it often allows one to guess (and retain) the meaning of a new verb that is related to one already known. Originally, the forms in -āpe- were double causatives, and some of them still have that meaning. Thus in addition to māreti 'kills' from marati 'dies' there is mārāpeti 'causes to kill.'

7. PRE- AND POST-POSITIONS

As stated in II, 7, Pāli has both prepositions and postpositions. Some examples of each appear in this reading:

The preposition anto 'within, inside'does not require any specific case on the noun that it precedes,but rather forms a compound with it, so that the entire compound takes the case required by the construction in which it appears:

antogāmaṃ pavisati	'goes into the village'
antonivesanaṃgato	'(he) who has gone into the house'
antonagare viharanti	'(they) live (with)in the city'

Several new postpositions appear in this lesson, and they require specific cases on their dependent nouns.

paṭṭhāya '(beginning) from' takes the ablative. Thus:

ajjato paṭṭhāya	'from today on'
ito paṭṭhāya	'henceforth'

nissāya 'because (of), owing to,' takes the accusative:

idaṃ kammaṃ nissāya	'because of this action'
dhanaṃ nissāya	'because of (by means of')wealth'

heṭṭhā 'beneath' may take the genitive:

rukkhassa heṭṭhā	'beneath the tree'

But heṭṭhā may also behave like anto:

heṭṭhāmañcaṃ 'beneath the bed' (mañco 'bed')

Postpositions often come from verb forms like gerunds or case forms of nouns which have been "frozen in" to idiomatic use as postpositions. Thus nissāya is actually the gerund of a verb nissayati 'leans on, relies on,, and paṭṭhāya is similarly related to paṭṭhaḥati 'puts down, sets down.' Similarly, the form santikā, 'from (the vicinity of)', which occurs in this lesson, is the ablative of santikaṃ 'vicinity', but could be regarded as a postposition taking the genitive.

8. REPEATED FORMS (REDUPLICATION)

Forms of several kinds may be repeated ("reduplicated") to give a distributive sense:

tattha tattha 'all over, here and there'
yattha yattha 'wherever'
icchit'icchitāni 'whatever (things) are/ were desired'

9. ādi, ādīni 'ETCETERA'

ādi 'beginning, starting point' when added to a noun or a list has the sense 'etcetera, and so forth'. In this usage, it commonly appears with neuter plural inflection:

hatthirūpakādīni 'images of elephants, etc'
kasigorakkhādīni 'agriculture, tending cattle, etc'
(kasi 'ploughing, agriculture')

10. SANDHI

When a form beginning in u- follows one ending in -a, the result may be -o-, particularly when they are closely joined in a compound. thus uṇha 'warm, hot' plus udakaṃ 'water' results in uṇhodakaṃ 'hot water'.

11. katapūño

In most compounds (except co-ordinate ones) the last element expresses the type of thing that the compound refers to, and the preceding element, which may stand in any of several relationships to it, such as subject, object, adjective, etc., but generally modifies or qualifies it in some way. thus Buddhadesito 'preached by the Buddha,' kasigorakkha 'agriculture'(literally:"ploughing-cattle protection/maintaining', with a co-ordinate compound as first member) kammakaro 'worker, work/deed-doer,' pubbakammam 'former action', kalyānamitto 'good friend' etc. However, Pali has a few compounds in which the first element is participle, that reverse this order. Thus diṭṭhapubbo 'seen before' or katapuñño 'doer of merit' in this reading (compare English "aforesaid' or "spoilsport'). There are a number of others formed with kata-, the past participle of karoti; thus katâparādho' doer of guilt, transgressor,' katakalyano 'one who has done good deeds, etc.'

LESSON X: FURTHER READINGS

1. Ath'eko makkaṭo taṃ hatthiṃ divase divase tathāgatassa upaṭṭhānaṃ karontaṃ disvā 'ahaṃ pi kiñcideva karissāmī' ti vicaranto ekadivasaṃ nimmakkhikaṃ daṇḍakamadhuṃ disvā daṇḍakaṃ bhañjitvā daṇḍaken'eva saddhiṃ madhupaṭalaṃ satthu santikaṃ āharitvā kadalipattaṃ chinditvā tattha ṭhapetvā adāsi. Satthā gaṇhi. Makkaṭo "karissati nu kho paribhogaṃ, na karissatī" ti olokento, gahetvā nisinnaṃ disvā "kinnukho" ti cintetvā daṇḍakoṭiyaṃ gahetvā parivattetvā olokento aṇḍakāni disvā tāni sanikaṃ apanetvā adāsi. Satthā paribhogamakāsi. So tuṭṭhamānaso taṃ taṃ sākhaṃ gahetvā naccanto aṭṭhāsi. Tassa gahita-sākhā'pi akkantasākhā'pi bhijji. So ekasmiṃ khāṇumatthake patitvā nibbiddhagatto satthari pasannena cittena kālaṃkatvā tāvatiṃsabhavane nibbatti.

(Rasv.)

2. Atīte eko vejjo gāmanigamesu caritvā vejjakammaṃ karonto ekaṃ cakkhudubbalaṃ itthiṃ disvā pucchi: "kiṃ te aphāsukaṃ" ti?

"Akkhīhi na passāmī" ti.

"Bhesajjaṃ te karomî"ti.

"Karohi sāmî" ti.

"Kimme dassasī" ti?

"Sace me akkhīni pākatikāni kātuṃ sakkhissasi, ahaṃ te putta-dhītāhi saddhiṃ dāsī bhavissāmī" ti. So bhesajjaṃ saṃvidahi. Ekabhesajjene'va akkhīni pākatikāni ahesuṃ. Sā cintesi "ahaṃ etassa 'puttadhītāhi saddhiṃ dāsī bhavissāmī ti paṭijāniṃ: vañcessāmi naṃ" [3] ti.

Sā vejjena "kīdisaṃ bhadde?" ti puṭṭhā "pubbe me akkhīni thokaṃ rujiṃsu, idāni atirekataraṃ rujantī" ti āha.

(Rasv.)

3. Atīte kira eko vejjo vejjakammatthāya gāmaṃ vicaritvā kiñci kammaṃ alabhitvā chātajjhatto nikkhamitvā gāmadvāre sambahule kumārake kīḷante disvā 'ime sappena ḍasāpetvā tikicchitvā āhāraṃ labhissāmī' ti ekasmiṃ rukkhabile sīsaṃ nīharitvā nipannaṃ sappaṃ dassetvā "ambho kumārakā, eso sāḷikapotako; gaṇhatha nan'ti āha. Ath'eko kumārako sappaṃ gīvāya daḷhaṃ gahetvā nīharitvā tassa sappabhāvaṃ ñatvā viravanto avidūre ṭhitassa vejjassa matthake khipi. Sappo vejjassa khandhaṭṭhikaṃ parikkhipitvā daḷhaṃ ḍasitvā tatth'eva jīvitakkhayaṃ pāpesi.

(DhAk.)

---

[3] Alternate form of taṃ

4. Atīte Bārāṇasiyaṃ Brahmadatte rajjaṃ kārente bodhisatto Bārāṇasiyaṃ vāṇijakule nibbatti. Nāmagahaṇadivase ca'ssa Paṇḍito'ti nāmaṃ akaṃsu. So vayappatto aññena vāṇijena saddhiṃ ekato hutvā vāṇijjaṃ karoti. Tassa Atipaṇḍito'ti nāmaṃ ahosi. Te Bārāṇasito pañcahi sakaṭasatehi bhaṇḍaṃ ādāya janapadaṃ gantvā vaṇijjaṃ katvā laddha-lābhā [4] puna Bārāṇasiṃ āgamiṃsu. Atha tesaṃ bhaṇḍa-bhājanakāle Atipaṇḍito āha; "Mayā dve koṭṭhāsā laddhabbhā" ti.

"Kiṃ kāraṇā?".

"Tvaṃ Paṇḍito, ahaṃ Atipaṇḍito; paṇḍito ekaṃ laddhuṃ arahati, atipaṇḍito dve" ti.

"Nanu amhākaṃ dvinnaṃ bhaṇḍamūlam'pi goṇādayo'pi sama-samā yeva? kasmā tvaṃ dve koṭṭhāse laddhuṃ arahasi?" ti.

"Atipaṇḍitabhāvenâ" ti.

Evaṃ te kathaṃ vaḍḍhetvā kalahaṃ akaṃsu.

Tato Atipaṇḍito 'atth'eko upāyo'ti cintetvā attano pitaraṃ ekasmiṃ susira-rukkhe pavesetvā "tvaṃ amhesu āgatesu "Atipaṇḍito dve koṭṭhāse laddhuṃ arahatī" ti vadeyyāsî ti vatvā bodhisattaṃ upasaṃkamitvā "samma mayhaṃ dvinnaṃ koṭṭhāsānaṃ yuttabhavaṃ vā ayuttabhāvaṃ vā esā rukkhadevatā jānāti, ehi naṃ pucchissāmâ" ti, taṃ tattha netvā "ayye rukkhadevate, amhākaṃ aṭṭaṃ pacchindâ" ti āha. Ath'assa pitā saraṃ parivattetvā "tena hi kathetha" ti āha.

"Ayye, ayaṃ Paṇḍito, ahaṃ Atipaṇḍito. Amhehi ekato vohāro kato; tattha kena kiṃ laddhabban" ti.

"Paṇḍitena eko koṭṭhāso, Atipaṇḍitena dve laddhabbā" ti.

Bodhisatto evaṃ vinicchitaṃ aṭṭaṃ sutvā "idāni devatābhāvaṃ vā adevatābhāvaṃ vā jānissāmî" ti palālaṃ āharitvā susiraṃ pūretvā aggiṃ adāsi. Atipaṇḍitassa pitā jālāya phuṭṭhakāle addhajjhāmena sarīrena upari āruyha sākhaṃ gahetvā olambanto bhūmiyaṃ patitvā imaṃ gāthaṃ āha:

"sādhuko Paṇḍito nāma,
natv'eva [5] Atipaṇḍito."

(Jāt)

GLOSSARY

akkamati	steps upon, treads upon; present participle akkanta
akkhiṃ	eye

---

[4] Here the object follows the participle and the entire form is plural, agreeing with te, which it modifies.

[5] na+tu+eva

aṭṭaṃ	question, problem, lawsuit, case
aṭṭhāsi	past of {tiṭṭhati}
aṇḍakaṃ	egg
atipaṇḍito	a name (‹ ati 'very, exceedingly' + paṇḍito)
atirekataraṃ	much more
addhajjhāma	half-burnt
apaneti	removes, leads away
aphāsukam	difficulty, disease
ambho	look here, hey, hello
ayyā	worthy one, honorable one
arahati	deserves
avidūre	vicinity, nearby
ādāya	having taken (ger. of ādāti 'takes'
āruhati	climbs
āhāra	food
idāni	now
upaṭṭhānaṃ	attendance, waiting upon
upari	above, on, upon, upper
upāyo	method, way out, trick
ekato	together
olaṃbati	hangs (from), is suspended
kadalipattaṃ	banana leaf
kāraṇaṃ	reason, cause
kiñcideva	something or other (kiṃ+ci(d)+eva)
kidisa	how, in what manner
kīḷati	plays
kumāraka	young boy
koṭi	end
koṭṭhāso	share
khandhaṭṭhikaṃ	backbone, back
khāṇu	stake, spike
gattaṃ	body
gīvā	neck, throat
goṇo	ox
chātajjhatta	be hungry
jālā	blazes, flames
ḍasāpeti	causes to bite or sting
tāvatiṃsabhavanaṃ	realm of the thirty-three gods
tikicchati	treats (medically)
tu	however, indeed
tuṭṭhamānasa	delighted, with delight
thokaṃ	little
daṇḍakamadhuṃ	a bee-hive on a branch
daṇḍako	branch, stick
dassasi	future 2 Sg. of deti

daḷhaṃ	tightly, hard, strongly
dāsī	maid-servant
dubbala	weak
dhītar	daughter
naccati	dances, plays
nāmagahanaṃ	naming, taking a name
nāmaṃ karoti	gives a name
nigamo	market-town, small town
nipanna	to lie or sleep
nibbattati	is born, arises
nibbiddha	pierced
nimmakkhika	without bees or flies
nīharati	puts out,stretches or takes out
pacchindati	settles, decides
paṭijānāti	promises
patati	falls, ger. patitvā
parikkhipati	coils around, encircles
paribhogo	enjoyment, use, partaking
parivatteti	turns, changes
paveseti	causes to enter, puts inside
palālaṃ	straw, dry leaves
pasanna	pleased, clear, bright
pākatika	natural state, state as before
pāpeti	brings about, brings to
puṭṭha	past participle of (pucchati)
phuṭṭha	touched (past participle of phusati 'touches')
bilaṃ	hollow
bodhisatto	aspirant to Buddhahood, a Buddha-to-be in an earlier life
Brahmadatto	a name of a king
bhañjati	breaks
bhaṇḍaṃ	goods
bhaṇḍammūḷaṃ	capital
bhadde	dear one, lady, term of address for women
bhājanaṃ	dividing
bhāvo	nature, fact, -ness
bhijjati	breaks, gets broken
bhūmi	ground, earth
bhesajja	medicine
makkaṭo	monkey
matthaka	top, head, surface
madhu	honey
madhu paṭalo	honeycomb
mānasa	with a mind, of the mind

mūlaṃ	price, capital, money
yutta	proper, befitting, to have a right to
rajjaṃkaroti/ kāreti	reigns
rukkhadevatā	a tutelary deity of a tree
rujati	pains or aches
laddhabba	future passive past participle of labhati
laddhuṃ	infinitive of labhati
lābho	profit, gain
vañceti	cheats
vaḍḍheti	increases (something), cultivates
vatvā	gerund of vacati
vayappatta	come of age
vinicchita	decided, settled
viravati	shouts, screams
vejjakammaṃ	medical practice
vejjo	a physician
saṃvidahati	arranges, applies, prepares, provides
sakaṭo(aṃ)	cart
sanikaṃ	slowly, gradually
sappo	a serpent
sama-sama	equal(ly)
sambahula	many
samma	friend, term of address for a friend
saro	voice, sound
sākhā	branch
sādhuka	good or righteous (one)
sāmi	lord, sir, husband
sāḷikapotako	a young bird (Mynah bird)
sīsaṃ	head
susirarukkho	hollow tree
hutvā	gerund of hoti/bhavati

LESSON XI

1. Atīte Jambudīpe Ajitaraṭṭhe eko gopālako vasi. Tassa gehe eko paccekabuddho nibaddhaṃ bhuñjati. Tasmiṃ gehe eko kukkuro ca ahosi. Paccekabuddho bhuñjanto tassa nibaddhaṃ ekaṃ bhattapiṇḍaṃ adāsi. So tena paccekabuddhe sinehaṃ akāsi. Gopālako divasassa dve vāre paccekabuddhassa upaṭṭhānaṃ gacchi. Sunakho'pi tena saddhiṃ gacchi.

Gopālo ekadivasaṃ paccekabuddhaṃ āha: "bhante, yadā me okāso na bhavissati, tadā imaṃ sunakhaṃ pesessāmi; tena saññāṇena āgaccheyyāthâ" ti. Tato paṭṭhāya anokāsadivase sunakhaṃ pesesi. So ekavacanen'eva pakkhanditvā, paccekabuddhassa vasanaṭṭhānaṃ gantvā, tikkhattuṃ bhussitvā attano āgatabhāvaṃ jānāpetvā ekamantaṃ nipajji. Paccekabuddhe velaṃ sallakkhetvā nikkhante, bhussanto purato gacchi. Paccekabuddho taṃ vīmaṃsanto ekadivasaṃ aññaṃ maggaṃ paṭipajji; atha sunakho tiriyaṃ ṭhatvā bhussitvā itaramaggameva naṃ āropesi.

Ath'ekadivasaṃ aññaṃ maggaṃ paṭipajjitvā, sunakhena tiriyaṃ ṭhatvā vāriyamāno'pi anivattitvā, taṃ pādena apanetvā pāyāsi. Sunakho tassa anivattanabhāvaṃ ñatvā, nivāsanakaṇṇe ḍasitvā ākaḍḍhanto gantabbamaggam' eva pāpesi. Evaṃ so sunakho tasmiṃ paccekabuddhe balavasinehaṃ uppādesi.

Aparabhāge paccekabuddhassa cīvaraṃ jīri. Ath'assa gopālako cīvaravatthāni adāsi. Paccekabuddho "phāsukaṭṭhānaṃ gantvā cīvaraṃ kāressāmî" ti gopālakaṃ āha. So'pi "bhante, mā ciraṃ bahi vasitthâ" ti avadi. Sunakho'pi tesaṃ kathaṃ suṇanto aṭṭhāsi. Paccekabuddhe vehāsaṃ abbhuggantvā gacchante bhuṃkaritvā ṭhitassa sunakhassa hadayaṃ phali.

Tiracchānā nām'ete ujujātikā honti akuṭilā.

Manussā pana aññaṃ cintenti, aññaṃ vadanti.

(Rasv.)

2. Evaṃ me sutaṃ. Ekaṃ samayaṃ bhagavā Āḷaviyaṃ viharati Āḷavakassa yakkhassa bhavane. Atha kho Āḷavako yakkho yena bhagavā ten'upasaṃkami, upasaṃkamitvā bhagavantaṃ etadavoca:

'Nikkhama, samaṇâ'ti.
'Sādhâvuso'ti bhagavā nikkhami.

'Pavisa, samanâ'ti.
'Sādhâvuso'ti, bhagavā pāvisi.

Dutiyaṃ pi kho Āḷavako yakkho bhagavantaṃ etadavoca

'Nikkhama' .. pāvisi.

Tatiyaṃ pi kho Āḷavako yakkho bhagavantaṃ etadavoca:

'Nikkhama' ... pāvisi.

Catutthaṃ pi kho Āḷavako yakkho bhagavantaṃ etadavoca:

'Nikkhama, samaṇâ'ti.
'Na khvâhaṃ taṃ āvuso nikkhamissāmi: yante karaṇīyaṃ, taṃ karohî'ti.

"Pañhaṃ taṃ, samaṇa pucchissāmi. sace me na vyākarissasi, cittaṃ vā te khipissāmi, hadayaṃ vā te phālessāmi, pādesu vā gahetvā pāragaṃgāya khipissāmî'ti.

'Na khvâhaṃ taṃ, āvuso passāmi sadevake loke sabrahmake sassamaṇa-brāhmaniyā pajāya sadevamanussāya yo me cittaṃ vā khipeyya, hadayaṃ vā phāḷeyya, pādesu vā gahetvā pāragaṃgāya khipeyya. Api ca tvaṃ āvuso puccha yad ākaṅkhasî'ti.

Atha kho Āḷavako yakkho bhagavantaṃ gāthāya ajjhabhāsi:

'Kiṃ sū'dha vittaṃ purisassa seṭṭhaṃ?
Kiṃ su suciṇṇaṃ sukhamāvahāti?
Kiṃ su have sādutaraṃ rasānaṃ?
Kathaṃjīviṃ jīvitamāhu seṭṭhaṃ?'

'Saddhîdha vittaṃ purisassa seṭṭham.
Dhammo suciṇṇo sukhamāvahāti.
Saccaṃ have sādutaraṃ rasānaṃ.
Paññājīviṃ jīvitamāhu seṭṭhaṃ.'

(SN.)

3. Na antalikkhe na samuddamajjhe - na pabbatānaṃ vivaraṃ pavissa
Na vijjati so jagatippadeso - yatthaṭṭhito muñceyya pāpakammā.

Na antalikkhe na samuddamajjhe - na pabbatānaṃ vivaraṃ pavissa
Na vijjati so jagatippadeso - yatthaṭṭhitaṃ na-ppasahetha maccu

Sukhakāmāni bhūtāni - yo daṇḍena vihiṃsati
Attano sukhamesāno - pecca so na labhate sukhaṃ

Sukhakāmāni bhūtāni - yo daṇḍena na hiṃsati
Attano sukhamesāno - pecca so labhate sukhaṃ

Parijiṇṇamidaṃ rūpaṃ - roganiḍḍhaṃ pabhaṃguṇaṃ
bhijjati pūtisandeho - maraṇantaṃ hi jīvitaṃ.

(Dhp.)

4. Atha kho bhagavā pañcavaggiye bhikkhū āmantesi: 'Rūpaṃ bhikkhave anattā. Rūpaṃ ca hidaṃ bhikkhave, attā abhavissa, nayidaṃ rūpaṃ ābādhāya

saṃvatteyya; labbhetha ca rūpe 'evaṃ me rūpaṃ hotu, evaṃ me rūpaṃ mā ahosî 'ti. Yasmā ca kho bhikkhave, 'rūpaṃ anattā, tasmā rūpaṃ ābādhāya saṃvattati. Na ca labbhati rūpe 'evaṃ me rūpaṃ hotu, evaṃ me rūpaṃ mā ahosî'ti.

"Vedanā bhikkhave, anattā. Vedanā ca hidaṃ bhikkhave, attā abhavissa, nayidaṃ vedanā ābādhāya saṃvatteyya; labbhetha ca vedanāya 'evaṃ me vedanā hotu, evaṃ me vedanā mā ahosî 'ti. Yasmā ca bhikkhave, vedanā anattā, tasmā vedanā abādhāya saṃvattati. Na ca labbhati vedanāya 'evaṃ me vedanā hotu, evaṃ me vedanā mā ahosî'ti.

"Saññā bhikkhave, anattā. Saññā ca hidaṃ bhikkhave, attā abhavissa, nayidaṃ saññā ābādhāya saṃvatteyya; labbhetha ca saññāya 'evaṃ me saññā hotu, evaṃ me saññā mā ahosî'ti. Yasmā ca bhikkhave, saññā anattā, tasmā saññā abādhāya saṃvattati. Na ca labbhati saññayā 'evaṃ me saññā hotu, evaṃ me saññā mā ahosî'ti.

"Saṃkhārā bhikkhave, anattā. Saṃkhārā ca hidaṃ bhikkhave attā abhavissiṃsu, nayime saṃkhārā ābādhāya saṃvatteyyuṃ; labbhetha ca saṃkhāresu 'evaṃ me saṃkhārā hontu, evaṃ me saṃkhārā mā ahesun'ti.. Yasmā ca kho bhikkhave, saṃkhārā anattā, tasmā saṃkhārā ābādhāya saṃvattanti. Na ca labbhati saṃkhāresu 'evaṃ me saṃkhārā hontu, evaṃ me saṃkhārā mā ahesun'ti.

"Viññāṇaṃ bhikkhave, anattā. Viññāṇañca hidaṃ bhikkhave, attā abhavissa, nayidaṃ viññāṇaṃ ābādhaya saṃvatteyya; labbhetha ca viññāṇe 'evaṃ me viññāṇaṃ hotu, evaṃ me viññāṇaṃ mā ahosî'ti. Yasmāca kho bhikkhave viññāṇaṃ anattā, tasmā viññāṇaṃ ābādhāya saṃvattati. Na ca labbhati viññāṇe 'evaṃ me viññāṇaṃ hotu. Evaṃ me viññāṇaṃ mā ahosî'ti.

(Mhvg.)

GLOSSARY

Ajita	a name of a country
ajjhabhāsati	addresses, speaks
anta	end, goal
X anta	having X as its end
antalikkhaṃ	atmosphere
apaneti	leads away, removes
aparabhāgo	later time, later
abhavissa	conditional of bhavati (see this grammar 2)
ākaṃkhati	desires
ākaḍḍhati	drags, pulls
āropeti	leads up to
ābādho	disease, affliction.
āvahāti	=āvahati 'brings, entails' with length for the poetic meter

Āḷavako	a name of a demon
Āḷavī	a place name
itara	other
ujujātika	straightforward, honest
uppādeti	produces, makes, gives rise to
esāna	searching for, eager for
okāso	occasion, time
kathaṃ jīviṃ	leading what kind of life, which way of living?
kukkuro	dog
kāreti	constructs, makes
kuṭila	crooked, dishonest
khattuṃ	times
tikkhattum	three times
gopālako	cowherd
catutthaṃ	for the fourth time
cittaṃ khipati	confuses (someone's) mind
jagati	(in) the world (locative of jagati- 'world'
jānāpeti	informs
jīrati	decays, is worn out
ṭhāti	stands
ḍasati	bites, chews, gnaws
tiracchāno	animal
tiriyaṃ	across
nikkhanta	ppl. of nikkhamati
niḍḍham	nest, place
nipajjati	lies down
nibaddhaṃ	always
nivattati	turns back
nivāsanakaṇṇaṃ	hem of the robe
pakkhandati	springs forward, jumps up
paccekabuddho	Individual or silent Buddha (see this grammạr 8)
pañcavaggīyā (bhikkhū)	the group of five monks to whom the Buddha preached his first sermon
paññājīviṃ	life of wisdom, insight
pañho	question
paṭipajjati	enters upon
padeso	province, part, region
pabbato	mountain, range of mountains
pabhaṃguna	easily destroyed
payāti	goes forward, proceeds
parijiṇṇa	decayed
pavissa	gerund of pavisati
pasahati	subues, oppresses
pāpeti	brings to, causes to attain

pāragaṃgāya	beyond the Ganges, the other side of the Ganges
purato	in front of, before
pūtisandeho	accumulation of putrid matter, mass of corruption
peseti	sends
phalati	splits, breaks open
phāleti	rends asunder
phāsuka	easy, comfortable
balavant	great, powerful; compound stem balava
bahi	outside, outer, external
brāhmaṇī pajā	generation (progeny) of Brahmins
bhattaṃ	boiled rice, food, meal
bhavanaṃ	abode, residence
bhijjati	is broken
bhuṃkaroti	barks
bhussati	barks
bhūtaṃ	living being
majjha	middle
muñcati	releases, is relieved
yakkho	demon, devil
rogo	disease, sickness
labbhati	is available, is obtained
vatthaṃ	cloth
vasati	lives, abides, dwells
vasanaṭṭhānaṃ	place of residence
vāriyamāna	being prevented, obstructed
vāro	time, occasion
vijjati	appears, seems
vittaṃ	property, wealth
vivaro(aṃ)	cavity, hole, hollow
vīmaṃsati	tests, considers
velā	time
vehāso	sky, air
vyākaroti	explains, clarifies, answers
saññāṇaṃ	token, mark, sign
saddhā	determination, faith
samuddo	ocean, sea
sallakkheti	observes, considers
sassamaṇa-brāhmaṇa	including religious teachers and brahmins
sādutara	sweeter, more pleasant
sineho	affection
su	indeed, verily
sukhakāma	desirous of happiness
suciṇṇa	well-practiced
sunakho	dog

seṭṭha	noble, best, excellent
hadayaṃ	heart, mind
have	indeed, certainly, surely
hiṃsati	oppresses

GRAMMAR XI

1. IMPERATIVES:

Several imperatives have occurred so far. The second person singular and plural imperatives were given in III, 5, and the third person in VII, 1. In addition, it was noted that the optative can occur as a polite imperative (III, 4.2) and that the third person imperative is also used as a respectful second person imperative(VII, 2.2).

In this reading, an alternate form of the second person imperative without the suffix -hi occurs. This bare form of the imperative is found primarily with verbs with a present stem in -a or -ā. Recall that final -a of the stem was lengthened before -hi if not already long. In the imperative without -hi, it is always short, even if long in the present:

PRESENT TENSE	-hi IMPERATIVE	BARE IMPERATIVE
labhati 'obtains'	labhāhi	labha
suṇāti 'hears'	suṇāhi	suṇa

NOTE: Another formation of the imperative is given under the Middle Voice in 4 below.

2. THE CONDITIONAL:

2.1 Formation:

Pāli has a conditional form of the verb. It looks like a blend of the future and past tense forms and is formed as follows :

(1) Adding the prefix a-. This is the same "augment ' that appears in the past tense (VI, 5);

(2) adding the affix -iss- that is used in the future (IX, 3), but followed by the following endings:

	Singular	Plural
1 Pers:	-aṃ	-āma
2 Pers:	-a	-atha
3 Pers:		-aṃsu

Note that these resemble the endings of of the past tense (VI, 6; IX, 2), except that the third person singular ends in short -a rather than -ā, and the third person plural has -ṃsu like the "-is aorist " type past .

The forms are illustrated below with the conditional of bhavati 'be, exist, become':

	Singular	Plural
1 Pers:	abhavissaṃ	abhavissāma
2 Pers:	abhavissa	abhavissatha
3 Pers:		abhavissaṃsu

2.2 Use: The conditional is used in forming "If...(then)" constructions. Usually, the verb of the "if" clause is in the conditional, and the sense is commonly strongly hypothetical or counter to fact ; that is, there is an implication that the situation described has not or could not take place. The verb of the "then" clause may be in the optative, and the implication is then that the whole situation is hypothetical:

no ce taṃ abhavissa ajātaṃ abhūtaṃ...nayidha jātassa bhūtassa nissaraṇam paññāyetha
(paññāyati 'appears, is clear, is evident' nissaraṇaṃ 'escape,departure')
'If there were not the not-born and the not-become, there would not appear an escape from the born and the having become.'

This reading gives an excellent example of this in Main Reading 4. Note the contrast between the sentences with the conditional - optative sequence and those with the present -past sequence.

3. THE PROHIBITIVE PARTICLE mā

The particle mā 'don't' usually occurs with the imperative, the past, or the optative.

With the imperative, mā forms a negative imperative:

mā gaccha 'don't go'
mā evaṃ dānaṃ detha 'do not give alms thus'

With the past verb, it forms a prohibitive, or a negative exhortation:

mā saddaṃ akāsi 'Do not make noise'

alaṃ, Ānanda, mā soci mā paridevi
(alaṃ '(that's) enough')
'Enough, Ananda, do not grieve, do not weep.'

With the optative, it means that something should not be done, as we would expect:

mā pamādaṃ anuyuñjetha 'Do not indulge in indolence.'

4. MIDDLE VOICE

Sanskrit had a system of of "middle" or "reflexive" endings, in contrast with the "active" endings. The middle inflections, in general, occurred with verbs that indicated actions done for the subject's own benefit, or which reflected back on or affected the subject. These endings were also required in passive verbs. In Pāli, the descendants of these endings sometimes occur, but they are relatively rare, particularly in prose, and are clearly dying out. The line between active and middle forms in meaning is also blurred, and often the middle endings seem to be used simply to give an elevated or archaic flavor, or, in poetry, to suit the meter. They are thus essentially remnants, but where found, may still be associated with verbs with a "middle" sense. Also, although they are much less common than the more familiar active endings, they do differ from them in shape, and thus the student should be prepared to encounter and recognize them. As with the active endings, there are different sets that occur with different tenses and moods, and here we simply give the endings, with examples of different verbs, so that the student may recognize them or refer to the charts where necessary.. (It is difficult if not impossible to find an actually occurring complete or even nearly complete set with any single verb.)

4.1 Present and Future Tense Middle Forms;

The following middle endings occur with present and future tense forms:

	Singular	Plural
1 Pers:	-e	-mhe/-mhase
2 Pers:	-se	-vhe
3 Pers:	-te	-ante/ -re

Examples:

mañne 'I think, suppose'; labhe 'I obtain'; labhate 'he obtains'; gamissase 'you will go'; karissare 'they will do'.

4.2 Past Tense Middle Forms:

The following endings occur with the past tense:

	Singular	Plural
1 Pers:	-aṃ	-mase/-mhase
2 Pers:	-(t)tho	-vho/ -vhaṃ
3 Pers:	-(t)tha	-re /-ruṃ

Examples:

maññitha 'he thought'; maññitho 'you thought'; abhāsittha 'he spoke (note the augment); pucchittho 'you asked'

4.3 Optative Middle Forms: The optative endings below are strictly speaking (or more accurately, historically speaking) middle endings. However, since these endings have been mixed to a great degree with other optative endings, they are not generally distinguishable in use, and some have been given before simply as optative forms.

	Singular	Plural
1 Pers:	-eyyaṃ	-(eyy)āmase
2 Pers:	-etho	-eyyavho
3 Pers:	-etha	-eraṃ

Examples: labhetha 'he should/might obtain'; bhajetha 'he should/ might associate with' jāyetha 'he/it should be born/ come into being'. labbhetha 'might be obtained'

4.4 Middle Imperative:

There are also imperative middle voice forms, as follows. The second singular form appears to be more common than the others, especially with certain verbs in fixed expressions.

	Singular	Plural
2 Pers:	-ssu	-vho
3 Pers:	-taṃ	-antaṃ

Examples: labhataṃ 'let him obtain'; gaṇhassu '(you) take'!; bhāsassu 'speak!'

4.5. Present Participle:

As described in IV,4 and IX, 5, the -māna present participle was originally a middle form, but in Pāli it has greatly extended its use, and has become primarily an alternate for the -ant participle.

5. LOCATIVE OF REFERENCE AND LOCATIVE OF CONTACT

The locative case may be used with a sense 'in reference to', with relation to', or 'concerning':

kathaṃ mayaṃ Tathāgassa sarire paṭipajjāma?
what shall we do with regard to the Tathagata's body?'
(sarīro, body'; paṭipajjati 'enters a path, follows a method')

Used with a verb of seizing, grasping, etc, the locative may signify the point of contact:

taṃ kesesu gaṇhāti '(he) takes him by the hair (used in the plural in Pāli)'

6. labbhati

labbhati is the passive form of labhati 'gets, obtains'. It may have the expected meaning 'be obtained, be received', but it also has a use in which it means 'come about', or even 'exist'. (recall the similar use of vijjati with ṭhānaṃ in

Grammar 7 of Lesson 5). In this use it may occur with the locative of reference (5 above), as in the reading here.

6. COMPARATIVE AND SUPERLATIVE

The most common way in which Pāli expresses the comparative (English "-er") is with the affix --tara added to an adjective:

ADJECTIVE	COMPARATIVE
piya 'dear'	piyatara 'dearer'
sādu 'sweet'	sādutara 'sweeter
bahu 'much'	bahutara 'more'
sīlavant 'virtuous'	sīlavantatara 'more virtuous'
balavant 'powerful'	balavatara 'more powerful'

As the last two examples show, adjectives in -(v)ant may add -a- or lose the final consonants when -tara is added.

There is also a superlative ("-est) affix -tama, as in sattama 'the best' (< santa), piyatama 'dearest' but it is rarer, and in Pāli the comparative often has a superlative sense.

There are also irregular comparatives and superlatives. Many of these are descended from Sanskrit forms in -īyas ans -iṣṭha. Sound change has disguised them, but in Pāli, they commonly end in -iya or -yya and (i)ṭṭha: Thus seyya 'better', seṭṭha 'best', bhiyyo 'more', pāpiṭṭha ' the worst', jeṭṭha 'the eldest', etc.

8. "PACCEKA BUDDHA"

A Pacceka , "Individual" or "Silent" Buddha" is an arahant who has attained Nibbāna by himself, without hearing the doctrine.from another, as opposed to those arahants who have learned by instruction. He does not have the capacity to teach others and awaken them to the doctrine of the four noble truths, as opposed to a Sammāsambuddha "Universal or Perfect Buddha" (Glossary, lesson VI), as represented, for example, by Gotama Buddha . The term Pacceka Buddha is not much used in the Pāli Canon, and the concept becomes more important in Mahāyāna contexts.

FURTHER READINGS XI

1. Na tvaṃ addasā manussesu itthiṃ vā purisaṃ vā āsītikaṃ vā nāvutikaṃ vā vassasatikaṃ vā jātiyā, jiṇṇaṃ gopāṇasīvaṃkaṃ bhoggaṃ daṇḍaparāyanaṃ pavedhamānaṃ gacchantaṃ āturaṃ gatayobbanaṃ khaṇḍadantaṃ palitakesaṃ vilūnaṃ khalitaṃsiro valitaṃ tilakāhatagattan'ti?

Tassa te viññussa sato mahallakassa na etad ahosi: "Ahaṃ pi kho'mhi jarādhammo jaraṃ anatīto. Handâhaṃ kalyāṇaṃ karomi kāyena vācāya manasâ"ti.

Na tvaṃ addasā manussesu itthiṃ vā purisaṃ vā ābādhikaṃ dukkhitaṃ bāḷhagilānaṃ sake muttakarīse palipannaṃ semānaṃ aññehi vuṭṭhāpiyamānaṃ aññehi saṃvesiyamānan'ti?

Tassa te viññussa sato mahallakassa na etad ahosi: "Ahaṃ pi kho'mhi vyādhidhammo vyādhiṃ anatīto. Handâhaṃ kalyāṇaṃ karomi kayena vācāya manasā"ti.

Na tvaṃ addasā manussesu itthiṃ vā purisaṃ vā ekâhamataṃ vā dvîhamataṃ vā tīhamataṃ vā uddhumātakaṃ vinīlakaṃ vipubbakajātan'ti?
Tassa te viññussa sato mahallakassa na etadahosi:
"Ahaṃ pi kho'mhi maraṇadhammo maraṇaṃ anatīto. Handâhaṃ kalyāṇaṃ karomi kāyena vācāya manasā"ti.

(-A. N.)

2. Katamā ca bhikkhave sammā-diṭṭhi?

Yaṃ kho bhikkhave dukkhe ñāṇaṃ dukkhasamudaye ñāṇaṃ dukkhanirodhe ñāṇaṃ dukkhanirodha gāminiyā paṭipadāya ñāṇaṃ ayaṃ vuccati bhikkhave sammā-diṭṭhi.

Yato kho āvuso ariyasāvako akusalañca pajānāti akusalamūlañca pajānāti, kusalañca pajānāti kusalamūlañca pajānāti, ettāvatā pi kho āvuso ariyasāvako sammā-diṭṭhī hoti, dhamme aveccappasādena samannāgato, āgato imaṃ saddhamman'ti.

Katamaṃ panâvuso akusalaṃ, katamaṃ akusalamūlaṃ, katamaṃ kusalaṃ, katamaṃ kusalamūlan'ti?

Pāṇâtipāto kho āvuso akusalaṃ
adinnâdānaṃ akusalaṃ
kāmesu micchâcāro akusalaṃ (kāya-kammaṃ)

musāvādo akusalaṃ
pisuṇā vācā akusalaṃ
pharusā vācā akusalaṃ
samphappalāpo akusalaṃ (vacī-kammaṃ)

abhijjhā akusalaṃ
byāpādo akusalaṃ
micchādiṭṭhi akusalaṃ (mano-kammaṃ)

Idaṃ vuccatâvuso akusalaṃ.
Ime dasa dhammā "akusalakammapathâti nāmena pi ñātabbā.

Katamañcâvuso akusalamūlam?

Lobho akusalamūlaṃ
doso akusalamūlaṃ
moho akusalamūlaṃ
Idaṃ vuccatâvuso akusalamūlaṃ.

Katamañcâvuso kusalaṃ?

Pāṇâtipātā veramaṇī kusalaṃ
adinnâdānā veramaṇī kusalaṃ
kāmesu micchâcārā veramaṇī kusalaṃ (kāya-kammaṃ)

musāvādā veramaṇī kusalaṃ
pisuṇā vācā veramaṇī kusalaṃ
pharusā vācā veramaṇī kusalaṃ
samphappalāpā veramaṇī kusalaṃ (vacī-kammaṃ)

anabhijjhā kusalaṃ
abyāpādo kusalaṃ
sammā-diṭṭhi kusalaṃ (mano-kammaṃ)

Idaṃ vuccatâvuso kusalaṃ.

Ime dasa dhammā "kusalakammapathâ'ti nāmena pi ñātabbā.

Katamañcâvuso kusalamūlaṃ?

Alobho kusalamūlaṃ
adoso kusalamūlaṃ
amoho kusalamūlaṃ.
Idaṃ vuccatâvuso kusalamūlaṃ.

(M.N.)

3. Pañcahi bhikkhave aṃgehi samannāgato mātugāmo ekantâmanāpo hoti purisassa.

Katamehi pañcahi?

Na ca rūpavā hoti, na ca bhogavā hoti, na ca sīlavā hoti, alaso ca hoti, pajañcassa na labhati.

Imehi kho bhikkhave pañcahi aṃgehi samannāgato mātugāmo ekantâmanāpo hoti purisassa.

Pañcahi bhikkhave aṃgehi samannāgato māṭugāmo ekantamanāpo hoti purisassa.

Katamehi pañcahi?

Rūpavā ca hoti, bhogavā ca hoti, sīlavā ca hoti, dakkho ca hoti analaso, pajañcassa labhati.

Imehi kho bhikkhave pañcahi aṃgehi samannāgato mātugāmo ekantamanāpo hoti purisassa.

Pañcahi bhikkhave aṃgehi samannāgato puriso ekantâmanāpo hoti mātugāmassa.

Katamehi pañcahi?

Na ca rūpavā hoti, na ca bhogavā hoti, na ca sīlavā hoti, alaso ca hoti, pajañcassa na labhati.

Imehi kho bhikkhave pañcahi aṃgehi samannāgato puriso ekantâmanāpo hoti mātugāmassa.

Pañcahi bhikkhave aṃgehi samannāgato puriso ekantamanāpo hoti mātugāmassa.

Katamehi pañcahi?

Rūpavā ca hoti, bhogavā ca hoti, sīlavā ca hoti, dakkho ca hoti analaso, pajañcassa labhati.

Imehi kho bhikkhave pañcahi aṃgehi samannāgato puriso ekantamanāpo hoti mātugāmassâti.

(S. N.)

4. Pañcimāni bhikkhave mātugāmassa āveṇikāni dukkhāni yāni mātugāmo paccanubhoti aññatr'eva purisehi.

Katamāni pañca?

Idha bhikkhave mātugāmo daharo va samāno patikulaṃ gacchati ñātakehi vinā hoti. Idaṃ bhikkhave mātugāmassa paṭhamaṃ āveṇikaṃ dukkhaṃ yaṃ mātugāmo paccanubhoti aññatr'eva purisehi.

Puna ca paraṃ bhikkhave mātugāmo utunī hoti. Idaṃ bhikkhave mātugāmassa dutiyaṃ āveṇikaṃ dukkhaṃ yaṃ mātugāmo paccanubhoti aññatr'eva purisehi.

Puna ca paraṃ bhikkhave mātugāmo gabbhinī hoti. Idaṃ bhikkhave mātugāmassa tatiyaṃ āveṇikaṃ dukkhaṃ yaṃ mātugāmo paccanubhoti aññatr'eva purisehi.

Puna ca paraṃ bhikkhave mātugāmo vijāyati. Idaṃ bhikkhave mātugāmassa catutthaṃ āveṇikaṃ dukkhaṃ yaṃ mātugāmo paccanubhoti aññatr'eva purisehi.

Puna ca paraṃ bhikkhave mātugāmo purisassa pāricariyaṃ upeti. Idaṃ kho bhikkhave mātugāmassa pañcamaṃ āveṇikaṃ dukkhaṃ yaṃ mātugāmo paccanubhoti aññatr'eva purisehîti.

Imāni kho bhikkhave pañca mātugāmassa āveṇikāni dukkhāni yāni mātugāmo paccanubhoti aññātr'eva purisehîti.

(S. N.)

5. Atha kho rājā Pasenadīkosalo yena bhagavā ten'upasaṃkami. Upasaṃkamitvā bhagavantaṃ abhivādetvā ekamantaṃ nisīdi. Atha kho aññataro puriso yena rājā Pasenadīkosalo ten'upasaṃkami. Upasaṃkamitvā rañño Pasenadīkosalassa upakaṇṇake ārocesi. "Mallikā deva devī dhītaraṃ vijātâti. Evaṃ vutte rājā Pasenadīkosalo anattamano ahosi. Atha kho bhagavā rājānaṃ Pasenadikosalaṃ anattamanataṃ viditvā tāyaṃ velāyaṃ imā gāthāyo abhāsi:

Itthîpi hi ekaccī yā - seyyā posā janādhipa
medhāvinī sīlavatī- sassu-devā patibbatā
tassā yo jāyati poso - sūro hoti disampati
tādiso subhariyāputto - rajjaṃ pi anusāsatîti

(S. N.)

GLOSSARY

aññatr'eva	outside of, exclusive of
atīta	past, free from
anatīta	not past, not free from
anattamana	displeased
anattamanatā	displeasure
analạsa	not lazy
alasa	lazy, idle
aveccappasāda	perfect faith, perfect clearness
ātura	sick, diseased, miserable
ābādhika	sick person
āroceti	tells, informs
āveṇika	inherent, peculiar, special
āsītika	eighty years old
utunī	a menstruating woman
uddhumātaka	swollen, bloated, puffed up
upakaṇṇake	secretly
ekaccī	some, certain
ekanta	complete, thoroughly
ekāhamata	a day after death (eka 'one' +aha'day(s)' + mata Ppl of miyyati/mīyati 'dies')
ettāvatā	so far, to that extent
kammapatho	way of action, doing
karīsaṃ	excrement
khaṇḍadanta	with broken teeth
khalita	bald
gatayobbana	past youth, aged
gatta	body, limbs
gabbhinī	a pregnant woman
gāthā	verse, stanza
(X)gāmin	leading to X, going to X (fem. -inī)
gopānasī	rafter, gable
-vaṃka	crooked (like a gable)
janādhipo	king (of men)
jāta	of the nature of
X jāta	having become X
jātiyā	since birth, from birth
jiṇṇa	frail, decrepit
ñātaka	relation, relative
tādiso (-a)	such, of such quality
tilaka	spot, freckle
tīhamata	three days after death (< ti+aha+mata)
dakkho (-a)	clever, able, skilled
daṇḍa	stick, staff, cane
-parāyana	leaning on, tottering on

daharo	young in years
disampati	king
dukkhita	afflicted
X deva	having X as god, highly respecting
devī	goddess (also used for a queen)
dvîhamata	two days after death (dvi+aha+mata)
nāvutika	ninety years old
paccanubhoti	undergoes, experiences
pajā	progeny, offspring
pañcama	fifth
paṭipadā	way, means, path, method, course
patikula	husbands family
patibbatā	a devoted wife
palāpo	prattle, nonsense
palitakesa	having grey hair
palipanna	=paripanna, ppl. of paripajjati: 'falls into, sinks into, wallows'
pavedhati	tremble
pāricariyā	serving, waiting on, attendance
pisuna	calumnious, backbiting, malicious
poso	man, male
pharusa	rough, harsh, unkind
bāḷhagilāna	grievously sick
bhariyā	wife
bhogavant	wealthy
bhogga	bent, crooked
mano	mind (inst. manasā)
mahallaka	old person
mātugāmo	woman
muttaṃ	urine
medhāvinī	wise woman
rajja	kingdom, realm
rañño	gen. sg.of rājan (see VI, 3)
rūpavant	beautiful
vaṃka	crooked
valita	wrinkled
vassasatika	hundred years old
vijātā	a woman who has given birth to a child
vijāyati	gives birth, brings forth
vinā	without
vinīlaka	bluish black, discolored
vipubbaka	full of corruption and matter, festering
vilūna	cut off (of hair), scanty
(v)uṭṭhāpiyamāna	-māna participle of uṭṭhāpeti 'lifts' (the v may appear in sandhi after vowels)

saṃvesiyamāna	< saṃvesiyati puts to bed
saka	one's own
sato	(genitive sg. of sant- pres part. of atthi)
samāno	being, existing
sampha	frivolous, foolish
sammādiṭṭhi	right understanding
-diṭṭhin	he who has sammādiṭṭhi
sassar	mother-in-law (compounding stem sassu)
siraṃ	head (accusative siram or siro)
sīavatī	virtuous woman
sīlavant	virtuous
subhariyā	good wife
sūro (-a)	valiant, courageous
semāna	-māna participle of seti 'lies'
seyya	better
handa	well then, now

LESSON XII

1. Evaṃ me sutaṃ. Ekaṃ samayaṃ Bhagavā Sāvatthiyaṃ viharati Jetavane Anāthapiṇḍikassa ārāme. Atha kho Bhagavā pubbaṇhasamayaṃ nivāsetvā pattacīvaramādāya Sāvatthiṃ piṇḍāya pāvisi. Tena kho pana samayena Aggikabhāradvājassa brāhmaṇassa nivesane aggi pajjalito hoti, āhutī paggahitā. Atha kho Bhagavā Sāvatthiyaṃ sapadānaṃ piṇḍāya caramāno yena Aggikabhāradvājassa brāhmaṇassa nivesanaṃ ten'upasaṃkami. Addasā kho Aggikabhāradvājo brāhmano Bhagavantaṃ dūrato'va āgacchantaṃ, disvāna Bhagavantaṃ etadavoca: "Tatr'eva, muṇḍaka, tatr'eva samaṇaka, tatr'eva, vasalaka, tiṭṭhāhī" ti. Evaṃ vutte Bhagavā Aggikabhāradvājaṃ brāhmaṇaṃ etadavoca: "Jānāsi pana tvaṃ, brāhmaṇa, vasalaṃ vā vasalakaraṇe vā dhamme" ti.

"Na khvâhaṃ, bho Gotama, jānāmi vasalaṃ vā vasalakaraṇe vā dhamme. Sādhu me bhavaṃ Gotamo tathā dhammaṃ desetu yathâhaṃ jāneyyaṃ vasalaṃ vā vasalakaraṇe vā dhamme" ti. "Tena hi, brāhmaṇa, suṇāhi, sādhukaṃ manasikarohi; bhāsissāmī"ti. "Evaṃ bho" ti kho Aggikabhāradvājo brāhmaṇo Bhagavato paccassosi. Bhagavā etadavoca:

"Kodhano upanāhī ca -- pāpamakkhī ca yo naro
vipannadiṭṭhi māyāvī -- taṃ jaññā 'vasalo' iti.
Ekajaṃ vā dijaṃ vā'pi -- yo'dha pāṇaṃ vihiṃsati
yassa pāṇe dayā natthi -- taṃ jaññā 'vasalo' iti.
Yo hanti parirundhati -- gāmāni nigamāni ca
niggāhako samaññāto -- taṃ jaññā 'vasalo' iti.

Yo mātaraṃ vā pitaraṃ vā-- jiṇṇakaṃ gatayobbanaṃ
pahu santo na bharati -- tam jaññā 'vasalo' iti.
Yo mātaraṃ vā pitaraṃ vā -- bhātaraṃ bhaginiṃ sasuṃ
hanti roseti vācāya -- taṃ jaññā 'vasalo' iti.

Rosako kadariyo ce -- pāpiccho maccharī saṭho
Ahiriko anottāpī -- taṃ jaññā 'vasalo' iti.
Na jaccā vasalo hoti -- na jaccā hoti brāhmaṇo
kammanā[1] vasalo hoti -- kammanā hoti brāhmaṇo...."

Evaṃ vutte Aggikabhāradvājo brāhmaṇo Bhagavantaṃ etadavoca:- "Abhikkantaṃ, bho Gotama, abhikkantaṃ, bho Gotama.' Seyyathâpi, bho Gotama, nikkujjitaṃ vā ukkujjeyya, paṭicchannaṃ vā vivareyya, mūḷhassa vā maggaṃ ācikkheyya, andhakāre vā telapajjotaṃ dhāreyya 'cakkhumanto rūpāni dakkhintī'ti; - evameva bhotā Gotamena anekapariyāyena dhammo pakāsito. Esâhaṃ bhavantaṃ Gotamaṃ saraṇaṃ gacchāmi dhammañca bhikkhusanghañca; upāsakaṃ maṃ bhavaṃ Gotamo dhāretu ajjat'agge pāṇ'upetaṃ saraṇaṃ gataṃ."ti.

(-SN)

---

[1] Alternative ablative of kammaṃ.

2. "Kacci abhiṇhasaṃvāsā -- nâvajānāsi paṇḍitaṃ?
ukkādhāro manussānaṃ -- kacci apacito tayā?'
'Nâhaṃ abhiṇhasaṃvāsā -- avajānāmi paṇḍitaṃ;
ukkādhāro manussānaṃ -- niccaṃ apacito mayā.'
'pañca kāmaguṇe hitvā -- piyarūpe manorame,
saddhāya gharā nikkhamma -- dukkhass'antakaro bhava.
Mitte bhajassu kalyāṇe -- pantañca sayanâsanaṃ
vivittaṃ appanigghosaṃ; -- mattaññū hohi bhojane,
Cīvare piṇḍapāte ca -- paccaye sayanâsane;
etesu taṇhaṃ mâkasi, -- mā lokaṃ punar 'āgami.
Saṃvuto pātimokkhasmiṃ -- indriyesu ca pañcasu
satī kāyagatā ty'atthu [2] -- nibbidābahulo bhava.
Nimittaṃ parivajjehi -- subhaṃ rāgûpasaṃhitaṃ,
asubhāya cittaṃ bhāvehi -- ekaggaṃ susamāhitaṃ
Animittañca bhāvehi -- mānânusayamujjaha:
tato mānâbhisamayā -- upasanto carissasī"ti.

Itthaṃ sudaṃ Bhagavā āyasmantaṃ Rāhulaṃ imāhi gāthāhi abhiṇhaṃ ovadati.

(SN)

3. Atha kho āyasmā Ānando yena Bhagavā ten'upasaṃkami; upasaṃkaṃitvā bhagavantaṃ abhivādetvā ekamantaṃ nisīdi. Ekamantaṃ nisinno kho āyasmā Ānando Bhagavantaṃ etadavoca:

"Tiṇ'imāni, bhante, gandhajātāni, yesaṃ anuvātaññeva gandho gacchati, no paṭivātaṃ.

Katamāni tīṇi?

Mūlagandho, sāragandho, pupphagandho. Imāni kho, bhante, tīṇi gandhajātāni, yesaṃ anuvātaññeva [3] gandho gacchati, no paṭivātaṃ.

Atthi nu kho, bhante, kiñci gandhajātaṃ yassa anuvātampi gandho gacchati, paṭivātampi gandho gacchati, anuvāta paṭivātampi gandho gacchatī" ti?

"Atth'Ānanda, kiñci gandhajātaṃ yassa anuvātampi gandho gacchati, paṭivātampi gandho gacchati, anuvātapaṭivātampi gandho gacchatī" ti.

"Katamañca pana, bhante, gandhajātaṃ yassa anuvātampi gandho gacchati, paṭivātampi gandho gacchati, anuvatapaṭivātaṃ pi gandho gacchatī" ti?

---

[2] te + atthu
[3] ṃ followed by -e may become -ññ- in sandhi.

ldhânanda, yasmiṃ gāme vā nigame vā itthī vā puriso vā buddhaṃ saraṇam gato hoti, dhammaṃ saraṇaṃ gato hoti, saṃghaṃ saraṇaṃ gato hoti. pāṇâtipātā paṭivirato hoti, adinnâdānā paṭivirato hoti, kāmesu micchācārā paṭivirato hoti, musāvādā paṭivirato hoti, surāmerayamajjapamādaṭṭhānā paṭivirato hoti, sīlavā hoti kalyāṇadhammo, vigatamalamaccharena cetasā agāraṃ ajjhāvasati ... tassa disāsu samaṇa brāhmaṇā vaṇṇaṃ bhāsanti -- 'asukasmiṃ nāma gāme vā nigame vā itthī vā puriso vā buddhaṃ saraṇaṃ gato hoti, dhammaṃ saraṇaṃ gato hoti, saṃghaṃ saraṇaṃ gato hoti, pāṇâtipātā paṭivirato hoti, adinnâdānā paṭivirato hoti, kāmesumicchâcārā paṭivirato hoti, musāvādā paṭivirato hoti, sīlavā hoti kalyāṇadhammo, vigatamalamaccharena cetasā agāraṃ ajjhāvasati ...'' iti.

Devatâpi'ssa vaṇṇaṃ bhāsanti -- 'asukasmiṃ nāma gāme vā nigame vā itthī vā puriso vā buddhaṃ saraṇaṃ gato hoti ... pe ... sīlavā hoti kalyāṇadhammo, vigatamalamaccharena cetasā agāraṃ ajjhāvasati'iti. Idaṃ kho taṃ, Ānanda, gandhajātaṃ yassa anuvātaṃ pi gandho gacchati, paṭivātampi gandho gacchati, anuvātapaṭivātampi gandho gacchatî'' ti.

"Na pupphagandho paṭivātam'eti
Na candanaṃ tagaramallikā vā
Sataṃ ca gandho paṭivātam'eti
Sabbā disā sappuriso pavāti"

(AN)

4. Sāvatthiyaṃ Adinnapubbako nāma brāhmaṇo ahosi. Tena kassaci kiñci na dinnapubbaṃ. Tassa eko'va putto ahosi, piyo manāpo. Brāhmaṇo puttassa pilandhanaṃ dātukāmo "sace suvaṇṇakārassa ācikkhissāmi, vetanaṃ dātabbaṃ bhavissatî" ti sayam'eva suvaṇṇaṃ koṭṭetvā, maṭṭāni kuṇḍalāni katvā adāsi; ten'assa putto 'Maṭṭakuṇḍalî'ti paññāyi.

Tassa soḷasavassakāle paṇḍurogo udapādi. Brāhmaṇo vejjānaṃ santikaṃ gantvā "tumhe asukarogassa kiṃ bhesajjaṃ karothâ'ti pucchi. Te assa yaṃ vā taṃ vā rukkhatacâdiṃ ācikkhiṃsu. So taṃ āharitvā bhesajjaṃ kari. Tathā karontass'eva tassa rogo balavā ahosi. Brāhmaṇo tassa dubbalabhāvaṃ ñatvā ekaṃ vejjaṃ pakkosi. So taṃ oloketvā "amhākaṃ ekaṃ kiccaṃ atthi; aññaṃ vejjaṃ pakkositvā tikicchāpehî"ti vatvā nikkhami.

Brāhmaṇo tassa maraṇasamayaṃ ñatvā "imassa dassanatthāya āgatâgatā antogehe sāpateyyaṃ passissanti, tasmā naṃ bahi karissāmî"ti puttaṃ nīharitvā bahi āḷinde nipajjāpesi. Tasmiṃ kālakate brāhmaṇo tassa sarīraṃ jhāpetvā devasikaṃ āḷāhanaṃ gantvā "kahaṃ ekaputtaka! kahaṃ ekaputtakâ"ti rodi.

(RasV.)

GLOSSARY

Aggikabhāradvājo	a name of a Brahmin
ajjhāvasati	inhabits
atipāta	slaying, killing

Anāthapiṇḍiko	the name of the chief male lay-donor of Buddha
animittaṃ	unaffected by outward signs or appearance; literally 'objectless'
anuvātaṃ	in the direction of the wind
anusayo	proclivity, disposition
aneka	many, various
antakara	putting an end to
anto	inside
apacita	respected
appanigghosa	without noise
abhiṇhaṃ	repeatedly, always
abhisamayo	realization, comprehension
avajānati	despises, disrespects
asuka	such and such
ahiriko	shameless one
ācikkhati	tells, informs
āharitvā	(from āharati) fetch, bring
ārāmo	park, resort for pastime, a private park given to the Buddha or the Sangha
āḷāhana	cremation ground
āḷinda	verandah
āhutī	oblation, sacrifice
ukkā	torch
ukkujjati	sets upright, rights (something)
ujjahati	gives up
upanāhī	one bearing ill-will or a grudge
upasaṃhita	possessed of
upasamati	is calm, is tranquil, ppl. upasanta
ekagga	calm, tranquil
eka-ja	once-born
kacci	'how is it, perhaps, I doubt' (indefinite interrogative particle expressing doubt or suspense)
kadariyo	one who is miserly, stingy
kāmaguṇā	sensual pleasures
kiccam	task, duty
kuṇḍalāni	earrings
koṭṭeti	pounds, beats
gatayobbanaṃ	old, aged (< gata 'gone'+yobbanaṃ 'youth')
gandha (jātānī)	(kinds of) perfumes, odors
gāthā	verse
cakkhukaraṇī	producing insight
cakkhumant	endowed with insight (lit. 'having eyes')
candana	sandal wood
cetasā	(Inst. of ceto mind)

jaññā	let one know (Optative 3 sg. of jānāti)
jiṇṇaka	frail, decrepit, old
Jetavana	Jeta's park, Jeta's grove
jhāpeti	burns
tagara	a fragrant shrub
taca	bark, hide, skin
tikicchāpeti	gets someone to cure (causative of tikicchati--see X, 6)
telapajjotaṃ	oil lamp
dayā	compassion, kindness
dija	twice-born one
dubbalabhāva	feebleness
devasika	occurring daily
nikkujjitaṃ	that which is turned upside down
niggāhako	one who rebukes, oppressor
nippajati	lies down, sleeps
nibbidā	indifference, disenchantment
nimittaṃ	(outward) sign, omen, cause
nīharati	takes out, drives out
pakāseti	makes known, illustrates
pakkosati	summons, calls
paggaṇhāti	holds up, ppl. paggahita
paccayo	requisite (of a monk) (as well as 'means, support, cause')
pajjalati	burns (forth), blazes up. ppl. pajjalita
paññāyati	appears, becomes clear
paṭicchannaṃ	that which is covered, concealed
paṭivātaṃ	against the wind
paṇḍurogo	jaundice, anemia
panta	remote, solitary, secluded
pariýāya	order, course, method
parirundhati	completely obstructs, imprisons
parivajjeti	avoids, shuns
pavāti	blows forth
pahu	able
pātimokkha	collection of disciplinary rules binding on a recluse
pāpamakkhī	one concealing sin
pāpiccho	one who has bad intentions, wicked one
piṇḍo	a lump of food, alms given as food
piya	dear
pilandhanaṃ	ornament
putto	son
balavā	(from balavant 'strong')
bahula	much, frequent
bhaginī	sister

bhajassu	2 sg. Imp. (middle) of bhajati 'keeps company with'
bharati	bears, supports, maintains
bhātar	brother
bhesajjaṃ.	medicine
macchara	avarice, envy
maṭṭa	polished, burnished
manorama	delightful
mala	impurity, stain
mallikā	jasmine
mātar	mother
māno	pride, arrogance, conceit
mānânusaya	predisposition or tendency to māno
māyāvin	deceitful person
muṇḍako	'a shaven-headed one'
mūḷha	gone astray, confused, ignorant (one)
rogo	disease, sickness
rodati	cries, laments
rosako	angry, wrathful one
roseti	irritates, annoys
vaṇṇaṃ bhāsati	speaks well (of), praises
vasalako	outcaste, wretch
vasalo	outcaste, person of low birth
vigata	gone away, ceased, bereft of
vipanna	gone wrong, lost
vipannadiṭṭhī	one with wrong views, heretic
vivareyya	(from vivarati open, uncover)
vivitta	secluded
vetanaṃ	wages, hire
saṃvāso	association, co-residency, intimacy
saṭho	fraudulent one
sati kāyagatā	mindfulness relating to the body
santo	peacefulness, calm
sapadānaṃ	in order, without interruption, without skipping any house (in alms-begging of a Buddhist monk)
samaññāta	designated, notorious
samaṇako	ascetic, recluse (may have a connotation of contempt)
sayanâsana	bed and seat, lodging
sasura	father-in-law (acc. sasuṃ)
sāpateyyaṃ	wealth
sāra	essence, heart of a tree
Sāvatthi	a place name
sudaṃ	indeed, just, even
subha	pleasant, good

suvaṇṇa	gold
suvaṇṇkāra	goldsmith
susamāhita	well-restrained, well composed
seyyathāpi	just as

GRAMMAR XII

1. ubho 'BOTH'

The form ubhaya 'both' that occurred in Lesson IX (Further Readings) is an adjectival form related to a pronominal form ubho, which occurs in this reading, and has the following case forms, for all genders. As we might expect, it takes plural agreement, since the dual of Sanskrit has been lost almost entirely in Pāli (ubho and ubhaya are themselves remnants of the dual).

Nom:	ubho / ubhe
Acc:	
Gen:	ubhinnaṃ
Dat:	
Inst:	ubhohi/ubhobhi /ubhehi / ubhebhi
Abl:	
Loc:	uhhosu /ubhesu

2. asu 'A CERTAIN'

asu has the sense 'a certain (one)' or 'such and such (a one/ ones)' It has both singular and plural forms:

SINGULAR			
	Masculine	Neuter	Feminine
Nom:	asu/amu /amuko	aduṃ	asu / amu
Acc:	amuṃ		amuṃ
Gen:	amuno /amussa		amuyā/amussā
Dat:			
Inst:	amunā		amuyā
Abl:	amunā /amumhā/amusmā		
Loc:	amumhi / amusmiṃ		amussaṃ/amuyaṃ

PLURAL			
	Masculine	Neuter	Feminine
Nom-Acc:	amū/amuyo	amū/amūni	amū/amuyo
Gen-Dat:	amūsaṃ / amūsānaṃ		
Instr-Abl:	amūhi / amūbhi		
Loc:	amūsu		

3. GEMINATE CONSONANT CASE FORMS: jaccā

Feminine -i and -ī stems with certain consonants before the -i or -ī may have alternate case forms with the consonant doubled (geminated). This occurs in those case forms in which the consonant is followed by -iy-. The consonants so affected belong to the the dental or retroflex series,[4] most commonly t, d, n or ṇ and when the gemination occurs, the -iy-is lost and the consonant is changed as follows:

-t-	becomes	-cc-
-d-	becomes	-jj-
-n-, -ṇ-	become	-ññ-.

The remaining case ending is added directly to the geminate consonant. Thus, for example, for jāti 'birth, caste', we may encounter the following forms (for the regular forms see I,1.23):

	Singular	Plural
Nominative-Accusative:		jacco
Instrumental, Ablative, Dative:	jaccā	
Locative:	jaccā, jaccaṃ	

Similarly, nadī 'river', has forms like najjo, najjā, etc.

4. GENITIVE ABSOLUTE:

The genitive absolute was introduced in X,1 with a temporal sense. The genitive absolute may also be used in the sense 'in spite of, even though' although'. In that use, the present participle is commonly used:

mama evaṃ vadantassa eva me mitto tam gāmaṃ pahāya gacchi.
'In spite of my saying that, my friend left the village'

mātāpitunnaṃ assumukhānaṃ rudantānaṃ so kumāro kesamassuṃ ohāretvā kāsāyāni vatthāni acchādetvā agārasmā anagāriyaṃ pabbaji.
'Despite his parents' crying with tearful faces, that prince shaving his hair and beard (kesamassu) and donning (acchādeti) saffron robes (kāsāyāni vatthāni) went forth from home to homelessness.'

[4] i.e., t, ṭ, d, ḍ, etc--see alphabet and pronunciation section.

evaṃ vadantiyā eva attano mātuyā sā kaññā vāpiyaṃ nahāyituṃ gacchi.
'Despite her mother's saying that, that girl went to the tank (vāpi) [5] to bathe.

(Note that here the subject of the genitive absolute attano mātuyā occurs after its verb, the genitive (feminine) participle vadantiyā. Such variable order is possible for effect.

5.COMPOUND PERFECTIVE FORMS:

5.1 The past participle plus hoti gives the sense that the action of the participle has been accomplished (much like English 'has gone, has done', etc). In this construction, the doer of the action will be in the nominative case if the verb is intransitive (i.e., has no object) and in the instrumental case if the verb is transitive, as in the instrumental subject sentence construction given in VI, 9. Both the participle and hoti will agree with the subject, or, in the instrumental construction, with the appropriate noun (i.e., the object), just as in the participial sentences without hoti:

so gehaṃ gato hoti 'He has gone home.'

ena puññaṃ kataṃ hoti
He has accumulated (literally 'done') merit' or:
Merit has been accumulated by him.'

sā tattha gatā hoti 'She has gone there.'

sabbe bhūtā matā honti 'All the beings have died (or: 'are dead.')

5.2 The past participle plus bhavissati (in the appropriate gender, person and number form) gives the sense 'might have', 'would have' or 'will have'. Note that although bhavissati is a future form, the sense of this construction is not necesarily future, but it may indicate a presumption that something has already occurred (compare English 'He will have gone by now.'). The case of the doer of the action will be the same as in the construction with hoti, as will the agreement pattern:

so adhunā gato bhavissati. 'He will have gone (by) now.'

tena idaṃ kataṃ bhavissati. 'He must/might have done this.'

bahujanā ettha āgatā bhavissanti. 'Many people will have come here.'

---

5 The term "tank" is commonly used in South Asia to refer to an irrigation reservoir or temple pond,

5.3 The future passive participle plus bhavissati gives the sense that the action should be or must be done. In this construction, the doer of the action will be in the instrumental case whether the verb is transitive or intransitive.

tvayā imaṃ kammaṃ kātabbaṃ bhavissati.

'This action should be done by you.'

mayā suve taṭtha gantabbaṃ bhavissati.
'I should/ must go there tomorrow (suve)'

6. AGREEMENT WITH vā 'OR' PHRASES:

6.1 When the relative demonstrative ya- occurs with a vā 'or' construction, it will agree with the noun that it most nearly precedes:

yā itthī vā puriso vā 'Whichever woman or man....',

but:

yo puriso vā itthī vā 'Whichever man or woman...'

6.2 When a vā construction is the subject of a participle, the participle will agree with the nearest noun (i.e., the last one in the series):

yadā itthī vā puriso vā Buddhaṃ saraṇaṃ gato hoti...
'When a woman or a man has gone to the Buddha-refuge...'

but:

yadā puriso vā itthī vā Buddhaṃ saraṇaṃ gatā hoti...
'When a man or a woman has gone to the Buddha-refuge...'

Note, however, that the verb hoti is singular, since both elements in the vā construction are singular.

7. eso ahaṃ

Unlike in English, the demonstrative (e)so may precede any of the personal pronouns to give emphasis, i.e., 'This (particular) I,' Therefore, eso ahaṃ, so ahaṃ, so tvam, etc.

FURTHER READINGS XII

DHAMMACAKKAPPAVATTANA SUTTA[6]

Evaṃ me sutaṃ:

Ekaṃ samayaṃ Bhagavā Bārāṇasiyaṃ viharati Isipatane Migadāye.Tatra kho Bhagavā pañcavaggiye bhikkhū āmantesi -

Dve'me, bhikkhave, antā pabbajitena na sevitabbā:

i Yo câyaṃ[7] kāmesu kāmasukhallikânuyogo - hīno, gammo, pothujjaniko, anariyo, anatthasaṃhito:

ii Yo câyaṃ attakilamathânuyogo - dukkho, anariyo, anatthasaṃhito

Ete te, bhikkhave, ubho ante anupagamma majjhimā paṭipadā Tathāgatena abhisambuddhā - cakkhukaraṇī, ñāṇakaraṇī, upasamāya, abhiññāya, sambodhāya, nibbānāya saṃvattati.

Katamā ca sā, bhikkhave, majjhimā paṭipadā Tathāgatena abhisambuddhā - cakkhukaraṇī, ñāṇakaraṇī, upasamāya, abhiññāya, sambodhāya, nibbānāya saṃvattati?

Ayaṃ'eva ariyo aṭṭhaṃgiko maggo - seyyathīdam:

Sammā diṭṭhi, sammā saṃkappo, sammā vācā, sammā kammanto, sammā ājīvo, sammā vāyāmo, sammā sati, sammā samādhi.

Ayaṃ kho sā, bhikkhave, majjhimā paṭipadā Tathāgatena abhisambuddhā - cakkhukaraṇī, ñāṇakaraṇī, upasamāya, abhiññāya, sambodhāya, nibbānāya saṃvattati.

Idaṃ kho pana, bhikkhave, dukkhaṃ ariyasaccaṃ:

Jāti'pi dukkhā, jarā'pi dukkhā, vyādhi'pi dukkhā, maraṇampi dukkhaṃ, appiyehi sampayogo dukkho, piyehi vippayogo dukkho, yamp'icchaṃ na labhati tam'pi dukkhaṃ, saṃkhittena pañcûpādānakkhandhā dukkhā.

Idaṃ kho pana, bhikkhave, dukkha-samudayaṃ ariya saccaṃ:

---

[6] This is the Buddha's first sermon after his enlightenment, in which he expounded his doctrine to five monks with whom he had been associated at an earlier time, and who had remained followers of strict asceticism.

[7] yo+ayaṃ = 'just this'

Yâyaṃ taṇhā ponobhavikā nandirāgasahagatā tatra tatrâbhinandinī - seyyathīdaṃ: - kāmataṇhā, bhavataṇhā, vibhavataṇhā.

Idaṃ kho pana, bhikkhave, dukkhanirodhaṃ ariyasaccaṃ:

Yo tassā yeva taṇhāya asesa-virāganirodho, cāgo, paṭinissaggo, mutti, anālayo.

Idaṃ kho pana, bhikkhave, dukkhanirodhagāminī paṭipadā ariyasaccaṃ:

Ayameva ariyo aṭṭhaṅgiko maggo - seyyathîdam: - sammā diṭṭhi, sammā saṃkappo, sammā vācā, sammā kammanto, sammā ājīvo, sammā vāyāmo, sammā sati, sammā samādhi.

* * *

1 (i) Idaṃ dukkhaṃ ariyasaccanti me, bhikkhave, pubbe ananussutesu dhammesu cakkhuṃ udapādi, ñāṇaṃ udapādi, paññā udapādi, vijjā udapādi, āloko udapādi.

(ii) Taṃ kho pan'idaṃ dukkhaṃ ariyasaccaṃ pariññeyanti me, bhikkhave, pubbe ananussutesu dhammesu cakkhuṃ udapādi,ñaṇaṃ udapādi, paññā udapādi, vijjā udapādi, āloko udapādi.

(iii) Taṃ kho pan'idaṃ dukkhaṃ ariyasaccaṃ pariññātanti me bhikkhave, pubbe ananussutesu dhammesu cakkhuṃ udapādi, ñaṇaṃ udapādi, paññā udapādi, vijjā udapādi āloko udapādi.

2 (i) Idaṃ dukkhasamudayaṃ ariyasaccanti me, bhikkhave, pubbe ananussutesu dhammesu cakkhuṃ udapādi, ñāṇaṃ udapādi, paññā udapādi, vijjā udapādi, āloko udapādi.

(ii) Taṃ kho pan'idaṃ dukkhasamudayaṃ ariyasaccaṃ pahātabbanti me, bhikkhave, pubbe ananussutesu dhammesu cakkhuṃ udapādi, ñāṇaṃ udapādi, paññā udapādi, vijjā udapādi, āloko udapādi.

(iii) Taṃ kho pan'idaṃ dukkhasamudayaṃ ariyasaccaṃ pahīnanti me, bhikkhave, pubbe ananussutesu dhammesu cakkhuṃ udapādi, ñāṇaṃ udapādi, paññā udapādi, vijjā udapādi, āloko udapādi.

3 (i) Idaṃ dukkhanirodhaṃ ariyasaccanti me, bhikkhave, pubbe ananussutesu dhammesu cakkhuṃ udapādi, ñāṇaṃ udapādi, paññā udapādi, vijjā udapādi, āloko udapādi.

(ii) Taṃ kho pan'idaṃ dukkhanirodhaṃ ariyasaccaṃ sacchikātabbanti me, bhikkhave, pubbe ananussutesu dhammesu cakkhuṃ udapādi, ñāṇaṃ udapādi, paññā udapādi, vijjā udapādi, āloko udapādi.

(iii) Taṃ kho pan'idaṃ dukkhanirodhaṃ ariyasaccaṃ sacchikatanti me, bhikkhave, pubbe ananussutesu dhammesu cakkhuṃ udapādi, ñāṇaṃ udapādi, paññā udapādi, vijjā udapādi, āloko udapādi.

4 (i) Idaṃ dukkhanirodhagāminī paṭipadā ariyasaccanti me, bhikkhave, pubbe ananussutesu dhammesu cakkhuṃ udapādi, ñāṇaṃ udapādi, paññā udapādi, vijjā udapādi, āloko udapādi.

(ii) Taṃ kho pan'idaṃ dukkhanirodhagāminī paṭipadā ariyasaccaṃ bhāvetabbanti me, bhikkhave, pubbe ananussutesu dhammesu cakkhuṃ udapādi, ñāṇaṃ udapādi, paññā udapādi, vijjā udapādi, āloko udapādi.

(iii) Taṃ kho pan'idam dukkhanirodhagāminī paṭipadā ariyasaccaṃ bhāvitanti me, bhikkhave, pubbe ananussutesu dhammesu cakkhuṃ udapādi, ñāṇaṃ udapādi, paññā udapādi, vijjā udapādi, āloko udapādi.

* * *

Yāva kīvañca me, bhikkhave, imesu catūsu ariyasaccesu evaṃ tiparivaṭṭaṃ dvādasâkāraṃ yathābhūtaṃ ñāṇadassanaṃ na suvisuddham ahosi, n'eva tāvâhaṃ, bhikkhave, sadevake loke samārake sabrahmake sassamaṇabrāhmaṇiyā pajāya sadevamanussāya anuttaraṃ sammā sambodhiṃ abhisambuddho paccaññāsiṃ.

Yato ca kho me, bhikkhave, imesu catūsu ariyasaccesu evaṃ tiparivaṭṭaṃ dvādasâkāraṃ yathābhūtaṃ ñāṇadassanaṃ suvisuddhaṃ ahosi, athâhaṃ, bhikkhave, sadevake loke samārake sabrahmake sassamaṇabrāhmaṇiyā pajāya sadevamanussāya anuttaraṃ sammā sambodhiṃ abhisambuddho paccaññāsiṃ.

Ñāṇañca pana me dassanaṃ udapādi, akuppā me cetovimutti ayaṃ antimā jāti, natthi'dāni punabbhavo ti.

Idamavoca Bhagavā. Attamanā pañcavaggiyā bhikkhū Bhagavato bhāsitaṃ abhinandanti.

Imasmiñ ca pana veyyākaraṇasmiṃ bhaññamāne āyasmato Koṇḍaññassa virajam vītamalaṃ dhammacakkhuṃ udapādi: "yaṃ kiñci samudayadhammaṃ sabbaṃ taṃ nirodhadhamman"ti.

Pavattite ca pana Bhagavatā dhammacakke bhummā devā saddamanussāvesuṃ:

Etaṃ Bhagavatā Bārāṇasiyaṃ Isipatane Migadāye anuttaraṃ dhammacakkaṃ pavattitaṃ appaṭivattiyaṃ samaṇena vā brāhmaṇena vā devena vā mārena vā brahmuṇā vā kenaci vā lokasminti.

Bhummānaṃ devānam saddaṃ sutvā Cātummahārājika devā[8] saddamanussāvesuṃ:

Etaṃ Bhagavatā Bārāṇasiyaṃ Isipatane Migadāye anuttaraṃ dhammacakkaṃ pavattitaṃ appaṭivattiyaṃ samaṇena vā brāhmaṇena vā devena vā mārena vā brahmuṇā vā kenaci vā lokasminti.

Cātummahārājikānaṃ devānam saddaṃ sutvā Tāvatiṃsā devā. - Yāmā devā - Tusitā devā - - Nimmānaratī devā - Paranimmitavasavattino devā - Brahmakāyikā devā saddamanussāvesuṃ:

Etaṃ Bhagavatā Bārāṇasiyaṃ Isipatane Migadāye anuttaraṃ dhammacakkaṃ pavattitaṃ appaṭivattiyaṃ samaṇena vā brāhmaṇena vā devena vā mārena vā brahmuṇā vā kenaci vā lokasminti.

Itîha tena khaṇena tena layena tena muhuttena yāva brahmalokā saddo abbhuggañchi. Ayañca dasasahassī lokadhātu saṃkampi sampakampī sampavedhi.

Appamāṇo ca uḷāro obhāso loke pāturahosi atikkamma devānaṃ devānûbhāvaṃ.

Atha kho Bhagavā udānaṃ udānesi:

Aññāsi vata bho Koṇḍañño, aññāsi vata bho Koṇḍaññoti.

Iti h'idaṃ āyasmato Koṇḍaññassa Aññā-Koṇḍañño tv'eva nāmaṃ ahosîti.

(-S. N.)

GLOSSARY

akuppa	unshakable
aññāsi	knew perfectly
aṭṭhaṃgika	eightfold, having eight constituents
atikkamma	passing beyond
attakilamatha	self mortification
ananussuta	not heard of
anālaya	free from attachment
anussāveti	proclaims
antima	last
anto	end, goal, extreme
appaṭivattiya	irreversible, not to be rolled back
appamāṇa	unlimited
abbhuggañchi	rose up
abhiññā	higher knowledge

8 Cātummahārājikā devā, Tāvatiṃsā devā., etc. are celestial beings that inhabit the deva and brahma realms.

abhinandati	rejoices, delights in
abhinandinī	finding pleasure in, delighting in (Fem.Sg.)
abhisambuddha	perfectly understood, fully realized
allīyati	clings to, is attached to
asesa	without residue, entire
ākāra	condition, state
udāna	emotional utterance, paean of joy
udānaṃ udānesi	uttered a paean of joy
upagamma	having approached
upasama	calmness
ubho	both
uḷāra	lofty, noble
khaṇa	moment, instant
gamma	low, vulgar, mean
gāminī	leading up
cāga	giving up
cetovimutti	mental emancipation
ñāṇakaraṇī	giving right understanding, enlightening
ñāṇadassana	perfect knowledge
nandirāga	passionate delight
paccaññāsiṃ	I realized perfectly
pariññata	well, fully understood
pariññeyya	what should be known, knowable,
parivaṭṭa	a circle
pahātabba	what ought to be given up
pahīna	abandoned, destroyed
pāturahosi	appeared
punabbhava	rebirth
pothujjanika	belonging to ordinary man
ponobhavika	leading to rebirth
brahma	Brahma, creator. Gen-Dat brahmuno; Instr. brahmunā
bhaññamana	being said
bhavataṇhā	craving for existence/rebirth
bhāvetabba	what ought to be developed
bhumma	earthly, terrestial
muhutta	moment
yathābhūtaṃ	as things really are
laya	brief measure of time
vata	surely, certainly
vāyāma	effort
vibhavataṇhā	craving for extinction
viraja	free from defilement
vītamala	stainless
veyyākaraṇa	explanation, exposition
saṃkappa	intention, purpose

saṃkampati	trembles
saṃhita	possessed of, consisting of
sacchikata	is realized
sacchikātabba	ought to be realized, experienced
samādhi	(state of) concentration, intense state of mind and meditation
sampakampati	trembles, is shaken
sampavedhati	shakes violently
sambodha	highest wisdom
sambodhi	enlightenment
sammā	properly, rightly
sevitabba	to be practiced

GENERAL GLOSSARY

Numerals refer to main readings of lessons, unless followed by .1, which indicates the further readings of that lesson. The alphabetical order, as in other glossaries, is:

a ā i ī u ū e o ṃ k kh g gh (ṃ) c ch j jh ñ ṭ ṭh ḍ ḍh ṇ t d th dh n p ph b bh m y r l v s h ḷ

(For more details, see the Introduction, Part II, Alphabet and Pronunciation.)

* * * * * * * * * * * * * * * *

aṃgam 'component, constituent part, limb, member' 2
akammaniya 'inactive, sluggish, slothful, lazy' 3.1
akaraṇaṃ 'non-doing' 2
akiñcano 'one who has nothing, one who is free from worldly attachment' 5
akuppa 'unshakable' 12.1
akubbant 'non-doer' 9
akusala 'bad, inefficient, sinful' 1
akusīta 'diligent, non-lazy' 2.1
akkamati 'steps upon, treads upon'; ppl. akkanta 10.1
akkhiṃ 'eye' 10.1
agandhaka 'having no fragrance' 5
agāraṃ 'house' 6
agāriyabhūta 'being a householder' 6.1
agutta 'unguarded' 1
aggaṃ 'tip, end' 10
aggi 'fire' 7.1
Aggikabhāradvājo name of a Brahmin 8.1
accāyata 'too long, too much stretched' 6.1
accāraddhaviriyaṃ 'over-exertion, too much exertion' 6.1
acchariya 'wonderful, marvelous' 6
acchariyaṃ 'a wonder, a marvel' 8
ajalaṇḍikā 'goat's dung' 10
Ajita name of a country 11
ajo 'a he-goat' 8
ajjatagge 'from today on' (< ajjato+agge) 5.1
ajjhattaṃ 'inwardly, internally, subjective(ly)' 5.1
ajjhabhāsati 'address, speak' 11
ajjhāvasati 'inhabit' 12
añjalikaraṇīya 'worthy of respectful salutation' 5.1
añña 'other' 1
aññatara 'one, somone, one of a certain number' 5.1
aññati 'comprehend, discriminate' 2
aññatra 'outside' 2
aññatreva 'outside of, exclusive of' 11.1
aññāsi 'knew perfectly' 12.1
añño 'another, other (one)' 3
aṭṭaṃ 'question, problem, lawsuit, case' 10.1
aṭṭhaṃgika 'eightfold, having eight constituents' 12.1
aṭṭhāsi past of {tiṭṭhati} 10.1
aṇḍakaṃ 'egg' 10.1
atakkāvacara 'beyond logic (or sophistry), beyond the sphere of thought, profound' 9.1
ati 'very, excessively' 10
atikkamma 'passing beyond' 12.1
Atipaṇḍito a proper name 10.1
atipāta 'slaying killing' 12
atipāteti 'kills, fells' 7
atirekataraṃ 'much more' 10.1
atirocati 'outshine, excel' 6
atisithila 'too loose, lax' 6.1
atīta 'past, free from' 11.1
atīto 'the past' 10
attakilamatha 'self mortification' 12.1
attan 'self' (reflexive) 6
acc. attānaṃ 4.1, 6, Iinstr sg. attanā 'by oneself' 3.1, gen.sg attano 'one's own' 7
attamana 'delighted, pleased, happy' 7
attānaṃ 'self, soul' (accusative singular of attan) 4.1
atthaññū 'one who knows what is useful, one who knows the correct meaning or proper goal' 4.1
atthaṃ gahetvāna 'having held back or given up profit or advantage' 6.1
atthaṃ vadati 'characterizes, gives the meaning to' 3
atthāya 'for the purpose of' < attho 8
atthi '(there) is' 3
attho (-aṃ) 'advantage, meaning, aim, usage, use, welfare, gain, sense, purpose, advantage, (moral) good, need' 1
atha 'now, then' 2
atha kho 'now, but, however' 2
atho = atha VI
adanta 'untamed' 1
adassana 'non-seeing, away from sight' 9.1
adinnaṃ 'ungiven thing' 3

adinnâdāna(ṃ) 'seizing or grasping that which is not given to one' 6
aduṭṭha 'free from malice or ill-will' not wicked 3.1
aduṭṭho 'one who is characterized by aduṭṭha 3.1
adoso 'non-ill-will, non-anger, non-hatred, non-malice' (a+doso) 2.2
addasā 'saw' (Third singular past tense of dakkhiti (passati) 'sees') 6
addhajhāma 'half-burnt' 10.1
addhā 'certainly, verily' 9
adhama 'low, base, wicked' 4
adhigacchati 'finds, acquires, attains, comes into possession of'; ppl. adhigata; inf. adhigaṇtuṃ 2
adhigaṇhāti 'excels, surpasses' 6
adhiṭṭhahati 'concentrate, fix one's attention on, undertake, practice' 6.1
adhiṭṭhāti 'attend to' 2 (=adiṭṭahati)
adhipajjati 'attains, reaches, comes to' 6.1
adhivāha 'bringing, entailing' 3.1
X-adhivāha 'entailing X' 3.1
anatīta 'not past, not free from' 11.1
anattamana 'displeased 11.1
anattamanatā 'displeasure' 11.1
anattā 'not a soul, without a soul, non-substantial' 7.1
anattho (aṃ) 'disadvantage, pointlessness, meaninglessness unprofitable situation or condition, harm, misery, misfortune' 1
ananussuta 'not heard of' 12.1
anabhijjhā 'absence of covetousness or desire' 3.1
anabhijjhālū 'one characterized by anabhijjā 3.1
analasa 'not lazy' 11.1
anavajja 'not blameworthy, not faulty' 2.2
anavaṭṭhita < an + ava + tthita 'not steady, not well composed' 8
Anāthapiṇḍiko name of the chief male lay-donor of Buddha 8.1
anādāno 'one who is free from attachment' 5
anādāya 'without taking or accepting' 6
anālaya 'free from attachment' 12.1
anāsavo 'one free from the four āsavas: (see glossary 9)
animittaṃ '"objectless" not affected by outward sense or appearance' 12
anutappa 'to be regretted' (from anutappati) 6
anutappati 'repents' 8
anuttara 'incomparable, excellent' 4.1
anudhammacārin 'one who acts in accordance with the Dhamma' nom. sing. anudhammacārī 4
anupādiyati < an +upādāti ('grasp) 'does not cling (to earthly things'), pres part. anupādiyāno, ger. anupādāya . 4
anuppatta 'having reached' (<anupāpuṇāti 'reach, attain') 6
anuppanna 'not having come into being' 1
anuppādo 'not coming into existence, non-existing' 1
anuyuñjati 'practises, gives oneself up to attends, pursues' 7
anuyogo 'application, practice, employment' 1.1
anurakkhati 'guard, protect, watch' 7.1
anuvātaṃ 'in the direction of the wind' 12
anusayo 'disposition, proclivity' 12
anusāsati 'advises, counsels, admonishes' 8
anussavaṃ 'tradition, hearsay' 7
aneka 'many, various' 12
anekaṃsikatā 'uncertaintly, doubtfulness' 7.1
anotappin 'reckless, not afraid of sin, remorseless' nom. sing. masc. anottappī (also anottāpī) 2.2
anta 'end, goal' 11
X anta 'having X as its end' 11
antakara 'putting an end to' 12
antarato 'from within (ablative of antara 'within') 6.1
antare 'in between, among' 10
antaradhānaṃ 'disappearance' 1.1
antalikkhaṃ 'atmosphere' 11
antima 'last' 12.1
anto 'inside' 12
anto 'end, goal, extreme' 12.1
antosāṇiyaṃ 'behind the curtain' 10
andhakāro(-aṃ) 'darkness' 7.1
andhatamaṃ 'deep darkness' 6.1
andhabhūta 'blinded, (mentally) blind, ignorant' 4
anveti 'enters, follows' 9
apagata 'is away from, desists from' 9.1
apacita 'respected' 12
apadeso 'argument, reason' ?
apaneti 'removes, leads away' 10.1
aparabhāgo 'later time, later' 11
apāyamukhaṃ 'cause of ruin' 9.1

apāyo 'calamity, a transient state of loss and woe after death' 7.1
api 'even, but, still' 5
api (pi) 'also' 7
apica (api + ca) 'further, moreover, furthermore' 7.1
appa 'little'
appasmim dadāti see Grammar 7
appaka 'little, few' 2
appaṃ '(a) little, not much' 4
appaṭivattiya 'irreversible, not to be rolled back' 12.1
appanigghosa 'without noise' 12
appamatto 'one who is diligent' 4.1
appamāṇa 'unlimited' 12.1
appamattakaṃ 'even a little' 10
appamādo 'diligence, earnestness' 1.1
appātamkatā 'freedom from illness' 9
appābādhatā 'good health' 9
appiya 'disagreeable or unpleasant (person or thing)' 3.1
appo 'a few' 4
aphalā 'fruitless' 5
aphāsukam 'difficulty, disease' 10.1
abbaṇa < a + vaṇa- 9
abbhuggacchati 'goes forth, goes out, rises into'; past abbhuggañchi 8.1
abbhuta 'exceptional, astonishing, marvellous, surprising' 8
abyāpannacitto 'one whose mind is free from malice or ill-will' 3.1
abyāpādo 'non-ill-will, benevolence, non-anger' 3.1
abhāvita 'uncultivated, not developed, untrained' 10
abhikkantaṃ 'excellent, superb, wonderful 5.1
abhijjhā 'covetousness' 3
abhiññā 'higher knowledge' 12.1
abhiṇhaṃ 'repeatedly, always' 12
abhinandati 'rejoices (over), delights in, approves of' 9
abhibhavati 'overcome' ger. abhibhuyya; ppl. abhibhūta 7
abhibhūta 'overcome,overwhelmed by'6.1
abhivaḍḍhati 'increases' 7
abhivassati 'rains (down, sheds rain' 6
abhivādeti 'salutes, greets, shows respect' 8
abhisambuddha 'perfectly understood, fully realized' 12.1
abhisambudhāno 'one who understands' 9.1
amataṃ 'ambrosia' or' the deathless state' 4.1
amatapadaṃ 'the region or place of ambrosia, the sphere of immortality' 4.1
amūḷho 'one who is not confused' 3.1
amoho 'non-confusion, clarity of mind' (<a+moho) 2.2
ambho 'look here, hey, hello' 10.1
ayaṃ 'this one' (also anaphoric) 3
ayoguḷo 'iron ball' 5.1
ayyā 'worthy one, honorable one' 10.1
arakkhita 'unprotected, unwatched' 1
araññaṃ 'forest, woods' 7
arahati 'deserves' 10.1
arahant 'deserving one, one who has attained absolute emancipation' nominative singular arahaṃ or arahā 4.1
ariya 'noble, distinguished' 2
ariyasaccaṃ 'noble truth' 7.1
ariyasāvikā 'a noble female devotee, a female disciple or devotee of the noble ones' 4
ariyassa vinaye 'in the teaching of the noble one' or 'the way of life of the noble ones' see glossary 9.1
ariyo 'noble one, exalted one' 4.1
aruṇ'uggamanaṃ 'dawnlight' 10
alasa 'lazy, idle' 11.1
aluddho 'non-covetous person' 3.1
alobho 'non-greed, non-covetousness' (< a+lobho) 2.2
alla 'wet' 9.1
allīyati 'cling to, attached to' 12.1
avakāso 'possibility, space, (there is a) possibility' 5
avaca 'said' 9.1
avacaro 'one at home in, conversant with' 7.1
avajānati 'despises, disrespects' 12
avabujjhati 'realize, understand' 6.1
avijjā 'ignorance' 3
avijjāgata 'ignorant (one)' 2
avijānanto 'not knowing, not understanding
< a + vijānanto
avidūre 'vicinity, nearby' 10.1
aviddasu 'ignorant, foolish' 4
aveccappasāda 'perfect faith, perfect clearness' 11..1
avoca third singular past of vatti, 'says, speaks' 5.1
asaṃvuta 'unrestrained' 1
asammoso 'non-bewilderment, non-confusion 1

asuka 'such and such 12
asesa 'entire, without remnant' 12.1
assa gen. sg. of ayaṃ 7
assa 3 sg. -ya optative of atthi. 8
assaddha 'not determined, not faithful' (<a+saddha) 2.2
assamiya 'belonging to a monastery or hermitage' 6
assamo 'monastery, hermitage, ashram' 6
assarūpakaṃ 'image or picture of a horse' 10
assumukha 'with a tearful face' 8
asso 'horse' 10
ahaṃ 'I' 1
ahitaṃ 'harm' 3
ahirika 'shameless, without modesty' 2.2
ahosi 'was, occurred' (past of hoti) 9.1
ākaṃkhati 'desires' 11
ākaḍḍhati 'drags, pulls' 11
ākāra 'condition, state' 12.1
ākāsadhātu 'space element, space, sky' 6
ākāso(aṃ) 'outer space, sky' 8.1
āgacchati 'comes' (pres part. āgacchanta) 3
ācariyo 'teacher' 10
ācikkhati 'tells, informs' 12
ājānāti 'grasp, understand' 9.1
ājiva 'life, living, livelihood' 4
ātura 'sick, diseased, miserable' 11.1
ādāti 'takes' ger. ādāya 10.1
ādātukāma 'eager to/ desirous of putting together (a ritual) 8
ādānaṃ 'grasping, putting up, placing' 8
ādāya 'taking, having taken' 10.1
ādi 'etcetera' 10
āditta 'burning, blazing' 5.1
ādiyati 'takes up, takes upon' 3
Ānandacetiyaṃ 'Ānanda monastery' 9
Ānando Ānanda, a disciple of Buddha 8
ānisaṃso(aṃ) 'advantage, good result/ good consequence' 8
āpajjati 'arrive at, reach,meet' 10
Āpaṇo place name 6
ābādho 'disease, affliction., 11
ābādhika 'sick person' 11.1
ābhā 'shine, luster, sheen' 6
āma 'yes' 3
āmanteti 'calls, addresses', past āmantesi 9
āmisaṃ 'material substance, food, flesh,sensual desire, lust ' 4.1
āmisagaruko 'one who attaches importance to material things, items of enjoyment or food,a greedy person' 7.1
āmisacakkhuka 'one intent on or inclined to material enjoyment' 7.1
āyasakyaṃ 'dishonor, disgrace, bad repute' 6.1
āyasmant 'venerable (one)', nom. sg.
āyasma (used as adjective as a respectful title of a Bhikkhu of some standing) 8
āyuṃ 'long life, vitality, longevity' 4 Instr. āyunā 'by longevity, duration of life' 6
ārati 'abstention' 5
āraddha 'begun, well begun, (well) undertaken' 9.1
āraddhaviriya 'energetic, resolute' 6.1
ārabhati 'begin' (viriyaṃ...'take effort, strive') 1
ārāmo 'park, resort for pastime, a private park given to the Buddha or the Sangha' 8.1
āruhati 'to climb' 10.1
āroceti 'tells, informs' 11.1
āropeti 'leads up to' 11
ālayarata 'lustful, delighting in desire' 9.1
ālayarāma 'clinging to lust' 9.1
ālayasamudita 'arisen from desire, craving' 9.1
āloko 'seeing, sight, light' 7.1
āvahāti 'for {āvahati} 'brings, entails' with metrical length 11
āvāho 'wedding (bringing the bride)' 6
āvila 'stirred up, agitated, stained, disturbed' 4
āvuso 'friend, brother, sir' a form of polite address (usually between monks) 9
āveṇika 'inherent, peculiar, special' 11.1
āsanaṃ 'seat' 6
āsavo 'that which flows (out or onto), clinging, desire' A technical term in Buddhist psychology for certain specified ideas which intoxicate the mind. 4.1
āsītika 'eighty years old' 11.1
āha 'said' 10
āharati 'bring' ger. āharitvā 10
āharāpeti 'cause to bring' 10
āhāra 'food' 10.1
āhu '(they) say or said' 6
āhutī 'oblation, sacrifice' 8.1
āhuneyya 'venerable, worthy of offerings' 5.1
Āḷavako name of a demon 11
Āḷavī a place name 11

ālāhana 'cremation ground' 12
ālindo (ālindo) 'verandah' 12
iṃgha 'come on, go on, look here, go ahead,' particle of exhortation 8.1
icchati 'desires, wishes, likes (for)' ppl. icchita 6.1
icchā 'desire' 3.1
itara '(the) other (one)' 10
itikirā 'hearsay, mere guesswork' 7
ito 'from here, hence' 8.1
ittara 'unsteady, fickle, changeable' 7.1
Ittaratā 'changeableness' 7.1
itthi 'woman' 1.1
itthirūpaṃ 'woman as an object of visual perception, female beauty 1.1
itthisaddo 'the sound of a woman, the word woman' 1.1
idaṃ 'this' 3
idapaccayatā 'having its foundation in this, causally connected' 9.1
idāni 'now' 10.1
idha 'here, in this world, now' 2
indriyaṃ 'faculty (of experience or perception), senses' 4.1
iva 'like, as' 4
issatthaṃ 'bow, archery' 5
iha 'here, now, in this world' 6.1
ukkā 'torch' 12
ukkujjati 'turns upright, rights (something)'
uggaṇhāti 'learns' 9
Uggatasarīro name of a Brahmin. Literally 'with upright body' 8
ucca 'tall, high, lofty' 8.1
uccayo 'heaping up, accumulation' 9
ujujātika 'straightforward, honest' 11
ujjahati 'give up' 12
uṭṭhahati 'rise, get up' (alternate form vuṭṭhahati,vuṭṭhati) 9.1
uṭṭhāpeti 'lifts' (alternate form vuṭṭāpeti) pres pl. uṭṭāpiyamāna 11.1
uṇha 'warm, hot' 10
utunī 'a menstruating woman' 11.1
uttama 'noble, best, highest' 4
uttara 'northern' 3.1
uttāna 'plain, open, evident, superficial, shallow' 4.1
udakaṃ 'water' 4.1
udapādi 'arose,' (preterite of uppajjati 'arise') 6.1
udabindu 'drop of water' 6.1
udāna 'emotional utterance, paean of joy' 12.1
udānaṃ udānesi uttered a paean of joy' 12.1
uddhaṃ 'up, above' 10
uddhaccam 'overbalancing, agitation, excitement, distraction, flurry' 6.1
uddhata 'unbalanced, disturbed, agitated' 4.1
uddhanaṃ 'fire hearth, oven' 6
uddharati 'raise, lift up' 7.1
uddhumātaka 'swollen, bloated, puffed up' 11.1
unnaḷa 'arrogant, proud, showing off' 4.1
upakaṇṇake 'secretly' 11.1
upakkileso 'defilement, taint, mental impurity' 4
upakkhaṭa 'prepared, ready, administered' pp. of upakaroti 8
upagamma 'having approached' 12.1
upajīvati 'lives on, depends on' 5
upaṭṭhānaṃ 'attendance, waiting upon' 10.1
upaddaveti 'cause trouble' 10
upadhi 'substratum (of rebirth), clinging to rebirth, attachment' 4.1
upaneti 'brings up to/into, offers, presents' ppl. upanita 8
upapajjati 'arises, is born, comes into existence, originates, gets to, is reborn in (alternate form uppajjati)' 7.1
upama 'like, similar' X-upama =' like X, similar to X' 9.1
upamā 'analogy, simile, example' 4.1
upari 'above, on, upon, upper' 10.1
uparima 'upper, above, overhead' 9.1
upasaṃkamati 'approaches, goes near'; past upasaṃkami 5.1
upasaṃhita 'possessed of' 12
upasanto 'being calm' 12
upasama 'calmness' 12.1
upasampajja 'having stepped onto, having arrived at having taken upon oneself 3.1
upasampadā 'acquisition, attainment, higher ordination of a monk' 2
upāyo 'method, way out, trick' 10.1
upāsako 'lay-devotee, practicing Buddhist' 5.1
upekkhaka 'indifferent, disinterested' 5.1
upeti 'approaches, attains, reaches' (the ppl. upeta has the sense'endowed' with') 5.1
uppajjati 'arises, is born, comes into existence, originates, gets to, is reborn in' (alternate form upapajjati) 1
uppajjamāna 'arising, being born' 7.1

uppanna 'having come into being', hence 'existing' 1
uppādeti 'produces, makes, give rise to' 11
uppādo 'arising, birth, coming into existence' 1
ubhaya 'both' 9.1
ubhayattha 'in both places' 10
ubho 'both' 12.1
uyyānaṃ 'park' 10
urabho 'a ram' 8
usabho 'bull, ox' 8
usukāro 'arrow-maker, fletcher' 4.1
ussāpanaṃ 'erection, putting up' 8
ussāpeti 'raise, lift up, erect' 8
uḷāra 'lofty, noble' 12.1
ūhanaṃ 'reasoning, consideration, examination' 6.1
eka 'one, single, only' 1
ekaka 'being alone' 10
ekagga 'calm, tranquil' 12
ekaggacitta 'of concentrated mind, of tranquil mind' 4.1
ekaghana 'compact, solid, hard' 4
ekaccī 'some, certain' 11.1
ekacce 'some, a few' 6
eka-ja 'once-born' 12
ekato 'together' 10.1
ekanta 'complete, thoroughly' 11.1
ekamantaṃ 'aside, on one side' 6.1
ekâsanabhojanaṃ 'taking only a single meal (solid food) a day'; (acc.) 9
ekāhamata 'a day after death (< eka 'one + aha 'day(s)'+ mata (ppl of miyyati/mīyati)' 11.1
eke 'some, a few' 4
eko 'alone' 7
etaṃ 'this, this thing' 2
etad =etaṃ 6
etadaggaṃ 'this (or this one) is best' 4.1
etadavoca < etad (=etam) + avoca 5.1
etadahosi 'such a thought occurred to one' 9.1
ettāvatā 'so far, to that extent' 11.1
ettha 'here, in this context, in relation to this' 4
etha 'come' Second person plural of eti 7
eva 'verily, indeed' (emphatic particle) 1
evaṃ 'thus' 1
evaṃ vutte 'when it was said thus' (loc. absolute) 8
evameva 'even so, just so, in similar manner, in the same manner, similarly' 2
evarūpa '(of this form), such, of this type' 7
esa 'that' alternate form of eso (nom. sg. masc. 2
esāna 'searching for, eager for' 11
eḷamūga 'not receptive to that doctrine, stupid' 2
okāso 'occasion, time' 11
otarati 'descends, enters into' 9
otāriyamāna 'that which is caused to be brought down' 9
otāreti 'bring down, lower' 9
ottappaṃ 'shrinking back from doing wrong, remorse' 6.1
otappin 'not reckless, afraid of sin, scrupulous' (nom. sing. masc. ottappī) 2.2
opammaṃ 'simile, example' 3
obhāso 'shine, splendour, luster, effulgence, appearance' 7.1
obhāsanaṃ 'shining' 7.1
olambati 'hangs (from) suspends' 10.1
oloketi 'looks (at) 10
ovadati 'advise, admonish, instruct, exhort' 8
kacci 'how is it, perhaps, I doubt' (indef.interrogative particle expressing doubt or suspense) 12
kaṭṭhaṃ 'wood, firewood, stick' 6
kata ppl. of karoti 10
katapuñño 'doer of pure deeds or good actions' 10
kataññutā 'gratitude' 5
katama 'which, what' 2
kattari 'pair or scissors' 10
katvā 'having done or made' 6
kathaṃ 'how' 3
kathaṃ jīviṃ 'leading what kind of life, which way of living?' 11
kathā 'story, speech, tale, talk' 10
katheti 'speak, talk' 10
kadariyo 'one who is miserly, stingy' 12
kadalipattaṃ 'banana leaf' 10.1
kammaṃ 'action, deed, action as related to rebirth' (among many meanings) 2.2
kammakileso 'depravity of action, bad works' 9.1
kammañña 'fit for work, ready for playing' 6.1
kammaniya 'ready, active' 3.1
kammantaṃ 'business, activity' 2
kammapatho 'way of action/doing' 11.1
kammin 'one who acts, doer' 9
karaṇa 'making, causing, producing';

X karaṇa = 'making X' 8.1
karīsaṃ 'excrement' 11.1
karoti 'does, makes'
2nd person imperative sing. karohi, 3
optative kāyira 9.
kalahajāta 'quarrelsome, disputing' 4.1
kalaho 'quarrel, dispute' 4.1
Kalandakanivāpa a place name
(literally, 'squirrel feed') 9.1
Kalasigāmo a place name 8.1
kalāpa 'a bundle, a bunch, a sheaf, a
row' 6.1
kilamatho 'fatigue, exhaustion' 9.1
kalyāṇa 'good, auspicious, morally
good' 4
kalla 'dexterous, smart, clever' 3.1
kasmā 'why' 7
Kasmīraṃ a place name, Kashmir 8.1
kassako 'husbandman, farmer,
cultivator' 5
kāmaguṇā sensual pleasures 12
kāmo (-aṃ) '(sense) desire' 4
kāyika 'felt by the body, physical' 4.1
kāyira optative of karoti 9 1
kāyo 'body' 3
kāraṇaṃ 'reason, cause' X.1
kāreti 'causes to do constructs, makes' 10
kālaṃ karoti 'pass away, die' 9.1
kālassa eva 'in early morning' 9.1
kālakata 'dead' 8.1
kālakiriyā 'death, passing away' 6
Kālāmā proper name, Kalamas, 7
kālaññū 'one who knows the proper
time' (for something)4
kālo '(proper) time, morning' 4
instr. kālena 'in time, at the proper
time' 6
kiṃ 'what' (neuter singular of ka
as an interrogative particle 3
kiṃlakkhaṇaṃ 'of what nature, of what
characteristic' (< kiṃ 'what'+lakkhaṇaṃ
'feature') 3.1
kiccam 'task, duty' 12
kiñcanaṃ 'any' 6.1
kiñcano 'worldly attachment, a trifle' 5.1
kittāvāta 'in what respect, in what
sense' 6.1
kitti 'fame, renown, glory' 8.1
kittisaddo 'sound of fame, praise,
renown' 8.1
kinnu 'why, but why, is it (that), how is
it that' (< kiṃ + nu) 3
kinnukho 'why, what for, what is it
then' (< kiṃ + nu + kho) 6
kira 'it is said,.truly, really'
(reportative particle) 10
kiriyā 'doing, action' 8.1
kiliṭṭhaṃ 'foulness, impurity' (neuter ppl.
of kilissati 10
kilissati 'becomes soiled', stained or
impure ,does wrong' 8
kileso 'defilement, impurity (in a moral
sense)' 6.1
kīdisa 'how, in what manner' 10.1
kīva 'how much, how many,
how great' 8.1
kīḷati 'to play' 10.1
kukkuro 'dog' 11
kujjhati 'be angry (with), be irritated' 7
kuñjaro 'elephant' 7.1
kuṭila 'crooked, dishonest' 11
kuṇḍalaṃ 'earring' 12
kuto 'whence, from where' 4
kudācana 'any day, ever' 2
kuddho 'angry one' 6
kubbanta 'doer, one that practices' 5
kumāraka 'young boy' 10.1
kumbho 'frontal lobes of an elephant' 10
kulaṃ 'lineage, clan, family, household' 6
kusala 'virtuous, good, efficient, skilled' 1
kusalaṃ 'virtue, good (action), merit' 2
kusīta 'indolent, lazy' 2.2
kuhiṃ 'where' 8.1
kūṭāgārasālā 'gabled house, pavilion' 8.1
Keniyo proper name 6
keso 'hair'(normally in the
plural, kesā) 9.1
ko 'who whichever person' 3
koci 'any (one), some (one)' (ko + ci) 3
kocideva 'some (one) or other'
(ko + ci + eva, with -d- inserted) 3
koṭi 'end' 10.1
koṭṭeti 'pound, beat' 12
koṭṭhāso 'share' 10.1
kodhana 'having anger, angry (one),
uncontrolled (one)' 6.1
kodho 'anger, ill will' 6.1
kosajjaṃ 'idleness, sloth, indolence' 1.1
khaṇa 'moment, instant' 12.1
khaṇati 'dig, uproot' 7
khaṇanto 'digging, one who digs' 6
khaṇḍadanta with broken teeth 11.1
khattiya 'of the warrior (Kshatriya)
caste' 8.1
khattuṃ 'times' (as in ti khattuṃ 'three
times') 11
khanti 'patience, forbearance' 5
khandhaṭṭhikaṃ 'backbone, back' 10.1

khamati 'is fitting, seems good 5.1
khayo 'end, cessation' 9.1
khalita 'bald' 11.1
khāṇu 'stake, spike' 10.1
khādanīya 'eatable' 10
khipati 'throws (away), puts, confuses (the mind)' 10
khippaṃ 'soon, quickly' 7.1
khīṇa 'exhausted, over, finished' 10
khīraṃ 'milk' 4.1
khīrodakībhūta 'like milk and water, (at harmony as milk and water blend 4.1
khuddaka 'small' 10
khettaṃ 'field, sphere' 5.1
kho 'emphatic particle' 2
gacchati 'go'; ppl. gata, ger. gantvā 1
gaṇayaṃ 'counting' 4
gaṇeti 'counts, reckons' 4
gaṇo 'group, multitude, crowd' 10
gaṇhāti 'picks up, takes'; ger. gahetvā 5.1
gatayobbana 'past youth, aged' 11.1
gattaṃ 'body, limbs' 10.1
gandho/aṃ 'odor, scent, smell' 1.1
gandha jātānī 'kinds of perfumes, odors' 12
gabbho 'womb' 7
gabbhinī 'pregnant woman' 11.1
gambhīra 'deep' 4
gamma 'low, vulgar, mean' 12.1
garahita 'despised, condemned, not approved' 3
garu 'venerable person, teacher' 7
garuka 'heavy, important, bent on, attaching importance to' 7.1
garukaroti 'respect, consider seriously' 9.1
gahapati 'householder, a man of private (i.e. not official) life' 8.1
gahapatika 'belonging to the rank of a householder, a member of the gentry' 8
gahapatiputto 'a man of the middle class, a nobleman, a householder' 9.1
gahetvā(na) ger. of gaṇhāti 6.1
gāthā 'verse, stanza' 11.1
X gāmin ' leading to, going to X (feminine -inī)' 11.1
gāminī 'leading up' 12.1
gāmo 'village' 5
gāravo 'reverence, respect, esteem' 5
gāvo accusative pl. (irreg.) of go 'cow' 4
gilati 'swallows' 10
gihin 'householder, layman'; compounding stem gihi 4.1
gīvā 'neck, throat' 10.1
guṇa 'quality, nature, component' 6.1
gutta 'guarded'; ppl. of gopeti 1
guyha 'to be hidden, that which is hidden, secret' 7.1
gehaṃ 'house, dwelling, household, hut' 7.1
gocara 'sphere, range' 4.1
goṇo 'ox' 10.1
Gotama 'one of the Gotama family, the family name of Buddha' 5
gottaṃ 'ancestry, lineage' 8
gopānasī 'rafter, gable' 11.1
gopānasīvaṃka 'crooked (like a gable)' 11.1
gopālako 'cowherd' 11
gopo 'cowherd' 4
gorakkhā 'cow-keeping, tending the cattle' 5
ghaṃseti 'to rub against' 10
ghaṭo(aṃ) 'pot' 10
ghātayati 'causes to kill' 4.1
ghānaṃ 'nose' 3.1
ghāyati 'smells' 3.1
ghoso 'noise, sound' 6
ca 'and, also' 1
cala 'unsteady, fickle' 7.1
cakkaṃ 'wheel, wheel as a symbol of conquering efficacy' 4.1
cakkavattin 'universal monarch' Nom. sing. cakkavattī 4.1
cakkhuṃ 'eye' 2
cakkhu karaṇī 'producing insight' ?
cakkhumant 'endowed with insight' (literally 'having eyes') ?
catu 'four' 4
catuttha 'fourth' 4
catutthaṃ 'for the fourth time' 11
candana 'sandalwood' 12
cando 'moon' 6
capala 'unsteady, fickle, vain' 4.1
capalatā 'fickleness,unsteadiness' 7.1
carati 'moves about, behaves, conducts (oneself), leads, , practices, carries out' 7
caritaṃ 'behavior, character' 7.1
carito 'one who has a character'; X-carita = 'one who has the character of X kind' 7.1
calita 'wavering, unsteady' 7.1
cavati 'fall (away)' 2.2
cāga 'giving up' 12.1
cāgo 'liberality, generosity' 6
cārikā 'wandering, journey, sojourn' 6

cāleti 'shake' 10
ci indefinite particle 3
cittaṃ 'mind' 1
cinteti 'think (of) 8.1
cirataraṃ 'rather long, longer, delayed' 8.1
cirena 'after a long time' 8.1
cuddasa 'fourteen' 9.1
ce 'if' 4
cetas 'mind' (Nom Sg.ceto, Instr. cetasā) 6.1
cetasika 'belonging to the mind, mental' 4.1
cetovimutti 'mental emancipation' 12.1
coro 'thief, robber' 5
cha 'six' 9.1
chaḍḍheti 'give up, discard' 9
chaddisā 'the six directions' (North, South, East, West, up, down) 9.1
chando 'desire, resolution, will' 1
chavi 'skin' 8
chātajjhatta 'be hungry' 10.1
chāyā 'shadow, shade, (light) image' 8.1
chiddaṃ 'hole, cut' 10
chindati 'cuts, severs, plucks, breaks' 6.1
chetvā(na) 'having cut off, having destroyed, having removed' (ger. of chindati, 'to cut, sever') 5
chedanaṃ 'cutting, severing, destroying' 6.1
-ja 'be born': X-ja = 'be born of X' 2.2
jagat 'world'; loc. jagati 11
jaññā 'let one know' (Optative 3 p. sg. of jānāti) 12
jaṭilo 'one who wears matted hair, a kind of ascetic' 6
janana 'causing, bringing, producing' 6.1
janapado 'province, locality, the country' 2
janādhipo 'king (of men)' 11.1
janeti 'generate, cause to be born' 1
jano 'man, people, individual' 6
jammī 'wretched, contemptible' 6.1
jarā 'old age, decrepitude, decay' 3.1
jahāti 'gives up, abandons' (root hā) ger. hitvā 7
jaḷa 'slow, stupid' 2
jaḷo 'a stupid person' 2
jāgarati 'to be awake, watchful' pres. part. jāgaranto 'one who is wakeful' 5
jāta 'born, arisen'; X jata = 'of the nature of' X', 'having become X' 6.1
jātarūpaṃ 'gold' 4
jāti 'birth, rebirth, possibility of rebirth' 3.1
jānāti 'knows, realizes, comprehends, understands' ger. ñatvā 3.1
jānāpeti 'informs' 11
jāni 'deprivation, loss' 6.1
jāyati' 'arises, is born' 4
jālaṃ 'net' 4
jālā 'blaze, flames' 10.1
jāleti 'kindle' 10
jiṇṇa /jiṇṇaka 'frail, decrepit',old 11.1
jivhā 'tongue 3.1
jīrati 'decays, is worn out' 11
jīvati 'lives' 4
jīvitaṃ 'life' 2
jīvo 'life' 4
Jetavana 'Jeta's park, Jeta's grove' 8.1
jhāpeti 'burn'; ger. jhāpetvā 12
ñatvā 'having known, having understood' ger. of jānāti 4.1
ñāṇaṃ 'knowledge, intelligence, insight, understanding' 7.1
ñāṇakaraṇī 'giving (right) understanding, enlightening' 12.1
ñāṇadassana 'perfect knowledge' 12.1
ñātako 'relative, kinsman' 5
ñāti 'a relation, relative' 6.1
(X) ṭṭhānaṃ 'condition or state of X' 6
ṭhapeti 'keeps, places, puts' 10
ṭhāti 'stand' 11
ṭhānaṃ 'place, locality, condition, cause, fact, principle, conclusion' 4
ṭhānaṃ...(vijjati) 'it is possible, it is conceivable' 5
ṭhitamajjhantike 'at midday, at noon' 10
ṭhiti 'persistence, continuity' 1
ḍayhati 'gets burned' 5.1
ḍasati 'bites, chews, gnaws' 11
ḍasāpeti 'cause to bite or sting' 10.1
takkara 'doing thus, acting accordingly 4
tagara 'a fragrant shrub' 12
taca 'bark, hide, skin' 12
tacchako 'carpenter' 4.1
taññeva < taṃ+ eva 5.1
taṇhā 'craving, thirst' 4
tatiya 'third' accusative tatiyaṃ used adverbally as 'thirdly','for the third time' 1
tato 'from this, thereupon, further thence, afterwards' 6.1
tato paṭṭhāya 'since then, from then onwards' 10
tatta 'heated, hot' 5.1
tattabhāvo 'hotness, the fact that it is warm/hot, warmth' 10
tattha 'there, in that' 6.1

tatra 'there' 8.1
tathattaṃ 'that state, thatness' Lit. 'the state of being so')', 3.1
tathā 'thus, so' 5.1
tathāgatappavedita 'expounded by the Tathāgata' 2
tathāgato' Tathagata, 'thus-gone-one', an epithet for a Buddha 2
tanuko 'a few' 4
tanti 'string or cord of a lute' 6.1
tantissara 'string music' 6.1
tapati 'shines, is bright, lustrous' 4
tappati 'suffer, be tormented' 10
taṃ third pers. singular pronoun (neut nominative-Accusative. or masc-fem. accusative) 2
tayidaṃ 'hence, therefore, so' (ītaṃ + idaṃ) 8
tasati 'fears' 4.1
tasmā 'therefore, hence' 3
tāto 'father, child, dear one' (vocative singular tāta) see glossary 9.1
tādisako 'of such a quality/nature'8
tādiso (-a) 'such, of such quality' 11.1
tāpayati 'torments, torture' 6
tārā 'star' 6.1
tārāgaṇo 'galaxy of stars, host of stars' 6
tālapakkaṃ 'palm fruit' 8
tāvatiṃsabhavanaṃ 'realm of the thirty-three gods' 10.1
-ti a form of iti, the quotation marker 1
tikicchati 'treats (medically)' 10.1
tikicchāpeti 'cause to cure, employ to cure' (Causative. of tikicchati 'cures' 12
tiṭṭhati 'stands, exists, is; remains' ppl. (ṭ)ṭhita, pres. part. tiṭṭhanta 1.1
tiracchāno 'animal' 11
tiriyaṃ 'across' 11
tilaka 'spot, freckle' 11.1
tīṇi 'three' (neut. nom. pl.) 2.2
tīhamata 'three days after death' (ti+aha+mata) 11.1
tu 'however, indeed' 10.1
tuṭṭha 'pleased, being happy/glad' 10
tuṇhībhāvo 'silence' 10
tuṇhībhūta '(being) silent' 8
tumhe 'you(plural)' (nominative plural of tvaṃ, 'you') 3.1
tejanam 'point or shaft of an arrow, arrow' 4.1
tena hi 'if so, in that case' 5.1
telapajjotaṃ 'oil lamp' 12
thanayati 'roars, thunders' 6
thalaṃ 'plateau, raised dry ground' 6
thūṇā 'pillar, post' 8
thūpāraha 'worthy of a stupa' 6
thūpo 'stupa, tope' 6
thero 'elder, senior (bhikkhu)' 5.1
thokaṃ 'little' 10.1
dakkhiṇa 'right (side),south, southern' 3.1
dakkhiṇeyya 'worthy of offerings or gifts' 5.1
dakkha 'clever, able, skilled' 11.1
dajjā Optative of deti (or dadati) 'give' 7
daṇḍakamadhuṃ 'a bee-hive on a branch' 10.1
daṇḍako 'branch, stick' 10.1
daṇḍaparāyana 'leaning on, tottering on a staff' 11.1
daṇḍeti 'punish' 5.1
daṇḍa 'stick, staff, cane, rod, punishment' 4.1
datvā 'having given'(ger. of deti /dadāti 'gives') 4
dadāti 'gives' Opt. dajjā, ger. datvā 7
danta 'tamed' 1
dabbī 'spoon, ladle' 8
damatho 'restraint, training, taming, control, silence' 4.1
damayati 'restrains,controls' 4.1
dayā compassion, kindness 12
dassasi future 2 Sg. of deti 11
dassanaṃ 'seeing, sight, insight, perfect knowledge' 2
dasseti 'show' 10
daharo 'young in years' 11.1
daḷhaṃ 'tightly, hard, strongly' 10.1
dāttaṃ 'sickle' 6.1
dānaṃ 'giving, charity' 5
dānapati 'a liberal donor' 8.1
dāyako 'giver, (lay) donor' 8.1
dārako 'child, youngster, boy' 7
dāruṃ 'wood' 4.1
dārukhaṇdakaṃ 'a piece of firewood, a stick' 10
dāsi 'maid-servant' 10.1
diguṇaṃ 'doubly, twofold' 5.1
dija 'twice-born one' 12
diṭṭha 'seen, witnessed' 7
diṭṭhaṃ 'a vision, that which is seen' 7
dippati 'shines, shines forth' 4.1
dibba 'divine' 4
divaso 'day' 10
disampati 'king' 11.1
disā 'direction' 9.1
disvā(na) 'having seen' (ger. of dis-/ passati 'sees') 5.1
dīgha 'long' 3

dīgharattaṃ 'for a long time' 3
dīpaṃ 'solid foundation, shelter, refuge' 6.1
du 'two' 8.1
dukkha 'painful, of suffering' 3.1
dukkhita 'afflicted' 11.1
dukkho/-aṃ 'sorrow, suffering, ill' 2.2
dugga 'rough ground, wrong way' 7.1
duggati 'unhappy existence, evil state, realm of misery' 7.1
duccaritaṃ 'bad behavior, incorrect behavior' 7
ducchanna 'ill-thatched, badly covered' 10
duṭṭha 'wicked, malicious' 7
dutiyaṃ 'second time' (accusative of dutiya, 'second,' used adverbally) 1
duddasa 'difficult to see, incomprehensible (by the ordinary)' 9.1
dunniggaha 'difficult to restrain' 8
duppañña 'not wise, foolish, ignorant' 2
dubbaṇṇa 'of bad color, ugly, of changed color' 6.1
dubbala 'weak' 10.1
dubbalabhāva 'feebleness' 12
dubbhāsita 'ill-spoken' 2
dummana 'unhappy, downcast' 5.1
duraccaya 'hard to remove, difficult to overcome' 6.1
duranubodha 'difficult to be understood' 9.1
dullabha 'rare, difficult to obtain' 6
dūra 'far' 8.1
deti 'gives, donates' (= dadāti) 4
future 2 Sg. dassasi 11
dentī 'one who gives' 4
X deva 'having X as god, highly respecting X 11.1
devasika 'occurring daily' 12
devo 'god'; also used as an epithet for king 5
deseti 'preach, declare' 9.1
doso 'anger, ill will, evil intention, wickedness, corruption, malice, hatred' 2.2
dvādasa 'twelve' 8.1
dvāraṃ 'door, gate' 10
dvīhamata 'two days after death (< dvi+aha+mata)' 11.1
dhanaṃ 'wealth, riches treasures' 6.1
X dhamma 'of the nature of X' 5.1
dhammakammaṃ 'righteous deed or activity, activities pertaining to the doctrine' 4.1
dhammacariyā 'righteous living' 5
dhammaññu 'knowing that which is proper, knowing the doctrine' 4.1
dhammapadaṃ 'word of righteousness' 9.1
dhammavinayo 'teachings of the Buddha, (Dhamma and Vinaya together)' 2
dhammo 'doctrine, physical or mental element or phenomenon; that which is true, righteous, proper and/or natural; factor; quality' (among many meanings) 1
dhātu (feminine.) 'element, relic, basis' 6
dhāreti 'holds, bears, accepts, contains, holds, holds back' 5.1
dhītar 'daughter' 10.1
dhovanto 'one who washes, one who cleans' 6
na 'not' 1
naṃ alternate form of the pronoun taṃ 5.1
nagaraṃ 'city, town' 3.1
nagaraguttiko superintendent of a city' 3.1
naccati 'to dance, play' 10.1
nanu (< na + nu) 'isn't it that' (as particle of interrogation), surely, certainly', (as particle of affirmation) 3
nandati 'rejoice, be happy' 10
nandirāga 'passionate delight' 12.1
namayati 'bends, fashions' 4.1
namassati 'salute, venerate, honor, do homage to' 9.1
nayati 'leads, takes' 4.1
naro 'man, individual' 6.1
nava 'nine' 7
navama 'ninth' 7
nahāyati 'bathe' 10
Nāgaseno proper name; vocative singular Nāgaseno 3
nāgo 'elephant' 7
nānāvidha 'various' 10
nāma 'just, indeed, for sure' 5
nāmaṃ 'name (for recognition)' 8
nāmaṃ karoti 'give a name' 10.1
nāmagahanaṃ naming, taking a name' 10.1
nāmagottaṃ 'the name (for recognition) and the surname (for lineage)' 8
nāvutika 'ninety years old' 11.1
nāḷi a measure of capacity, 'cupful' 10
nāḷimatta 'a cupful' (about a nāḷi)

nikkujjitam 'that which is turned upside down' 12
nikkhamati 'set forth, come out of' , ppl. nikkhanta 9.1
nigacchati 'go down to, enter, come to, suffer' 6.1
nigamo 'market-town, small town' 10.1
niggāhako 'one who rebukes, oppressor' 12
nicca 'permanent, constant, non- transitory' 5.1
nitthaṃ gacchati 'concludes, arrives at a conclusion' 9
niḍḍhaṃ 'nest, place' 11
nittharati 'concludes, ends, finishes 10
nidānaṃ 'source, cause, origin: = ' 2.2
X-nidāna 'having X as source or origin'
niddāyitā 'a sleepy person' 7.1
nindā 'blame' 4
ninnaṃ 'low land' 6
nipaka 'intelligent, mature' 7
nipajjati 'lies down, sleeps' 12
nipanna 'having lain down or slept' (ppl. of nipajjati) 10.1
nipuṇa 'efficient, subtle, abstruse, clever, skillful,accomplished' 9.1
nipphatti (f.) 'conclusion, end, completion' 10
nibbattati 'be born, arise' 10.1
nibbāṇaṃ 'emancipation' 9.1
nibbidā 'indifference, disenchantment' 12
nibbiddha 'pierced' 10.1
nibaddhaṃ 'always' 11
nimanteti 'invites' 6
nimittaṃ 'object of a thought' 6.1
nimmakkhika 'without bees or flies' 10.1
nirayo 'purgatory, hell' 7.1
nirāmisa 'not characterized by āmisa' 4.1
nirupadhi 'free from passions, or attachment, desireless' 4.1
nirodho 'cessation, emancipation, calming down' 2.2
nivattati 'turns back' 11
nivāto 'modesty, gentleness' 5
nivāpaputṭha 'fed on fodder' 7.1
nivāraṇatthaṃ 'for the purpose of preventing, to prevent' 10
nivāsanakaṇṇaṃ 'hem of the robe' 11
nivāseti 'dress oneself, put on clothes or robes' 8.1
nivesanaṃ 'settlement, abode, house' 8.1
niveseti 'established' 8
nisidati 'sits down, sit, is seated' ppl. nisinna 3 sg. past nisīdi 6.1
nissāya 'because of, on account of' 10
nīca 'low' 8.1
nīharati 'puts out, stretches out, drives or takes out'; ger. nīharitvā(na) 10.1
nu 'then, now' (interrogative particle) 3
nekkhammaṃ 'renunciation of worldliness, freedom from lust, craving and desires' 4.1
nettiko 'irrigator' 4.1
no 'verily not (na + u; negative emphatic - more emphatic than na) 3.1
pakata 'done, made:
X-pakata = done out of X' 2.2
pakāseti 'make known, illustrate' 12
pakopana 'upsetting, shaking, making turbulent' 6.1
pakopo 'agitation, anger' 7
pakkosati 'summons, calls' 12
pakkosāpeti 'summon, call' 10
pakkhandati 'springs forward, jump up' 11
pakkhipati 'throw, put' 10
paggaṇhāti 'uplifts, takes up, stretches forth, holds out/up, takes up, makes ready'' ppl. paggahita 1
paṃko (-aṃ) 'mud' 7.1
pacati 'cooks, bakes, heats' 10
paceti 'gathers' 9.1
paṭi(s)suṇāti 9
paccanubhoti 'undergoes, experience 11.1
paccakkhāya 'having given up, having abandoned' 6.1
paccaññāsiṃ '(I) realized perfectly' 12.1
paccati 'ripen' 9
paccatthika(o) 'opponent, opposing' 4.1
paccantima 'bordering, adjoining (near), countryside' 2
paccayo 'cause, motive, means, ground,motive, support' 8.1. 'requisite (of a monk) 12
X-paccaya 'having X as paccayo' 8.1
paccassosi 'assented, agreed'
3rd. sg. past of paṭi(s)suṇāti 9.1
3rd pl. past paccassosum 9
paccājāyati' 'is (re)born' 2
paccupaṭṭhāti 'is present' 6
paccekabuddho 'silent Buddha, individual Buddha. See glossary 6
pacchindati 'settle, decide' 10.1
pacchima 'west, western' 3.1
pajahati /hāti 'gives up, abandons, discards';infin. pajahitaṃ; ger. pahāya 3
pajā 'people, progeny, offspring' 9.1
pajānāti 'realizes, understands well' 5.1

pajjalati 'burns (forth), blazes up'; ppl. pajjalita 8.1
pañca 'five' 3.1
pañcama 'fifth' 11.1
pañc'upādānakkhandhā 'the five aggregates' See glossary 3.1
pañjalika 'with folded hands' 9.1
paññavant 'wise (one), insightful (person)' masc. nom. sg.paññavā nom. pl. paññavanto- 2
paññā 'wisdom, knowledge, insight' 2
paññācakkhuṃ 'eye of wisdom; eye of insight' 2
paññājīviṃ 'life of wisdom, insight' 11
paññāpeti 'indicate, point out, make known, declare' 8.1
paññāpento 'one who prepares or arranges' 6
paññāyati 'appear, be clear' 12
pañho 'question' 11
paṭikkosati 'blame, reject' 9
paṭigganhāti, 'receive, accept'; ppl. paṭiggahita 9
paṭiggahaṇaṃ 'acceptance, receiving' 4
paṭiggāhako 'recipient, he who receives' 4
paṭicchannaṃ 'that which is covered, concealed' 12
paṭiccasamuppādo 'arising on the grounds of a preceding cause, dependent origination' (theory of the twelve causes) 9.1
paṭicchādin 'covering, enveloping' 9.1
paṭijānāti 'to promise' 10.1
paṭinissaggo 'renunciation, giving up' 9.1
paṭinissagga 'rejection, forsaking' 12.1
paṭipanna 'stepped on to, entering on' 9.1
paṭipajjati 'enters upon' 11
paṭipadā 'way, means, path, method, course' 11.1
paṭibala 'competent, capable' 2
paṭipucchati 'asks in response, inquires in return' 5.1
paṭiyādeti 'prepares, arranges' 6
paṭilābho 'attainment' 2
paṭivattiya 'to be turned back, resistible' 4.1
paṭivātaṃ 'against the wind' 12
paṭivijjha 'having penetrated, intuited, acquired, comprehended' 6.1
paṭivirata 'restrained from, abstained from' 4
paṭisandahati 'is connected, is reunited, is reborn' 3
paṭisallīna 'secluded, retired, gone into solitude' 6.1
paṭisevati 'follows, pursues, indulges in, experiences' 4
paṭṭhāya 'beginning from, henceforth' (with Abl.)' 10
paṭhama 'first'; acc. sg. paṭhamaṃ used as adverb 'first(ly)' 4
paṭhamataraṃ 'as early as possible, (very) first' 8.1
paṭhavī 'earth' 8.1
paṇidahati 'puts forth, longs for, applies, directs', ppl. paṇihita 8.1
paṇīta 'exalted, excellent' 9.1
paṇḍako 'eunuch, weakling' 7.1
paṇḍitamānin 'one who thinks himself wise' 9.1
paṇḍitavedanīya 'to be understood by the wise' 9.1
paṇḍito 'wise one' 4
paṇḍurugo 'jaundice' 12
paṇṇaṃ 'leaf' 10
patati 'to fall', ger. patitvā 10.1
patikula 'husband's family' 11.1
patiṭṭhāpento 'one who places, one who keeps' 6
patiṭṭhita 'established, fixed, founded upon' 6
patiṭṭhāti (-ṭṭhahati) 'stands fast or firmly, stays, sets up, establishes oneself' 2.2
patinandita 'rejoiced, welcomed' 6
patibbatā 'a devoted wife' 11.1
patirūpa 'agreeable (status, position, state)' 8
patīta 'delighted, with delight' 8
patta 'attained, reached' 10
pattacīvaraṃ 'bowl and robe' 8.1
padaṃ 'word, foot, footstep' 9
padahati 'exert, strive, confront' 1
padīpeti 'lights, kindles' 3
padīpo 'lamp' 3
padeso 'province, part, fact, limited extent, indication' 9
pana 'verily, but' 3.1
panta 'remote, solitary, secluded' 12
papatati 'drops, falls down or off' 6.1
papupphakaṃ 'flowery arrows, flower-tipped arrows (of sensual passion)' 9.1
pabbajita 'renounced, ordained, gone forth (into holy life,)' 4.1
pabbato'mountain, range of mountains' 11
pabhaṃguna 'easily destroyed' 11
pamatto 'one who is lazy, not diligent' 4.1

pamādo 'indolence, sloth' 1.1
pamuñcati 'is let loose, liberated, set free', ppl. pamutta 8
pamodati 'rejoices, enjoys, finds pleasure in' 4
payāti 'goes forward, proceed' 11
payirupāsati 'associate' 8
para '(of) others' 4
paraṃ 'after' 7
paro 'other (person)' 6
paradāro 'someone else's wife' 3
parapessa 'serving others' 5
paramparā 'tradition' 7
parikkhipati 'to coil around, encircle' 10.1
parijiṇṇa 'decayed' 11
pariññeyya 'what should be known' 12.1
paritassati 'be excited, be worried, be tormented' 5
parinibbāti 'pass away, die without rebirth' 9
paripajjati: 'falls into, sinks into, wallows' 11.1
paripūrati 'be filled, attain fullness' 8
pariplava 'unsteady, wavering' 8
pariplavapasāda 'one whose tranquillity is superficial or wavering' 8
paribyūḷhya 'provided with' 6
paribhogo 'enjoyment, use' 10.1
paribhojanīya 'to be used (of water for washing)' 10
parimutto 'one who is completely freed, a fully-freed one' 3
parivajjeti 'shun, avoid' 7.1
pariyādāya 'having overpowered, taking up completely' 1.1
pariyādinnacitta 'with the mind completely overpowered by, with the mind completely taken over by' 7
pariyāya 'order, course, method' 12
pariyodapanaṃ/-a 'purification' 2
pariyodāta 'very clean, pure, cleansed' 8
parirundhati 'completely obstruct, imprison' 12
parivajjati 'avoids, shuns, gives up' 6.1
parivaṭṭa 'a circle' 12.1
parivatteti 'turns, changes' 10.1
parivitakko 'reflection, thought, consideration' 6.1
parivuta 'followed by, surrounded by' 6
parisā 'assembly, group, gathering, retinue' 4.1
parisaññu 'knowing or knower of the assembly' 4.1
parisuddha 'clear, pure, spotless, bright, perfect' 8
parissayaṃ 'obstacle' 7
parihāyati 'decrease, dwindle, deteriorate' 1
pare 'other, other (ones)' 6
paro 'another, next (one)' 3.1
palavati 'floats, swims, jumps' 6.1
palāpo 'prattle, nonsense' 11.1
palāyati 'flee, run away' 10
palālaṃ 'straw, dry leaves' 10.1
paveseti 'to cause to enter, to put inside' 10.1
palitakesa 'having grey hair' 11.1
pavatti 'manifestation, wielding, happening' 8.1
pavaḍḍhati 'grows (up), increases' 6.1
pavattati 'proceeds, goes on' 4.1
pavatteti 'sets in motion, keeps (something) going, turns, rolls (something) 4.1
pavāti 'blow forth' 12
pavisati 'enters, goes into'; ppl. paviṭṭha; ger. pavissa 8.1
pavedita 'pointed out, expounded, declared, made known' 2
pavedhati 'tremble' 11.1
paveseti 'make enter, procure, furnish, provide' 7.1
pasaṃsati 'praises'; ppl. pasattha 5
pasaṃsā 'praise' 4
pasanna 'pleased, clear, bright' 10.1
pasahati 'subdues, oppresses' 11
pasādo 'tranquility, serenity, clarity, purity' 8
passati 'sees, realizes' 3.1
paharati 'hit, strike, beat' 10
pahātabba 'what ought to be given up' 12.1
pahānaṃ 'avoidance' 1
pahāya ger. of pajahati 7
pahīna 'given up, abandoned, calmed down' (ppl. of pajahati) 3
pahu 'able' 12
paḷipanna =paripanna, ppl. of paripajjati: 'falls into, sinks into, wallows' 11.1
pākaṭa 'open, manifest, unconcealed' 7.1
pākaṭaṃ karoti 'makes manifest, makes appear' 7
pākata 'common, vulgar, uncontrolled' 4.1
pākatindriya 'of uncontrolled mind' 4.1
pākatika 'natural state, state as before' 10.1
pāṇa 'life, breath, living (being). 12

pāṇâtipāto 'destruction of life, taking life' 6
pāṇi (ṃ) 'hand' 9
pāṇin 'a living being', instrumental singular pāṇinā 4.1
pāṇupetaṃ 'for life' (literally 'possessed-with-breath-ly' < pāṇa(ṃ) 'breath + upetaṃ
neuter past participle of upeti approaches, obtains') 5.1
pāṇo 'breath, life' 3
pātimokkha 'collection of disciplinary rules binding on a recluse' 12
pātubhūta 'manifested, become manifest, appeared' 3.1
pāturahosi 'appeared' 12.1
pāteti 'fells makes fall'
(aggiṃ)pāteti = 'kindles (fire)' 10
pādo 'foot' 10
pānaṃ 'drink, drinking' 4
pānīyaṃ 'water for drinking' 10
pāpaṃ 'sin, evil, bad deed, wrong action' 2
pāpaka 'sinful, evil, wicked' 1
pāpakaṃ 'bad action' 9.1
pāpakammaṃ 'evil, sinful act' 5.1
pāpakārin 'evil-doer; (nom. sg. pāpakāri) 10
pāpaṇiko 'merchant, shopkeeper' 2
pāpiccho 'one who has bad intentions, wicked one' 12
pāpuṇati 'reaches' 10
pāpeti 'brings about, causes to attain 10.1
pāpo 'evildoer' 9
pāragaṃgāya 'beyond Ganges, the other side of the Ganges' 11
pāricariyā 'serving, waiting on, attendance' 11.1
pāripūri 'fulfillment, completion' 1
pārileyyako 'a name of an elephant' 10
pāroho 'side branch of a banyan tree descending roots from the branch of a banyan tree 10
pāsāṇo 'stone' 10
pāhuneyya 'worthy of hospitality' 5.1
pi 'emphatic particle' 1
piṭaka 'basket' a term used for the three main divisions of the Pāli canon 7
piṭakasampadāna 'piṭaka tradition, authority of the piṭakas' 7
piṇḍāya 'for alms (begging)' (dative of piṇḍo) 9.1
piṇḍo 'a lump of food, alms given as food' 8.1
pitā 'father' Compound stem pitu 9.1
piya 'dear' 12
piyaṃ 'pleasure, pleasant thing, dear thing, endearment' 4
piyo 'pleasant one, agreeable one dear one' 3.1
pivati 'drinks' 4
pilandhanaṃ 'ornament' 12
pisuna 'calumnious, backbiting, malicious' 11.1
pīṭhasappin 'a cripple' 10
puggalo 'person, individual' 6
pucchati 'questions, asks, ppl. puṭṭha' 8
puññaṃ 'merit, righteousness, meritorious act' 5.1
puṭṭha ppl. of pucchati 10.1
putto 'son, child' 6
puthu 'many, various, individual, diverse, separately' 5
puna 'again' 7
puna ca paraṃ 'furthermore, and again' 11.1
punappunaṃ 'again and again' 7.1
punabbhava 'rebirth' 12.1
pupphaṃ 'flower' 5
pubbaṇhasamayaṃ 'in the forenoon, in the morning' 2
pubbe 'previously, before, earlier, in the past' 6.1
purato 'in front of, before' 11
puratthima 'eastern' 9.1
purisapuggalo 'individual, man' 6
purisâdhamo 'wicked person' 4
purisuttamo 'noble, best person' 4
puriso 'man, male, person' 3
purohito 'the king's head-priest' 10
pūjanīyo 'respect-worthy person' 5
pūjā 'worship, offering' 5
pūjeti 'worship, adore, offer' 9.1
pūtisandeho 'accumulation of putrid matter, mass of corruption' 11
pūreti 'fill' 6
pe signal of repetition (ellipsis) 2
pecca 'having departed, after death' 6
pemaṃ 'love, affection' 4
peseti 'sends' 11
pessiko 'a messenger, a servant' 5
pokkharaṃ 'lotus leaf' 6.1
pothujjanika 'belonging to an ordinary man' 12.1
ponobhavika 'leading to rebirth' 12.1
porohiccaṃ 'office of a family priest' 5
poso 'man, male' 11.1
pharati 'spread, pervade 10

pharusa 'rough, harsh, unkind' 11.1
phalaṃ 'fruit, result, having the result' 6.1
phalati 'splits, breaks open' 11
phāti 'increase, development' 2
phāleti 'rends asunder, splits, cleaves' pres part. phālenta 6
phāsuka 'easy, comfortable' 11
phāsuvihāro 'comfort, ease' 9
phusati 'touches, feels' ; ppl. phuṭṭha 3.1
pheṇaṃ 'foam, froth' 9.1
pheṇûpama ‹phena(ṃ) + upama 9.1
phoṭṭhabbaṃ 'touch, contact' 1.1
badarapandum 'light yellow (fresh) jujube fruit' 8
bandhanaṃ 'bond, fetter; stalk' 8
balaṃ 'strength, power, force' 4
balakāyo 'army' 6
balavant 'great, powerful'; cmpd. stem balava; nom. sg. balavā 11
balikataraṃ 'more, more greatly' 5.1
bahi 'outside, outer, external' 11
bahu 'many' 8.1
bahu(ṃ) 'much, many' 4
bahutara 'many, more' 2
bahula 'much, frequent' 12
bahulīkata 'practiced frequently, exercised, expanded' 3.1
Bārāṇasī (proper name) Benares 10
bālo 'fool, ignorant one, stupid one' 5
bālyaṃ 'folly, idiocy' 9.1
bāhusaccaṃ 'learning, knowledge' 5
bāḷhagilāna 'grievously sick' 11.1
Bimbisāro proper name of a king 6
bilaṃ 'hollow' 10.1
bīraṇaṃ (proper name)the name of a plant 6.1
Buddho 'a Buddha, one who has reached enlightenment' 1
buddha 'enlightened, awakened' 4.1
bodhisatto 'aspirant to Buddhahood, a Buddha in an earlier incarnation' 10.1
byañjanaṃ 'syllable, consonant, sign, mark' 9
byākaroti 'explains, answers,brings to light' 5.1
byāpannacitto 'he whose mind is malevolent' 3
byāpado 'ill will, malevolence, revengefulness' 3
Brahmadatto proper name of a king 10.1
brahmaloko 'Brahma-world' 8.1
brahmā 'Brahma, Supreme God' Instr.sg. brahmunā) 4.1
Gen-Dat brahmuno.
brāhmaṇī pajā 'generation (progeny) of Brahmins 11
brāhmaṇo 'Brahmin'; in Buddhist texts, sometimes 'one who lives a noble life, without regard to caste' 4
brūti 'says, tells, calls, shows, explains' 5
Bhagavant 'fortunate one' (epithet for the Buddha) 5.1
bhaginī 'sister' 12
bhajati 'associates (with)'imper. 2 sg bhajassu 4
bhañjati 'breaks' 10.1
bhaññamāna'being said' 12.1
bhaṇati 'says, speaks' 3
bhaṇḍaṃ 'goods' 10.1
bhaṇḍanajāta 'quarrelsome' 4.1
bhaṇḍanaṃ 'quarrel, quarreling, strife' 4.1
bhattaṃ 'boiled rice, food, meal' 11
bhadante 'sir, sire' a form of address generally used (by monks) in addressing the Buddha 9
bhadde 'dear one, lady', term of address for women 10.1
bhadraṃ 'good, as good' 9
bhadro 'good one, (doer of good)' 9
bhante 'reverend sir, sire, sir, venerable one' 3
bhabba 'competent, able' 2
bhayaṃ 'fear, apprehension' 4
bhavaṃ 'individual, person' 5
bhavataṇhā 'craving for existence/rebirth' 12.1
bhavati 'becomes, exists, is' ger. bhutva/hutvā, third pers. fut. bhavissati 6
bhavatîha 'it is said (in this context)' (‹ bhavati+iha) 7.1
bhavanaṃ 'abode, residence' 11
bhavissati 'will be' (third pers. future of bhavati) 6
bharati 'bears, supports, maintains' 12
bhāgavant 'sharer, participant in' nominative singular bhāgavā 4
bhāginī 'participant, sharer' (feminine) 4
bhājanaṃ 'vessel, utensil' 6
bhājanaṃ 'dividing' 10.1
bhātar 'brother' 12
bhāyati 'fears' 4.1
bharati'bears, supports, maintains' 12
bhariyā'wife' 11.1
bhāvanā 'development' 1

bhāveti 'begets, produces, increases, cultivates develops' ppl. bhāvita 3
bhāvo 'nature, fact, -ness' 10.1
bhāsati 'says, speaks'
pres. part. bhāsamāno 6
bhāsati 'shines forth, is bright';
middle voice bhāsate 4
bhikkhave 'Oh, monks' (vocative plural of bhikkhu) 1
bhikkhavo vocative plural of bhikkhu, alternate for bhikkhave 9
bhikkhu '(Buddhist) monk' 1
bhikkhusaṃgho 'community of Buddhist monks' 6
bhijjati 'breaks, gets broken' 10.1
bhiyyo 'further, more' 8.1
bhiyyobhāvo 'increase, growth'
(from bhiyyo 'greater' + bhavo 'state' 1
bhīru 'coward' 7
bhīruko 'fearful one, coward, one who is shy' 7.1
bhuṃkaroti 'barks' 11
bhuñjati 'enjoys, eats' 5
bhumma 'earthly, terrestial' 12
bhussati 'barks' 11
bhūtaṃ 'living being' 11
bhūmi 'ground, earth' 10.1
bhedo 'breaking, splitting, disunion, decomposition' 7.1
bhesajja(ṃ) 'medicine' 10.1
bho 'friend, sir'(polite form of address) 5
Bhoganagaraṃ 'Bhoga'(city name) 9
bhogavant 'wealthy' 11.1
bhogo 'wealth, possession, enjoyment, item for enjoyment' 2
bhogga 'bent, crooked' 11.1
bhojanaṃ 'meal, nourishment' 4
bhovādin 'a brahmin' (according to the way he is addressed) 5
makkaṭo 'monkey' 10.1
maghavant 'Indra, king of the gods' 5
maṃkubhāvo 'downcast-ness, discontent, confusion, moral weakness' 10
maṃkubhūta 'discontented, troubled, confused' 8.1
maṃgalaṃ 'blessing, good omen, auspices, celebration, festival' 5
maccarin 'greedy one, selfish and avaricious one, stingy one' 6
maccu 'death, the god of death' 4.1
maccurājo 'king of death' 9.1
macco 'mortal, human being' 2
macchara 'avarice, envy' 12
majjaṃ 'intoxicating drink, liquor' 5
majjhanhikasamayaṃ 'during midday' 2
majjhima 'central, middle' 2
majjho 'middle, midst' 3.1
maññati 'think, deem, conceive, consider (as)' 2
maññati 'think know' 9.1
maṭṭa 'polished, burnished' 12
maṇikaṃ 'a big jar, pot' 6
maṇḍalamāla 'pavilion, a circular hall with a. peaked roof' 6
mata 'dead, one who is dead' 4.1
mattisambhava 'born of a mother' 5
matta 'about, only' 8.1
mattaññu 'knowing the right measure, moderate' 4.1
mattā 'measure, quantity, right measure' 4.1
matthaka 'top, head, surface' 10.1
madhu 'honey' 10.1
madhu paṭalo 'honeycomb' 10.1
manas 'mind'; nom. sg. mano
instr. sg. manasā 3.1
manasikaroti 'reflect upon, consider, bear in mind, recognize' 9
manasikāro 'attention, pondering, fixed thought' 6.1
manāpa 'agreeable, pleasing, pleasant, charming' 8.1
manujo 'man' 6.1
manussa paṭilābho 'being born as a human, attaining human status' 2
manussabhūta 'human (being), (one) in human form' 4.1
manusso 'man, human being' 2
manorama 'delightful' 12
mantitaṃ '(that which is) given as counsel, secret talk' 7.1
mando 'idiot, fool, stupid one' 7.1
maraṇaṃ 'death' 3.1
marīcidhamma 'nature of a mirage' 9.1
mala 'impurity, stain' 12
mallikā 'jasmine' 12
mahato 'great, big' (dative singular of mahanta, 'great, big') 1
mahant 'big, great'
mahanto 'great, big (one)' 6
mahagghaso '(one who) eats much, greedy, gluttonous' 7.1
mahant 'big, great' 10
mahallaka 'old person' 11.1
mahā 'big, great, large, huge';
(nom. sg. of mahant) 7.1
Mahāli proper name of a person 8.1
mahāmatto 'chief minister' 5.1

mahāyañño 'great sacrifice, big almsgiving' 6
mahārājo 'great king' 3
Mahāvana name of a park 8.1
mā prohibitive particle. 'do not' 7
Māgadha 'of the Magadha (country)' 6
māṇavako 'youth, young man' (especially a young Brahmin)' 6
mātango 'elephant, type of elephant' 7
mātar 'mother' 12
mātūgamo 'woman' 11.1
māno 'pride, conceit' 12
mānasa 'of the mind' 10.1
mānasaṃ 'intention, purpose of mind, mental action' 6.1
mānânusaya 'predisposition or bad tendency to pride 12
mānusa 'human' 4
māneti 'respect, honor' 9.1
māyāvin 'deceitful person' 12
māro 'Māra, death personified, death, god of death, tempter' 4.1
māluvā 'kind of creeping vine' 6.1
micchā' 'wrong, incorrect' 4
micchâcāro 'wrong behavior' 6
micchādiṭṭhi 'wrong views' ?
micchādiṭṭhiko 'he who has incorrect views' 1
mitto 'friend' 4
middhī 'slothful (one)' 7.1
mīyati 'dies' 4.1
mukhaṃ 'mouth, face' 10
mukhara 'garrulous, noisy, scurrilous' 4.1
mukharatā 'talkativeness, garrulousness' 10
muñcati 'releases, is relieved' 11
muṇḍako 'a shaven-headed one' 8.1
muta 'thought, what is thought, that which is thought' 7
mutta 'freed' 4
muttaṃ 'urine' 11.1
mutto 'one who is released, one who is freed' 3
musā 'falsely' 3
musāvādo 'lying, falsehood' 6
muhutta 'moment' 12.1
mūlaṃ 'root, origin' 7
mūlaṃ 'price, capital, money' 10.1
mūḷha 'gone astray, confused, foolish, ignorant (one)' 12
megho 'rain cloud' 6
methuna 'sexual' 4
methuna dhammo 'sexual intercourse' 4
medhāvin 'wise, wise one' 8
medhāvinī 'a wise woman' 11.1
merayaṃ 'fermented liquor' 4
modati 'rejoice, be happy' 10
moho 'delusion, ignorance, confusion' 2.2
yaṃ 'that, since, for, when (relative)' 5.1
yaṃ yadeva 'whichever' 8.1
yakkho 'demon, devil' 11
yañño 'sacrifice, almsgiving' 6
yato 'since, whence, because' 9.1
yathayidaṃ 'that is to say, namely, to wit'
(< yathā 'thus'+idaṃ 'this') 1
yathā 'just as, like' 3
yathākathaṃpana 'then how, how so then' 9.1
yathābhūtam 'as things really are' 12.1
yattha 'wherever' 8
yattha kāmanipātin 'that which falls/clings wherever it wishes'.1 8
yadā 'when' 3.1
yadidaṃ 'that is (to say), namely' 6
yannūna 'well, now' 'rather' 6.1
yamaloko 'world of Yama' 9.1
yavo 'barley, corn (in general); 6.1
yaso (yasas) 'fame, repute, glory' 6
yācita 'being requested, being begged for' 7
yājako 'one who sacrifices, a priest' 5
yāti 'go, proceed, go on' 9
yāva 'until, up to, as long as' 9
yāvajīvam 'as long as one lives' 8
yāvañc'idaṃ 'that is, namely, as far as, in so far as (yāvam + ca + idaṃ; cf. yadidam) 8
yutta 'proper, befitting, to have a right to' 10.1
yūpo 'a sacrificial post' 8
yo 'who' (relative pronoun) 3
yogâvacaro 'one who has applied himself to spiritual exercises (yoga) see glossary 6.1
yogo 'application' 7.1
yojanaṃ 'a measure of space, a distance of about 4 to 8 miles' 5
yodhâjīvo 'a warrior, a soldier' 5
yonija 'born of a womb' 5
yonisomanisikāro 'proper attention, correct reflection' 8.1
rakkhati 'guards, protects, takes care of, watches over'; ppl. rakkhita 7
rajataṃ 'silver', any non-gold coin' 4
rajjaṃ 'kingdom, realm' 11.1
rajjaṃkaroti 'to reign' 10.1
rañño genitive sg. of rājan 11.1

raṭṭhaṃ 'reign, kingdom, empire, country' 5
rata 'delighting in, intent on, devoted to' 4.1
rati 'love, attachment' 4
ratti 'night' 5
ratta 'infatuated, impassioned' 7.1
raso 'taste, savor' 3.1
rahado 'lake' 4
rahogata 'being alone, being in private' 6.1
rāgaggi 'fire of passion' 7.1
rāgo 'passion, exitement, lust, attachment' 4
Rājagaha place name 9.1
rājan 'king' genitive sg. rañño 1.1
rājaputto 'prince' 5.1
rukkhadevatā 'tutelary deity of a tree' 10.1
rukkho 'tree' 8.1
rucira 'agreeable, attractive' 5
rujati 'pains, aches' 10.1
rūpaṃ '(visual) form, object of visual perception' 1.1
rūpavant 'beautiful' 11.1
rogo 'disease, sickness' 11
rodati 'weep, lament, cry' 8
roseti 'irritates, annoys' 12
lakkhaṇaṃ 'feature, mark, characteristic, discriminating mark' 3.1
X lakkhaṇaṃ 'characterized or marked by X' 3.1
labhati 'gets, receives; get a chance to'; ppl laddha; inf. laddhuṃ; fut. pass. part. laddhabba 2
laya 'brief measure of time' 12.1
lahu 'flightly, light' 8
lahuṭṭhānaṃ 'lightness of body, bodily vigor, good health' 9
lābho 'profit, gain' 10.1
lāvako 'cutter, reaper' 6.1
Licchavi a clan name 8.1
luddha 'greedy, covetous' 3
lunāti 'cut, reap' 6.1
loko 'world, universe, people in general' 4
lobho 'avarice, greed, covetousness' 2.2
lolatā 'nature of being fond of or addicted to, longing, greed' 7.1
vagga 'dissociated, dissentious' 4.1
vacanaṃ 'utterance, word, saying, speech' 9
vaco 'speech, word'; compounding stem vacī (also appears as vacā)'6, 6.1
vacchagotta 'of Vaccha lineage' in reference to a Brahmin referred to by surname 8
vacchataro 'a weaned calf, a bullock' 8
vacchatari 'a weaned female calf, a heifer' 8
vañceti 'to cheat' 10.1
vaṭarukkho 'a banyan tree' 10
vaḍḍhati 'grows, increases (something), cultivates' 6.1
vaṇo 'wound' 9
vaṇṇaṃ bhāsati 'speaks well of, praises' 12
vaṇṇavanta 'colorful' 5
vaṇṇo 'color, complexion, outward appearance' 4
vata' surely, certainly' 12.1
vatthaṃ 'cloth, clothes' 9.1
vadati 'says, speaks' ppl. vutta 3
vadeti 'says, speaks' 6
vadho 'killing, destruction' 6.1
vanaṃ 'forest' 6.1
vanasaṇḍo(aṃ) 'jungle, forest' 10
vandati 'bow down at, salute' 10
vayappatta 'come of age' 10.1
varagāmo 'hereditary village, a village given as a gift' 10
varāho 'pig' 7
valita 'wrinkled' 11.1
vasati 'lives, abides, dwells' 11
vasanaṭṭhānaṃ 'place of residence' 11
vasalako 'outcaste, wretch' 12
vasalo 'outcaste, a person of low birth' 12
vasundharā 'earth' 6
vasena 'because of, on account of' 7.1
vassasatika 'hundred years old' 11.1
vā 'or' 1
vācā 'word, speech' 5
vāṇijo 'a merchant' 5
vāṇijjā 'trade, merchandise' 10.1
vāto 'wind' 4
vānaro 'monkey' 6.1
vāma 'left (side)' 6.1
vāyamati 'strive, endeavor, struggle' 1
vāyāma 'effort' 12.1
vāriyamāna 'being prevented, obstructed' 11
vāro 'time, occasion' 11
Vāseṭṭho a proper name 5
vāḷamigo 'a wild beast' 10
vigata 'gone away, ceased, bereft of' 12
vikkiṇṇavāca 'of loose talk' 4.1
vicarati 'move about' 10

vijayo 'victory, triumph' 9.1
vijāyati 'give birth, bring forth' 11.1
vijātā 'a woman who has given birth' 1.1
vijānanaṃ 'act of cognizing, discriminating' 3.1
vijānanta 'knowing clearly, understanding'
pres. part of vijānāti ' 5
vijānāti 'perceives, understands with discrimination, discriminates' 3.1
vijeti 'win, conquer'; ppl. vijita 9.1
vijjati 'appears, seems' 5
vijjā 'discriminative knowledge, insight, wisdom, higher knowledge' 3.1
vijjāgato 'one who has attained wisdom (vijjā)' 3.1
vijjumālin 'wearing a garland or row of lightning' (epithet for a cloud) 6.1
vijjobhāsa 'light of insight' (<vijjā + obhāsa) 7.1 .
viññāya 'having perceived or known' 5.1
viññāṇaṃ 'consciousness' 3.1
viññāta 'known, what is known, that which is known, what is perceived/ recognized/ understood' 7
viññū 'intelligent, wise(one)' 3
viññugarahita 'despised by the wise 3
vittaṃ 'property, wealth' 11
vidaṃseti 'shows, make appear' 7.1
viditvā 'know, realize' (gerund of vindati) 9.1
vidhameti 'destroy, ruin, do away with, dispel' 7.1
vinayakammaṃ 'ethical activity, activities pertaining to monastic discipline' 4.1
vinayo 'discipline, code of ethics', often 'monastic discipline' (referring to a large collection of rules governing the monastic life of the bhikkhus). See glossary 9
vinā 'without' 11.1
vinicchita 'decided, settled' 10.1
vinipāto 'great ruin, a place of suffering, state of punishment' 7.1
vinīlaka 'bluish black, discolored' 11.1
vindati 'knows, realizes' ger.
viditvā/vinditvā 9.1
vipanna 'lost, gone wrong' 12
vipannadiṭṭhī' one with wrong views, heretic' 12
vipariṇāma 'change' 5.1
vipassati 'sees clearly, insightfully, have spiritual insight' 4
Vipassi name of a Buddha previous to Gotama 9.1
X-vipāka 'having X as fruit or result' 2.2
vipāko 'result, fruition' 2.2
vipubbaka 'full of corruption and matter festering' 11.1
vippatimutto 'one who is freed' 4
vippayogo 'separation, dissociation' 3.1
vippasīdati 'is serene, tranquil, becomes calm' 4
vippasanna 'tranquil, calm, purified, clear, clean, bright, happy, pure, sinless' 8
vibbhantacitta 'with wandering or confused mind' 4.1
vibhavataṇhā 'craving for extinction' 12.1
vimala 'clear, clean, bright' 6.
vimuccati 'be freed' 6.1
viya 'like, as'(particle of comparison) 6.1
viraja 'free from defilement' 12.1
virati 'complete abstention' 5
viravati 'shouts, screams' 10.1
virāgo 'detachment' 9.1
viriyaṃ 'effort, exertion, energy' 1
viriyārambho 'taking effort' 1.1
virocati 'shines forth, is brilliant' 4
vilūna 'cut off (of hair), scanty' 11.1
vivaro(aṃ) 'cavity, hole, hollow' 11
vivaṭa #ppl of vivarati 10
vivaṭamatta 'as soon as it was open' (vivaṭa + matta) 10
vivadati 'disputes,quarrels'; pres. part. vivadamāna 4.1
vivarati 'open, disclose'; ppl. vivaṭa 7.1
vivādāpanna 'disputing, quarreling' 4.1
vivādo 'dispute, quarrel, contention' 4.1
vivāho 'marriage, wedding, carrying or sending away of a bride' 6
vivitta 'secluded' 12
visaṃ 'poison' 9
visaṃyutto 'he who is detached' 5
visattikā 'clinging to, adhering to. lust, desire' 6.1
visama 'unequal, disharmonious' 4.1
visārado 'self-possessed, confident, knowing how to conduct oneself, wise' 8.1
visuddhi 'purity' 10
visesato 'specially, particularly' 4.1
vihaññati 'suffer' 10
viharati 'live, reside, abide, lead a life' 3.1
vihiṃsati 'injures, hurts, oppresses' 6
vihesā 'vexation' 9.1
vīṇā 'lute' 6.1

vītamala 'stainless' 12.1
vīmaṃsati 'tests, considers' 11
vuccati 'is called, is said'
pres. part. vuccamāna 4.1
vuṭṭhahati 'rise, get up'
(alternate form uṭṭhahati, uṭṭhati) 9.1
vuṭṭāpiyamāna <pres part. of uṭṭhāpeti 'lifts', (alternate form uṭṭāpiyamāna) 11.1
vuṭṭhi 'rain' (feminine.) 10
vutta 'said, spoken' (ppl. of vadati) 7.1
ve 'verily, indeed, truly' 5
vejjekammaṃ 'medical practice' 10.1
vejjo 'doctor, physician' 10.1
vetanaṃ 'wages, hire' 12
vedanā 'feeling, sensation' 5.1
Venāgapura city name 8
Venāgapurika 'of Venagapura' 8
vepullaṃ 'fullness, abundance' 1
veyyākaraṇa 'explanation, exposition' 12.1
veraṃ 'enmity, ill-will' 2
veramaṇī 'abstinence' 6
velā 'time' 11
Vesālī place name 8.1
vehāso 'sky, air' 11
Veḷuvana place name 9.1
vohāro 'trade, business, merchandise' 5
vyākaroti 'explains, clarifies, answers' 11
vyādhi 'sickness, malady, illness, disease' 3.1
sa- 'one's own' 2
saṃkappa 'intention, purpose' 12.1
saṃkamati 'cross esover, transmigrates' ppl. saṃkanta 3
saṃkamanto 'one who crosses over, one who transmigrates' 3
saṃkampati 'tremble' 12.1
saṃkhāro 'essential condition, a thing conditioned, mental coefficient' (normally in plural saṃkhārā) 5.1
saṃkhittena 'in short, in brief' 3.1
saṃgaho 'assistance, protection, kind disposition' 5
saṃgâtigo 'he who has gone beyond (overcome) attachment' 5
saṃgho 'community, association, esp. community of Buddhist monks' 1
saṃyamo 'control, restraint' 5
saṃyojanaṃ 'bond, fetter' (that binds one to the wheel of transmigration) 5
saṃvattati 'lead to, be conducive to' 1
saṃvāso'association, co-residency, intimacy' 12
saṃvijjati 'seems to be, appears, exists' 6.1
saṃvidahati 'arranges, applies, prepares, provides' 10.1
saṃvuta 'controlled, restrained' 1
saṃvesiyati 'puts to bed'; pres. part. saṃvesiyamāna 11.1
saṃsāro 'life cycle' 5
saṃhita 'possessed of consisting in' 12.1
saka 'one's own' 11.1
sakaṭo (aṃ) 'cart' 10.1
sakiñcano 'one who has something, one who is full of worldly attachment' 5
sakuṇo 'bird' 8.1
sakúnto 'bird' 4
sakubbanto 'doer, one who practices' 5
sakkaccaṃ 'properly, well, carefully, thoroughly' 2
sakkaroti 'respect' 9.1
sakkā '(it is) possible' 3
sakkoti 'be able, can'; fut. sakkhissati 10
sakkharā 'pebble' 10
Sakya family name (lineage of the Buddha) 6
saggo 'heaven, celestial world, happy place' 4
sace 'if' 7
saccaṃ 'truth' 3.1
sacchikaroti 'realizes for oneself, experiences'; ppl. sacchikata fut. pass. part. sacchikātabba 12.1
sañjānāti 'know, recognize, be aware of' 9
saññā 'perception, recognition, signal, indication' 5.1
saññāṇaṃ 'token, mark, sign' 11
saṭho 'fraudulent one' 12
sata 'mindful' 5.1
sataṃ 'hundred'; compounding stem satu 6
satakkaku 'epithet for a cloud' 6
sati kāyagatā 'mindfulness relating to the body' 12
satīmant 'mindful one', nom. sg. satīmā) 7
sato 'being, existing' (genitive sg. of sant) 11.1
satta 'sunk' 7
satto 'being, living being, creature' 2
satthar 'teacher, the Buddha' 9
sadā 'always, forever' 5
sadevaka 'together with (that) of the gods' 9.1
saddo 'sound, word' 1.1
saddha 'determined, faithful, believing' 2.2
saddhā 'determination' 11

saddhiṃcaro 'constant companion, one who accompanies' 7
saddhammo 'true doctrine' 1.1
saddhiṃ 'with' 6
sanantana 'eternal, old, ancient' 2
sanikaṃ 'slowly, gradually' 10.1
santuṭṭhi 'contentment' 5
sant 'good person' nom. sg. santo 6
sant(a) 'existing, being' (pres.part. of atthi), genitive sg. sato 5.1
santa 'tranquil, calm' 9.1
santikaṃ 'the vicinity, near'; loc. santike 'to (the vicinity), abl. santikā 'from the vicinity (of)'.2 7
santo 'fatigued one, he who is tired' 5
santo nom. sg of sant 'good person'.
sandasseti 'compares with, shows (against)'; pres. part. sandassiyamāna 'that which something is compared with' 9
sandiṭṭhika 'visible, actual, of advantage to this life, empirical 5.1
sandissati 'tally with, agree with' 9
sandosaṃ 'defilement, pollution' 6.1
sapadānaṃ 'in order, without interruption, without skipping (in alms-begging of a Buddhist monk)' 8.1
sappo 'a serpent' 10.1
saphala 'fruitful' 5
sabaṭṭhaka 'a gift comprising eight of everything given' 10
sabba 'all' 2
sabbena sabbaṃ 'completely, entirely altogether' 8
sama 'even, equal, harmonious' 4.1
samakaṃ 'equally, (at the same time)' 8.1
samagga 'being in unity' 4.1
samaññāta 'designated, notorious' 12
samaṇako 'ascetic, recluse' (may have a connotation of contempt) 8.1
samaṇo 'recluse, mendicant' 4
samatā 'equality, evenness, normal state' 6.1
samativijjhati 'pierce through' 10
samatta 'completed, grasped, accepted, accomplished' 3.1
samatho 'calming down, cessation' 9.1
samanupassati 'sees, perceives correctly' 1
samannāgata 'endowed with, possessed of' 2
samayo 'time, period, season' 6.1
sama-sama 'equal' 10.1
samādapeti 'encourages, incites, rouses' 3.1
samādinna 'accepted' 3.1
samādiyati 'takes upon or with oneself'; ppl. samādinna 6
samādhi 'concentration' 12.1
samādhinimittaṃ 'object of meditation, object of concentration' 2
samāno 'being, existing' 11.1
samāhita 'collected, composed, settled, attentive' 4.1
samiñjati 'is moved, shaken' 4
samīrati 'is moved, blown' 4
samudayo 'origin, rise' 2.2
X samudayo 'having X as origin, arising from X 2.2
samuddo 'ocean, sea' 11
sameti 'correspond, agree' 8
sampakampati 'trembles, is shaken' 12.1
sampajāna 'thoughtful, mindful, attentive, deliberate' 4.1
sampajjalita 'ablaze, in flames' 5.1
sampati 'now, right now, just now' 8
sampayogo 'association' 3.1
samparāyika 'belonging to the next world' 8.1
samparivattasāyī 'one who sleeps turning to and fro' 7.1
sampavedhati 'shake violently' 12.1
sampha 'frivolous, foolish' 11.1
sambahula 'many' 10.1
sambodha 'highest wisdom' 12.1
sambodhi 'enlightenment' 12.1
samma 'friend', a term of address for a friend 10.1
sammajjati 'sweeps' 10
sammati 'be pacified, cease' 2
sammatta 'intoxicated (by/with), overpowered by' 6.1
sammada 'drowsiness, intoxication' 6.1
sammappaññā 'right knowledge, true wisdom' 7.1
sammappajāno 'fully comprehending one' 4
sammā 'properly, rightly' 12.1
sammādiṭṭhi 'right understanding' 11.1
sammādiṭṭhiko 'he who has right views' 1
sammādiṭṭhin 'he who has right understanding' 11.1
sammāsambuddho 'perfectly enlightened one, a universal Buddha' 6
sammukho 'face to face, in presence' 9
sammūḷha 'confused, confounded, stupid' 2

sammodati 'exchange friendly greetings, rejoices(together), delights' past sammodi 6.1
sammodamāna 'in agreement, on friendly terms, rejoicing together' 4.1
sammoso 'bewilderment, confusion' 1
sayanâsana 'bed and seat, lodging' 12
saraṇaṃ 'refuge, protection' 1
saravatī 'having resonance or melodiousness' 6.1
sarīram 'body' 10
saro 'voice, sound' 10.1
sallakkheti 'observes, considers' 11
sallapati 'talk, speak' 10
savaṇaṃ 'hearing, listening to' 2
sasuro father-in-law; acc. sasuṃ 12
sassamaṇa-brāhmaṇa'including religious teachers and brahmins' 12
sahate 'conquers, overcomes' 6.1
sahāyo 'friend' 7
sahitaṃ 'texts, scriptures taken as a whole' 4
sākacchā 'conversation, discussion' 5
sākhā 'branch' 10.1
sāṇi 'curtain' 10
sādiyati 'appropriate, take on oneself, enjoy' 4
sādutara 'sweeter, more pleasant' 11
sādhu 'good' 8
sādhuka 'good or righteous (one) 10.1
sādhukaṃ 'well' (adverb), thoroughly' 9
sādhuvihāridhīro 'one who is of noble behavior, one who is steadfast' 7
sāpateyyaṃ 'wealth' 12
sāmaṃ 'of oneself, by oneself' 6
sāmaññaṃ 'state of an ascetic or monk, the holy life 4
sāmi 'lord, sir, husband' 10.1
sâmisa 'characterized by or having āmisaṃ' 4.1
sāyaṃhasamayaṃ 'in the evening' 2
sāyati 'tastes, eats' 3.1
sāra 'essence, heart of a tree' 12
sārada 'autumnal, fresh' 8
sālittakasippaṃ 'art of slinging stones' 10
sāvako 'disciple' 6
sāvajja 'blameable, faulty' 2.2
Sāvatthi place name 8.1
sāveti 'announce, tell, declare' 8
sāsanaṃ 'teaching, message, (Buddhist) order' 9
sâsava 'with, having, or characterized by āsavo 4.1
sāḷikapotako 'a young bird (Mynah bird)' 10.1
Sāḷho proper name 3
siṃghāṭako(-aṃ) 'cross, cross-roads' 3.1
sikkhā 'study, training, discipline' 6.1
sikkhāpadaṃ'precept, rule, instruction' 6
Sigālaka proper name 9.1
sineho 'affection' 11
sippaṃ 'craft,science, art, technical knowledge' 5
sippiko 'artisan, craftsman' 5
siraṃ 'head accusative siraṃ or siro' 11.1
sīghataraṃ 'faster, sooner' 8.1
sīlavatī 'virtuous woman' 11.1
sīlavant 'virtuous' 11.1
sīlasampanno 'one endowed with virtue, one who practices morality, virtuous one' 6
Sīvako proper name 5.1
sīsaṃ 'head' 10.1
Sīho a proper name 8.1
su 'indeed, verily' 11
sukhaṃ 'happiness, comfort, ease, well-being' 2.2
sukhakāma 'desirous of happiness' 11
sukhâvaha 'bringing happiness' 8
sugati 'happiness, bliss, happy fate, happy state, a realm of bliss' 8.1
sugatin 'righteous one' 9
suggati =sugati 10
sucaritaṃ 'good behavior' 7
suciṇṇa 'well-practiced' 11
succhanna 'well-thatched, well-covered' 10
suṇāti 'hears, listens'; ppl. suta; ger. sutvā(na) 3.1
suta 'heard, that which is heard' (ppl. of sunāti) 7
suttaṃ discursive part of Buddhist scripture (Sanskrit sūtra) 9
sutvāna 'having heard, having listened to' (gerund of suṇāti) 4
sudaṃ 'indeed' 12
sududdasa 'exceedingly difficult to see/grasp' 8
sudesita 'well-proclaimed' 9.1
sunakho 'dog' 11
sunipuṇa 'very subtle' 8
Suppavāsā proper name (feminine); vocative Suppavāse 4
subha 'pleasant, good' 12
subhariyā 'good wife' 11.1
subhāvita 'well-developed,cultivated,trained' 10
subhāsita 'well spoken' 2

subhāsitadubbhāsitaṃ 'things well and badly spoken, things proper to say and not proper to say' 2
sumana 'of a happy mind, of a pleased mind' 5.1
surā 'liquor' 4
suvaṇṇa 'gold' 12
suvaṇṇakāra 'goldsmith' 12
suvimuttacitto 'one with a well-freed mind' 4
susamāhita 'well-restrained, well composed' 12
susikkhita 'well-trained, well-practiced' 5
susirarukkho 'a tree having a hollow' 10.1
suhajjo 'friend, good-hearted one' 6.1
sūpa 'soup, broth, curry' 8
sūro (-a) 'valiant, courageous' 11.1
sekho 'one still in training, a learner' 9.1
seṭṭha 'noble, best, excellent' 11
seṭṭhatā 'excellence, foremost, place' 5
seti 'sleeps, dwells, lives' 6.1
senāpati 'a general' 8.1
Seniya a clan name (literally: 'belonging to the army') 6
semāna 'lying (down)' (pres. part. of seti 'lies') 11.1
seyyathā 'just as, just like, as if' 8
seyyathāpi 'just as (if)' (seyyathā + pi) 12
seyyo 'better' 11.1
selo 'rock' 4
Selo proper name 6
sevati 'serve, practice, take upon oneself' fut. pass. part. sevitabba 7.1
sevanā 'association' 5
so 'he, that one (male)' (nominative singular of sa) 3
soko 'sorrow, grief' 4
socati 'grieve' 10
Soṇo proper name 6.1
soṇḍā 'elephant's trunk' 10
soṇḍiko 'drunkard' 7.1
soṇḍī 'a natural tank in a rock' 10
soṇḍo 'one who is addicted to drink, a drunkard' 7.1
sotaṃ 'ear' 3.1
sodheti 'to clear, to clean' 10
sovacassatā 'gentleness, obedience' 5
svātanāya 'for tomorrow, for the following day' 6
hatthaṃ 'hand, trunk of an elephant' 10
hatthi 'elephant' 10
hatthirājā 'elephant-king, chief of elephants' 10
hatthirūpakaṃ 'elephant's image or picture' 10
hattho 'hand' 6.1
hadayaṃ 'mind, heart' 11
hanati 'kills, strikes' (also hanti) 3
handa 'well then, now' 11.1
harati 'take away, remove'
have 'indeed, certainly, surely' 11
hiṃsati 'oppresses' 11
hitaṃ 'benefit, welfare, good' 3
hitvā ger. of jahāti 7
hirimā 'modest' (masculine nominative singular of hirimant) 2.2
hirī 'sense of shame, bashfulness' 6.1
hīna 'low, base' 6.1
hīnāya āvattati literally 'turn to the lower'. hence:'give up orders, return to secular life' 6.1
hutvā ger. of hoti / bhavati 10.1
hurāhuraṃ 'from existence to existence' 6.1
heṭṭhā 'below, beneath, underneath' 10
heṭṭhima 'lower, below' 9.1
hetu 'basis, cause' 7.1
X hetu 'for the sake of X for the purpose of X by reason of X' 7.1
hoti 'is, becomes' ger. hutvā 3
huraṃ 'in the other world, in another existence' 4

GRAMMATICAL INDEX

This grammatical index has two sections. The first has entries according to the Pāli forms, and is arranged by the Pāi alphabetical order. It includes affixes, particles, clitics, etc. It also includes the forms that were used to illustrate classes of nouns and verbs, since that may assist the student in accessing those classes.

The second part of the index is according to English entries for tenses, cases, etc. and is thus in English alphabetical order.

GRAMMATICAL INDEX SECTION 1: PALI ENTRIES:

-a stem nouns (masculine and neuter) I, 1.21
a- negative I,6.2
aggi 'fire' (masculine -i stem)
añña '(an)other' VI,13
aṭṭhānaṃ and ṭhānaṃ V,7
attan 'self' (masculine -an stem) VI,1, (as reflexive) VIII,3
atthi 'is ,exists' III,2.1, optative VII,1
attho 'purpose' compounds VIII,8
addasā (root aorist)VI,7.1
-an stems(masculine) VI,1
-ant present participle III,6.12, V.3
-anīya future passive participle VII,2.1
ayaṃ 'this,that' (masc. and fem.) II,2.4, IV,1
-ar stem nouns IX,1
arahant (forms) V,4
avoca (past of vac- 'say, speak') VI,8, VIII,4
-as stem nouns VI,5
asu 'a certain' XII,2
assosi past tense (-s aorist) IX,2.1
ahaṃ 'I' V,1.1
-ā stem nouns (feminine) II,1
ādi,ādīni 'etcetera' X,9
-āpe- causatives X, 6.3
āha, āhu VI,11
-iṭṭha superlative XI,7
-itabba future passive participle VII,2.1
-i stem nouns (masculine) VIII,1
-i stem nouns (feminine) I,1.23
(i)ti I,3.3
- in stem nouns VI,2
ima- 'this, that' II,2.14, IV,1
imaṃ 'this,that' (neuter) II,2.4, IV,1
-iya comparative XI,7
iva 'like, as' IV,10
-iss- future tense IX,3,
-iss- conditional XI,2.1
-ī stem nouns (feminine) I,1.23
upasamkami (-is aorist) VI,7.2
ubho 'both' XII,1
-u stem nouns (feminine) VI,6
-e- stem verbs III,7, VIII,6; (-e- causatives) X,6.1
-e- optative IV,6
eka 'one' IV,7.2
etaṃ 'this' II,2.12
etamatthaṃ(vadāmi) III,13
eti 'comes' VII,5
-eyy- optative III,4
eva emphatic III,10.23
eso ahaṃ XII,7
-o- stem verbs III,7
ka interrogative pronoun III,1
kaṭapuñño compound type X,11
katama interrogative II,3
kayirā(tha) (optative of karoti) IX,7
karaṇīya (future participle of karoti) VII,2; X,5
karoti 'does' (-o stem verb) III,7.2
kā feminine interr. pronoun III,1
kāma 'desiring' VIII,9
kiṃ neuter interr. pronoun III,1
ko masculine interr. pronoun III,1
kho emphatic III,10.21
gacchati past tense IX,2.2
go 'cow' IV,2
ca 'and' I,3.2

cakkhu 'eye' (neuter -u stem) II, 1.3
catu 'four' IV,7.3
ci indefinite III,10.1
ce 'if' IV,11
cetas 'thought' (-as stem) VI,5
jaccā (case forms of jāti) XII,3
ṭhānaṃ and aṭṭhānaṃ V,7
-ṭhānaṃ compounds VI, 15
-(i)ṭṭha superlative XI,7
-ta past participle V,5.11
-tabba future passive participle VII,2.1
taṃ third pers. pronoun II,2.11
-tama superlative XI,7
-tara comparative XI,7
ti 'three' IV,7.3
tuṃ infinitive II.4
tumhe 'you (plural)' V,1.2
te 2nd pers. sing.. enclitic V,1,3
-to ablative ending III,15
tvaṃ 'you (singular)' V,1.2
-tvā(na) gerunds IV,3.11; X,3
dis- /passati 'sees' II,4.13
dvi 'two' IV,7.4
dhamma (masculine -a stem) I,1.21
-dhamma compounds VI, 15
dhātu 'element'(-u stem) VI,6
na- negatives I,6.1
-na past participle V, 5.12
natthi 'is not' III,3
nadī (feminine -ī stem) I,1.23
nivesaye (alternate -e verb endings) VIII,6
-nīya future passive participle VII,2.1; X,5
nu interrogative emphatic III,10.24
no negative VII,4
no first pers pl. enclitic V,1,3
pañca 'five' IV,7.5
para 'other' IV,8; VI,13
parivuta VI,14
passati /dis- 'sees' II,4.13
pitar 'father' (relationship -ar nouns) IX,1.12
-pe- causatives X, 6.2
pe(yyālaṃ) discourse substitute II,8
brahman 'god Brahma' VI,1,2
bhavati 'be, become' III,2.3; future forms IX,3.1 (see also hoti)
bhavant- address form VI,4; VIII,5
bhavissati with past part. XI,5.2, with future passive part. XI,5.3
bhāveti 'increases, develops (-e stem verb) III,7.1
bhikkhu '(Buddhist) monk' (masculine -u stems) II,1.2
bhoto < bhavant ' (vocative) VI 4
maccarin 'miser' (-in stem noun) VI,2
mahant 'great' VI, 3
manas (-as stem) VI,5
-mant nouns and adjectives V.2
mā negative VII,4; prohibitive XI,3
mātar 'mother' (relationship -ar nouns) IX,1.12
-māna present participle IV,4 with passive verbs IX,5
me first pers sing. enclitic V,1,3
-ya gerunds IV,3.12
-ya optatives VII,1
ya/yaṃ (relative pronoun) II.2.13
yadi 'if' III,9.1
yasmā III,12
yā (feminine relative pronoun) II,2.13
yāti 'goes' IX,6
yena....tena VI,10
yo (masculine relative pronoun) II,2.13
yohi koci 'whosoever' V,6
-yya comparative XI,7
ratti (feminine -i stem) I,1.23
rājan 'king' (forms) VI,1.3
rūpa (neuter -a stem) I,1.22
labhati 'obtains, receives' (-a stem verb) I,2
labbhati 'comes about, exists' XI,6
vac- 'say' (past) VI,8; VIII,4
vatti 'speaks'(past) VIII,4
-vant nouns and adjectives V.2
vā 'or' I,3.2, agreement of forms with XII,6
vo 2nd pers. pl.. enclitic V,1,3

sa/taṃ 'third pers. pronoun' II,2.11
sa- reflexive prefix II,9
sakkā ' is possible' III,11
sace 'if' VII,6
sati (locative absolute) X,2
satthar 'teacher' (agent -tar nouns) IX,1.11
saddhiṃ VI,14
sante (locative absolute) X,2
santo 'virtuous one' VI,3
sabba 'all' IV,8
sā feminine pronoun II,2.1
sālā 'hall' (feminine -ā stem)
silavant (-vant adjective/noun) V,2
so masculine pronoun II,2.1
hā- (root) 'decrease' VII,8
hi emphatic III,10.22
hoti 'is, becomes' III,2.2,
with past participle XII,5.1
hotu 3 Sg. imperative VIII,2

GRAMMATICAL INDEX SECTION 2: ENGLISH ENTRIES

ABLATIVE IN -to III,15
ACCUSATIVE I,142
destination I,8
manner III,8
time II,10
ADDRESS FORM bhavant VI,4; VIII,5
ADJECTIVES IN -vant and -mant V,2
AGENT NOUNS IX,1.11
AGREEMENT
of adjectives I,7
with vā 'or' phrases XII,6
CASES I,14
use of cases VIII,7
(see also under specific cases)
CAUSATIVE VERBS X,6
CLITICS I,3
COMPARATIVE AND SUPERLATIVE XI,7
COMPOUNDS I,10 ;II,12 ;III,14
with-gata II,11.2
co-ordinate II,11.1
kaṭapuñño type X,11
CONDITIONAL XI,2
CONJOINING IN SERIES I,9
CORRELATIVE CONSTRUCTION II,6
DISCOURSE SUBSTITUTE
pe(yyālaṃ) II,8
EMPHATICS hi, kho, eva, nu III,10.2
ENCLITIC PRONOUN FORMS V,1.3
EQUATIONAL SENTENCES II,5
FEMININE NOUNS
-ā stems II,1.1
-i AND -ī stems I,1.23
-u stems VI,6
FIRST AND SECOND PERSON PRONOUNS V,1
FUTURE PARTICIPLES
see under 'participles'
FUTURE TENSE III,6; IX,3
GEMINATE CONSONANT CASE FORMS: jaccā XII,3
GENDER I,12
GENITIVE
absolute X,1; XII,4
of fear IV,9
GERUND -tvā(na), -ya IV,3
use IV,3.2; X,3
'HUNDREDS' VI,12
'IF' III,9
IMPERATIVE III,5; XI,1
third person VIII,2
INDEFINITE ci III,10.1
INFINITIVE IN -tuṃ II,4
use of II,4.2
INTERROGATIVES
katama 'which' II,3
ka(ko/kiṃ/kā) III,1
'LIKE, AS' -iva IV,10
'LIVE BY' V,10
LOCATIVE CASE VII,7
absolute VIII,3
among' or 'in' VI,16
reference and contact XI,5
MASCULINE NOUNS
-a stems I,1.21
-an stems VI,1
-i stems VIII,1
-u stems II,1.2
MIDDLE (VOICE) XI,4
imperative XI,4.1
past tense XI,4.2
present and future tense XI,4.1
NEGATIVES I,6
no and mā VII,4
NEUTER -a STEMS I,1.22
NOMINATIVE I,141
NOUNS 1.1
forms II,1
(see also under 'cases')
numbers I,13
types I,1.2
agent nouns IX,1.11
-vant and -mant nouns V,2
(see also under 'masculine', feminine', and 'neuter')
NUMERALS I.13, IV,7

OPTATIVE III,4, IV,6, VII,1
  use III,4.2
  middle endings XI,4.3
PARTICIPLES
  modifying nouns X,4
  future (passive) participle VII,2
    in -nīya X,5
  past (perfective) participle V,5
    past participial sentences with instrumental subjects VI,9
  present participle III,6; XI,4.5
    -māna IV,4; IX,5
    feminine in -ī AND -ā IV,5
PARTICLES III,10
PASSIVE VERBS IX,4
PAST (PERFECTIVE) PARTICIPLE
  see under 'participles'
PAST TENSE ('AORIST') VI,7
  addasā type
    ('a- and root aorists' VI,7.1
  assosi type ('-s aorist') IX,2
  upasaṃkami type ('-is aorist')
  of vac- 'SAY' VI,8; VIII,3.1
PERFECTIVE FORMS (COMPOUND) XII,5
PARTICLES (CLITICS) I,3
PREFIX sa- 'WITH' V,8
POSTPOSITIONS II,7; X,7
PREPOSITIONS II,7; X,7
PRESENT TENSE I,2.2
  stem I,2.1
  middle forms XI,4.1
PRESENT PARTICIPLE
  see under 'participles'
PROHIBITIVE PARTICLE mā- XI,3
PRONOUNS II,2
  enclitic forms V,1.3
  first and second person V,1
  relative I,4; II,2
  third person II,2.1
REFLEXIVE attan VIII,3
REFLEXIVE PREFIX sa- II,9
RELATIONSHIP NOUNS IX,1.12
RELATIVE PRONOUN ya-/yaṃ I,4; II,2.13
  see also under 'correlative'
REPEATED FORMS (REDUPLICATION) X,8
SANDHI I,5; II,12; III,17; VIII,10; VI;17; X,10
SERIES (conjoining in) I,9
SUPERLATIVE XI,7
STEM FORM (nouns) I,1.1
'THIS, NOT THAT' V,9
VERBS I,2
  root and present stem I,2.1
  -a verbs I,2
  -e VERBS VIII,6
  -o verbs VIII,6
  'be' and 'become' III,2
  causative verbs X,6
  passive verbs IX,4
  root hā- VII,8
  root vac- VI,8; VIII,4
  root dis- II,4.13
  (see also under specific forms: participles, tenses, etc.)
VOCATIVE I,143